TRANSPORTATION
TO THE SEABOARD

Contributions in American History

Series Editor: Stanley I. Kutler

TRANSPORTATION TO THE SEABOARD

The "Communication Revolution" and American Foreign Policy, 1860–1900

Howard B. Schonberger

Contributions in American History
Number 8

Greenwood Publishing Corporation
Westport, Connecticut

Library of Congress Catalog Card Number: 75-105979
SBN: 8371-3306-8

Greenwood Publishing Corporation
51 Riverside Avenue, Westport, Connecticut 06880

Printed in the United States of America

Contents

v

PART THREE

Trunk-line Railroad Executives
in Quest of World Markets

PART FOUR

Conclusion

Acknowledgments

I WAS PROVIDED the financial help needed to complete this manuscript by the University of Wisconsin Graduate School, the Carl Russell Fish Fellowship, and the Ford Foundation. My thanks to the editors of *Minnesota History* for permission to use material for Chapter 8 from my article in the Winter 1968 issue (vol. 4). I am very grateful to the staffs of many research libraries which I used, especially The State Historical Society of Wisconsin, the Minnesota State Historical Society, and the Newberry Library.

I owe personal and professional debts to my colleagues Edward Crapol, James Erlenborn, Patrick Hearden, Dennis Nordin, and Tom Terrill for their encouragement and criticisms. My largest debt is to Professor William Appleman Williams, now at Oregon State University, who guided this book at the dissertation stage and inspired me with his teaching, intellect, and friendship.

Finally, I wish to express my appreciation to my wife Ann, for the reasons that every researcher and author knows.

Introduction

THE OVERSEAS empire that Americans controlled in 1900 was not the result of a sudden absence of mind, and was not forced upon the United States by other nations. Intellectuals, missionaries, military leaders, spokesmen for economic interest groups, and government policy makers after the Civil War helped to build that empire with conscious purpose and after much debate. The rapid agricultural and industrial transformation of the nation brought on severe domestic crises and pushed forward foreign policy issues. Far from being isolationist, the United States emerged as an imperial nation in the 1890s as the natural culmination of its own internal economic and ideologic development.

The conviction that the United States would become a supreme world power is easily discerned in the thoughts and actions of such key early foreign policy figures as William Henry Seward, President Ulysses S. Grant, and James G. Blaine. During the 1860s, Secretary of State Seward purchased Alaska, hoped to annex Canada and Hawaii, and sought colonies in the Caribbean. For the Orient, Seward urged a policy of commercial expansion a generation before the Open Door notes. In the next decade, President Grant paved the way for American expansion in the Pacific. The reciprocity treaty with Hawaii in 1875 made the islands wholly dependent upon the United States and laid the economic groundwork for later annexation. In 1872, a minor naval officer claimed the island of Samoa for the United States and led American diplomacy into its first imperial difficulties and involvement with the major European powers. Secretary of State James G. Blaine become a symbol of the new aggressiveness of American diplomacy during the 1880s. Obsessed with displacing the British from the Western Hemisphere, Blaine championed unilateral control over any isthmian canal, fathered the notion of a Pan-American Union dominated by the United States, successfully pressed for the adoption of the coercive tactic of reciprocity treaties with Latin American countries, and engaged in a major diplomatic confrontation with the British during the Chilean crisis of 1891–1892.[1] Clearly, long before the crucial developments of the Spanish-American War and its aftermath, the United States had become committed to and embroiled in overseas activities.

The dynamics of the enlarged concerns of American diplomacy after the Civil War were primarily related to internal economic forces and issues. Three principal groups influenced the making of foreign policy decisions—farm businessmen, the merchant and shipping interests, and the industrial and financial community. Historians have focused upon the latter group as virtually the exclusive source of domestic influence upon the emerging imperial foreign policy. Abundant investment and market opportunities within the country for manufacturers, railroad entrepreneurs, and bankers, according to orthodox interpretations, reduced American interest and activities in world affairs to a minimum until the economic depression of the 1890s. Only then did the concerted search for foreign markets for industrial surpluses and social stability at home launch America on an imperial course.[2]

Although the industrial-financial community greatly expanded and consolidated its share of the total wealth of the nation after the Civil War and dominated both political parties and Congress, one must not overlook the crucial role of the vast majority of Americans in the inception of the overseas expansionist drive. Americans who live in small towns and rural areas increased in population by almost 80 percent from 1865 to 1900. Relative to the growth of urban areas, rural population did decrease but remained over 50 percent of the total population of the country as late as 1900. Encouraged by the rapidly extended railroad net, farmers put more new land under cultivation from 1865 to 1900 than had been opened during the first 250 years of American history. Agricultural production of every sort increased spectacularly, more rapidly, as almost all contemporary observers acknowledged, than the domestic market could absorb. The secular price index for farm products showed a steady decline throughout these years, and agrarians suffered from severe depressions in each of the last three decades of the nineteenth century. Viewing their problems as businessmen geared to the market logic of Adam Smith, agrarians attempted to extend the free marketplace to the world at large and thereby ensure their own prosperity and freedom at home. The agrarian conception of a world marketplace, rather than a continental one, redefined the strategic boundaries of the United States and provided the criteria for determining international friends and enemies.[3]

The development of the market expansionist mentality of the agrarian majority during the post-Civil War period becomes crucial to an understanding of why the United States embarked on an imperial course with the cooperation of a broad consensus of the people. As early as the 1860s, agrarians of the South and West felt a humiliating sense of dependence upon the Northeast and England as sources of capital and as vital markets for agricultural exports. They explicitly defined their position as colonial and frequently compared their plight to other colonial societies, such as India and Ireland. They complained incessantly of their inferior status as the colonial end of an imperial relationship, with the Northeast and England serving as the metropolis.

Farm businessmen demanded in strident tones their own and the nation's commercial, financial, and political freedom and independence. They chafed under the limitations imposed by having the prices of their goods and the cost of their money determined in a foreign metropolis. Northeastern manufacturers, railroad men, middlemen, bankers, and politicians were seen as stifling the farmers' market outlets abroad by their strategy of working within rather than challenging the British imperial system. By the 1870s, the agrarians were no longer satisfied with being simply "tail to the London kite," and they asserted that the United States could independently assume the commercial and monetary hegemony of the world.[4]

The expansionist outlook of the agrarian majority, and its adoption and modification by metropolitan interests, can be traced through several key economic issues which entered prominently into the political arena of the post-Civil War decades. Generally the recurrent public debates over such matters as the tariff, the remonitization of silver, subsidies to the merchant marine, internal improvements, railroad regulation, and alien land legislation are viewed simply as part of domestic political or economic history. But these debates invariably gave rise to expressions of economic nationalism and shaped American attitudes toward foreign policy. Whatever the motives of special interests, the tariff was used consciously as a weapon of diplomacy and directly influenced the economic and political relations of the United States with foreign countries. The free-silver campaign of the Populists did not originate solely out of a desire to increase the money supply and thereby create higher prices for farm commodities. As they pointed out repeatedly, the acceptance of the gold standard by metropolitan businessmen and politicians made the whole economy dependent upon Great Britain and hindered trade prospects with silver backed currency countries in Latin America and Asia. Many Americans believed that the decline in the American merchant marine affected the competitive advantage of American goods in foreign markets and that its reconstruction was vital to a more vigorous foreign policy.[5]

The following pages examine the issue of transportation to the seaboard in the post-Civil War era. This may seem remote from economic nationalism and foreign policy. Yet, to a surprising extent, the debates over internal improvements, government regulation of the railroads, and the role of trunk-line railroads in the transportation of American agricultural exports were shaped by, and in turn contributed to, America's broader struggle for world power. To avoid misunderstanding, three caveats are entered at the outset. First, to the majority of railroad managers and shippers, the effect of transportation conditions on day-to-day profit-making was vastly more important than broad considerations of the balance of trade or growing nationalism. Second, nationalistic arguments often were used during transportation debates to achieve primarily domestic and not foreign policy objectives. Railroad interests, for example, very effectively raised the specter of Canadian railroad competition to modify the Interstate Commerce Act. Finally, among those who stressed the nationalistic aspects of transportation policy, from the dirt farmer to the President, the suggestion of a concrete foreign policy vis-à-vis specific countries was seldom given. The main point throughout these years was that such assertions of economic nationalism deepened the awareness of influential policy makers of the world market problem confronting American capitalism. And they helped define which foreign nations were rivals and which were allies in the American pursuit of world power.

This study has been divided into three parts. The first and longest part considers the years 1860 to 1880, when the transportation issue was at the center of national attention. The issue first rose in the 1850s among western farmers and merchants who became increasingly oriented toward the sale of surplus foodstuffs to distant markets in the East and abroad. And that trend accelerated during the Civil War decade. One result was a mania for railroad construction in the West financed largely by eastern and foreign investors. As long as commodity prices remained high, westerners paid scant regard to the abuses of the railroad system. But as soon as prices dropped, the problems of transportation rose inevitably to the foreground.

The rise and fall of commodity prices appeared closely related to demand in the international market. "As is well known," stated the president of the Chicago Board of Trade in 1869, "the markets of England fix the price at which nearly all the productions of our country are sold, whether for export or consumption."[6] Cheaper transportation of foodstuffs to the seaboard, it followed, would enlarge foreign demand and sustain a higher level of prices at home. The development of facilities for the handling of agricultural products and the reduction of freight rates were an essential precondition for transforming local markets into a prosperous world market. And this concern for marketplace expansion made western farmers and merchants acutely aware of worldwide transportation developments: European railway regulation and nationalization of railroads, the completion of the Suez Canal, the construction of railroads and improvement of waterways in India and Russia. All directly affected their well-being and stimulated demands for government assistance to improve American transportation.

Western farmers and merchants insisted on measures to improve their competitive position in the export market. They hoped to win a larger share of the returns from that trade by curtailing the dominance which eastern interests exercised in the West through their control of the railroad network. Farmers tended to be much more explicit than merchants in their analysis of the problem of the colonial bondage—to use their expression—in which organized capital held them, since the western merchants were more often financially and politically beholden to eastern interests. Rapidly organized into Granges after 1869, the farmers discussed and debated various strategies for loosening the grip of the East and improving their position in the political economy. Diversified agriculture, more processing plants, the introduction of manufacturing—all were considered. But as long as agricultural surpluses increased, the problem of transportation to distant markets was inescapable. At the state level, regulatory laws establishing maximum rates would cheapen transportation and make railroad companies answerable to the public. Both Grangers and merchants pushed vigorously in the 1870s for such regulation of the railroads in the West.

At the national level, regulation of the railroads appeared impractical. The Grangers proposed alternative means to obtain access to foreign markets and end the domination of private railroads in the West. The improvement of the Mississippi, the widening of the locks of the Erie Canal, the use of the St. Lawrence River, and the construction of a double-track freight railway from the interior to the Atlantic coast were projects proposed by the Grangers and supported by merchants to provide cheaper transportation to the seaboard and weaken the grip of the eastern metropolis. The abortive effort of the Grangers to organize the Mississippi Valley Trading Company is symbolic of the force of these ideas.

An examination of the movement for cheap transportation in the South concludes Part One. There the issue was never as crucial as in the West because of the high value of cotton relative to its weight. Nevertheless, the South—a devastated and occupied society after the Civil War—sought increased railway construction and large appropriations for internal improvements as an important remedy to its economic ills.

Such improvements would cheapen the costs of shipping cotton and other goods to distant markets; also, a portion of the agricultural exports of the West would be channeled through southern ports.

Great state-level efforts were made to attract capital for the rehabilitation of the railroads after the Civil War, but southern Congressmen returned to Washington with hopes of federal assistance, too. By 1875, a coalition of southern Democrats and northwestern Republicans was organized and annually increased the amount of appropriations for internal improvements and enlarged the proportion given to the South. The demands of that alliance grew out of the argument that the agricultural products of the South and West supplied 80 percent of total exports, enabling the economy (and the government) to enjoy a favorable balance of trade. Unless appropriations for the desired improvements were forthcoming, these Congressmen argued, other nations would maintain control of overseas markets, agricultural exports would decline, and the government would lose a principal source of revenue from a decreased level of dutied imports.

Part Two attempts to demonstrate how the issue of transportation to the seaboard entered into the 1880s debate over federal regulation of the railroads. The rapid decline in railroad rates during the massive depression of the 1870s, especially for the highly competitive export products of the West, diverted traffic from the waterways. As a consequence, improved waterways seemed less important as either regulators of rail rates or carriers of export products. Moreover, railroad mileage in the 1880s increased enormously, further complicating the transportation problem.

Demands for federal regulation came from nearly all groups and from every region of the country. To many farmers, local rates appeared exorbitant in contrast to competitive through rates. To many merchants, railroads disregarded the commercial interests of their cities. And to many railroad managers, the collapse of voluntary pooling agreements to maintain rates led them to seek a political solution to the industry's problems. That some regulation was inevitable from such a chorus of advocates was clear as early as 1878. Charles E. Perkins, president of the Chicago, Burlington & Quincy and a laissez-faire diehard, commented that year that "the public will regulate us to some extent—and we must make up our minds to it."

But one question unsettled all the participants in the national debate over what kind of federal legislation was necessary. How would regulation affect rates on agricultural exports and the commercial strength of the United States generally? Spokesmen for the trunk-line railroads in the East were largely responsible for focusing attention on this question and setting the terms of the future debate. In their campaign against the Reagan bill, the perennial regulatory measure in Congress from 1878 to 1885, they argued that its provisions would increase rates on export commodities and destroy foreign trade. Farmers and merchants and their congressional representatives were forced to deal with this issue. But it was the railroad men who most effectively appealed to nationalistic sentiments to oppose, modify, or escape federal regulation to their own benefit. In so doing, the regulation issue contributed to the growing national consciousness of American commercial and political power.

Part Three consists of three case studies of the major railroads' role in transporting to the seaboard exports of agricultural surpluses. It examines the importance which the leadership of the Baltimore & Ohio Railroad, the Illinois Central Railroad, and the Great Northern Railroad placed on that trade, the cooperation of merchants and farmers along the line of these roads in expanding that trade, and the involvement, if any, of these railroad men in national issues which affected agricultural surplus exports.

The trunk-line roads from the major Atlantic coast ports were the first to carry the bulk commodities of the West to the seaboard for export in the 1870s. Of all the traffic handled by these roads, the agricultural products destined for foreign markets produced the greatest competition. John W. Garrett, president of the B&O at the time, looked to agricultural export figures—though only a small percentage of total business—as a reliable index of the well-being of his enterprise. Not only did he engage in frequent rate wars to increase the road's share of that business, but he actively, though privately, sought to extend that market.

As the center of the production of agricultural staples moved steadily westward during the 1880s, the railroads with terminals on the Gulf and Pacific coasts took an increasing interest in the export of those items and their by-products. Unlike the trunk lines to Atlantic ports, the railroads on the Gulf coast and the transcontinentals often opened the way to new markets in Latin America and Asia. Their efforts were made considerably easier by the intense animosity that developed around the Populist movement in the South and West towards eastern interests. One popular solution for weakening the hold of the East involved increasing the direct sale of agricultural surpluses in the new markets of Latin America and the Orient. Stuyvesant Fish, president of the Illinois Central, and James J. Hill, president of the Great Northern, worked vigorously with merchants and farmers to extend overseas markets, attempting on numerous occasions to influence American foreign policy directly.

Traditional accounts of American foreign policy often overemphasize the dramatic outburst of the Spanish-American War as a contrast with the supposed quiescence of the preceding decades. But when foreign policy is redefined in terms of the influence of so-called domestic issues, the overt imperialism at the end of the nineteenth century appears more like the tip of the proverbial iceberg. The force behind that outward thrust lay in the economic nationalism which had developed around various arguments for the expansion of overseas markets for American surpluses in the post–Civil War era. The continued agitation by farmers, merchants, and railroad men that transportation problems be considered as part of a broader struggle of America to extend its economic and political power to the rest of the world is only one small example of the need to revise our view of nineteenth-century American foreign policy.

NOTES

1. Julius W. Pratt, *A History of United States Foreign Policy* (Englewood Cliffs: Prentice-Hall Inc., 1955), pp. 172–190, 201–212.

2. Walter LaFeber, *The New Empire: An Interpretation of American Expansion, 1860–1898* (Ithaca: Cornell University Press, 1963), pp. 6–24, 150–196. See also Ernest R. May, *Imperial Democracy* (New York: Harcourt, Brace & World, 1961), pp. 267–270; Wayne S. Cole, *An Interpretive History of American Foreign Relations* (Homewood, Ill.: Dorsey, 1968), pp. 122–165.

3. William A. Williams, *The Roots of the Modern American Empire* (New York: Random House, 1969), pp. 22–25.

4. Ibid., pp. 14–16.

5. Ibid., pp. 385–404.

6. *Country Gentleman*, 22 April 1869.

PART ONE

Cheap Transportation
to the Markets of the World

1

The Granary of
the World and the Fight
Against Isolation

THE FUNDAMENTAL changes that took place in the transportation of commodities and the transmission of information in the last half of the nineteenth century have been aptly characterized as a "communication revolution." New inventions, new materials, and new methods produced vast improvements in railroads, ocean and inland shipping, and cable telegraphy. The extension of those services to most parts of the world bound ever tighter the global strands of commerce.[1] The international exchange of commodities and services in 1900 took place on a scale hardly imaginable only fifty years earlier. Even such a prescient observer as William Henry Seward confessed difficulty in comprehending the long-term impact of technological changes in transportation and communication. But he did point out, in numerous speeches, their importance for the future strength of the nation in the world competition for commercial supremacy.

The construction of a transcontinental railroad and a national program of internal improvements, both of which Seward forthrightly advocated, had widespread political appeal among the farmers and merchants of the West. They understood the necessity of selling American agricultural surpluses in the markets of the world and argued that cheaper transportation was essential to that end. By extending the area of commercial agriculture, however, cheaper transportation created even larger surpluses and contributed to the fall in commodity prices.[2]

The actual decline in transportation costs and commodity prices in the United States from 1860 to 1880 was part of a worldwide phenomenon. It only increased the agitation of westerners for internal improvements, railroad construction, and railroad regulation in order to compete more successfully with other nations in foreign markets. In the view of many in the West, the Republican party, which controlled state and national governments in the post-Civil War decade, failed to keep pace with this global acceleration of the communication revolution. The organization of third parties and the revival of the Democratic party during the 1870s reflected the discontent and inaugurated a new approach to the transportation problem.

Seward, Prophet of the American Empire

Born and nurtured in the West, the Republican party rose to prominence by combining an antislavery platform with the economic aspirations of the West for a program of internal improvements. River and harbor improvements, canals, and transcontinental railroads for the westerner largely depended upon funds from the national treasury. Only $6 million had been spent on western rivers and the Great Lakes in the entire period from 1790 to 1860.[3] And sectional differences over the route (or routes) of a transcontinental railroad had defeated a common interest in the consummation of the project. The

Republicans unequivocally favored rivers and harbors appropriations of a "national character" and a transcontinental railroad in their platforms of 1856 and 1860.[4]

By 1856, the Democratic party had scuttled John C. Calhoun's earlier attempts to square states-rights doctrines with support for a national program of internal improvements. The dream of the reestablishment of the alliance of the South and West had been shattered by the slavery question and the commercial pull of the Erie Canal and trunk-line railroads.[5] President Buchanan, a northern Democrat, and Congress followed Democratic party dictum with the result that, except four small relief acts, not one piece of rivers and harbors legislation reached the statute books during his term of office. Both the Charleston and Richmond conventions of the Democratic party in 1860 were silent on the question of internal improvements.[6]

Though the importance of internal improvements to the West, and to the rise of the Republican party, has long been acknowledged, the element of economic nationalism that was tied to this issue has not been carefully considered. This is surprising, for during the Civil War decade William Henry Seward, a leading spokesman for the Republicans and Secretary of State in two administrations, perhaps best symbolizes the concern to manipulate the internal transportation system to establish overseas commercial power. Moreover, it was in the new states of the West that Seward, a New Yorker, had his strongest appeal and where, according to Frederic Bancroft, his biographer, he was regarded as the "greatest American statesman."[7]

In his 1860 presidential campaign tour through the West, Seward talked of the tremendous growth of the region, the necessity for its continued expansion with free labor, and its future role as part of the American Empire. In the age of industrial societies, Seward argued, empires expanded more rapidly than in ancient times. He opined that, even in 1860, the power of the empire of the Atlantic states was passing away to the Mississippi Valley.[8] He emphasized the importance of having a strong economic and unified political base at home in order for the American Empire to extend further westward to its final goal, the Orient, there to struggle with other commercial powers.

Seward advocated four concrete and interrelated policies to realize such a base of power: a protective tariff, the sale of public lands, unrestricted immigration, and an extensive program of internal improvements.[9] Though Seward believed that agriculture was the main wheel of national prosperity, he greatly feared an excessive reliance on the production of a few staples and the neglect of home manufactures in favor of cheaper goods from abroad. A protective tariff would diversify industry, create a demand for the use of new natural resources, and establish a true basis for American economic independence from England. The sale of public lands, quickly and at low prices, and unrestricted immigration, would attract and provide cheap labor for the production of agricultural products that formed the basis of American commercial strength. Finally, Seward hearkened back to the statesman he admired most, John Quincy Adams, for a program of internal improvements at government expense. Canals, improved rivers and harbors, and one or more transcontinental railroads would effectively unite the home base and prepare the nation for its commercial expansion abroad.[10]

While serving as a Senator, Seward found great perplexity in the public mind over the proper role of government in internal improvements. Questions of practicality, of expediency, and of constitutionality hindered or altogether defeated the appropriation bills for such measures. Yet Seward remained hopeful that a campaign of public education would ensure that all works essential to the improvement of internal commerce and the public defense would be constructed by the federal government with federal money. Such propaganda ought to single out the need for transcontinental railroads,

Seward thought, for those, of all enterprises, were clearly of vast utility and practicality. Once the public had accepted the use of federal power to unite the continent with railroads, it would accept other internal improvements by the government.[11]

There was no project that Seward cherished so persistently as that of a transcontinental railroad. In his first year in the Senate, for example, he promised to aid that project, and as Secretary of State he recalled that it had been the first and best of all the measures he supported while in public service.[12] Like many advocates of a transcontinental railroad, Seward insisted that such roads were the technological instruments for the American control of the markets of the Orient. In his view, the commerce of Asia had been the foundation of all commerce since the earliest ages, controlling the rise and fall of nations and furnishing the basis for Britain's greatness. A transcontinental railroad would grasp the Asiatic trade for the United States and bring it to the peak of world power.[13] When the Union Pacific and Central Pacific were joined in 1869, Seward was prompted to remark that Japan, China, and Australia were "already adjacent, and commercially bound to the American Pacific coast."[14]

The highway to the Pacific was potentially more than the means for conducting trade with Asia. Seward also felt that it could become an instrument of production, or at least create the facilities for production, in the area through which it passed. For that and for obvious political reasons, Seward favored the northern route in continuation of the northwestern track of migration. In the broad plains of the Northwest, where "state after state is yet to rise," Seward predicted that the transcontinental railroad would develop a region "whence the production for the support of human society in other crowded states must forever go forth."[15]

In the helpful terms of Henry Nash Smith, Seward represents the tension between an outward-looking as against an introspective conception of empire. No longer was the transcontinental railroad project merely a means of extending the maritime commerce of the United States to Asia; it had also become a means of developing the trans-Mississippi region. Strong weight was given to the latter argument, for when the first transcontinental road in 1869 failed to draw the trade with the Orient which Seward and other promoters had predicted, and American imports and exports proved to be a negligible part of the freight carried by the transcontinentals, the idea of a continental empire emerged temporarily triumphant. Empire had lost its "transitive reference. It no longer beckons onward toward the Pacific and the Far East."[16] It was not until the completion of the Canadian Pacific Railway in 1886 and the fears that it aroused in the United States, that the interest in Asia as the ultimate destiny of the American West once again became paramount in the discussion of transcontinental railroads.[17]

In Seward's view, more than transcontinental railroads were needed to strengthen the home base and prepare for overseas expansion. In his biography of John Quincy Adams published in 1851, Seward suggested his agreement with Adams that roads and canals were "the most essential means of improving the condition of nations." He praised Adams for giving the largest share of his attention as President to problems of internal improvements and the protection of domestic manufactures. The more completely the internal resources of the country were developed, the less dependent America would be on foreign powers and the greater would be its public and private prosperity.[18]

Seward followed the example set by his mentor. He frequently had responsibility for internal improvement bills in the Senate, and he favored granting all that was requested. When he could not get that, he accepted what he could obtain by compromise. "I prefer internal improvements somehow to internal improvements nohow," Seward said in 1854. "I prefer internal improvements anyway to a defeat and subversion of the system."[19] It was his vigorous advocacy of internal improvements, more than any other issue, that brought Seward his popularity in the Northwest. William B. Allison introduced Seward to a Dubuque, Iowa, crowd in 1860 as the man who had "ever aided in the improvement of our own western rivers and harbors," and Gov. Alexander W. Randall of Wisconsin contended that in all the great measures of public policy for the benefit of the West, Seward's voice and vote had been given with gratitude.[20]

In attempting to conceptualize the full impact of railroads, canals, and telegraphs upon the United States and the world, Seward often confessed to great bewilderment; yet few men so well articulated the significance of these developments. On the domestic front they obliterated state boundaries and produced a "physical and moral centralism" more complete than that of an absolute monarch. These same instruments also allowed for the continual expansion of American interests abroad. Telegraphs and railroads across the rivers and boundaries of Canada would inevitably draw that nation to the United States. Steamers on the lakes of Nicaragua, the railroad across the Isthmus of Panama, and the negotiations for an isthmian canal, all indicated to Seward that "the motives to enlargement" were "gaining new vigor."[21]

The Civil War
Cuts Outlets to the Sea

Although such men as Seward were able to recognize the advent of steam and electricity as a revolutionary force, they seemed unable to comprehend the drastic changes still to come. The accelerated expansion of American agriculture, facilitated by the extensive and cheaper modes of transportation developed during and after the Civil War, brought a continuous growth in crop acreage and production that continued until the end of the century. A large, steady surplus of grain and livestock was created, and a growing commitment was made to the production of staple crops for distant markets. The self-sufficient farmer of the agrarian ideal, if he ever existed, was transformed into a commercial businessman increasingly subject to the fluctuations of freight rates and international commodity prices.[22] The impact of these changes was forcefully impressed upon the consciousness of westerners in the opening years of the Civil War by the disruption of familiar patterns of trade and the flood of export traffic. The issue of internal improvements rose to new prominence.

The West had, by the end of 1860, largely recovered from the disasters of the Panic of 1857 and, with an abundant wheat and corn crop, looked forward to a period of great prosperity. The states bordering on the Great Lakes anticipated an especially bright future on the grounds that the eastern markets would not be greatly affected by the secession crisis. But southern Ohio, Indiana, Illinois, and Missouri were not in so fortunate a position. Continued commercial and financial relations with the South appeared threatened by the political movement for secession. A small incident three months before war broke out was a harbinger of worse to come for the lower West.

Authorities in Mississippi ordered a battery of artillery to be placed on the banks of the Mississippi River at Vicksburg to stop passing boats which were then ordered to land for inspection. Boats not destined for Vicksburg were compelled to pay wharfage fees. The action provoked a strong friend of the South, Stephen Douglas, to complain that "Illinois, situated in the interior of the continent, can never acknowledge the right of the states bordering on the seas to withdraw from the Union at pleasure and form alliances by which we shall be excluded from all access to the ocean." In the Indiana legislature, Democrats and Republicans agreed that such interference with commerce would be considered an offense against the whole Northwest.[23]

The outbreak of the war created dislocations in the existing pattern of trade and severe economic distress. The blockade of the Ohio and Mississippi rivers and the closing of the Baltimore & Ohio Railroad most seriously affected farmers and merchants in the lower West and in the region beyond Lake Michigan. Producers who had generally sold in the South could not pay the freight rates to eastern markets. The great demand for supplies to the rapidly mobilizing armies offset the decline in some places, but war prosperity did not come in large measure until 1862. Wheat, flour, packed pork, and corn liquor, the principal cash crops of these two areas, went unsold. Hard times fanned the coals of western sectionalism and provided the backdrop for the growing "copperhead movement."[24]

Bitterest complaints in the West were reserved for the eastern trunk lines which, it was generally felt, were making excessive wartime profits. The closing of the Mississippi, the tremendous demand for railroad cars, and high operating costs stemming from inflation caused transport rates to soar at twice the rate of commodity prices from October 1860 to May 1861. Further increases in freight rates were made throughout the war, though not so rapidly.[25] As a result, dissatisfaction and discontent with the transportation system prevailed in the West well into 1863.

By the summer of 1862, moreover, the situation had developed strong political overtones. President Lincoln dispatched Gen. John A. McClernand to tour the West. McClernand reported that the antiadministration sentiment was due to excessive freight rates and low farm prices. He urged immediate military operations to reopen and regain New Orleans in order to secure an outlet for western farm surpluses. Gov. Oliver P. Morton of Indiana gave Lincoln a similar warning. Only a vigorous military movement to open the Mississippi River could save the West for the Republican party in the November elections.[26]

Although the opening of the Mississippi did not come until

September 1863, the sudden reversal of the economic recession early in the fall of 1862 helped avert a complete rout of the Republican party in the congressional elections. Most of Ohio, Indiana, and Illinois swung over to the Democrats and three of Wisconsin's six districts elected Democrats. Michigan, Iowa, and Minnesota, however, remained Republican, adding to Lincoln's slim eighteen-vote margin in the House. The continued economic recovery after 1862, and the Union victories on the battlefield, assured the Republicans of an easier election in the West in 1864.[27]

The wartime boom had belied the dire predictions of dissidents in the West. The demand for goods from the southward movement of Union armies and a shift in trade from southern to eastern markets were important elements in advancing prices. But the large export demand for American foodstuffs attracted the critical attention of most observers. Henry Varnum Poor, editor of the *American Railroad Journal,* concluded from a comparison of British and American export statistics at the close of 1861 that "the superiority of the United States over other nations in its commercial position or strength, is now fully demonstrated." The war had proven that cotton was no longer necessary to the maintenance of foreign trade and that "we are self-sustaining, while they are more or less dependent" upon American foodstuffs.[28] One newspaper editor in Minnesota exclaimed, in 1862, that the large exports meant that the "scepter of power passes from King Cotton to King Grain of the West."[29] Chicago enjoyed spectacular growth in wealth and population from the new trade.[30] In fact, exports of wheat, the most important cash crop of the West, jumped from $4 million in 1860 to $38 million in 1861, $43 million in 1862, and $47 million in 1863 before falling to $19 million in 1865.[31]

The Lincoln administration took early note of the importance of this trend and the need for efficient transportation of these exports to the seaboard. Isaac Newton, Commissioner of Agriculture, emphasized that grain production was the pivot around which all other interests revolved, and argued that agricultural prosperity depended on the "continued and increased demand for our products, both at home and abroad." The export of foodstuffs would allow the United States "to command the precious metals and the respect, if not the fear of mankind." A more ready access to these markets was possible only with good roads, canals, and railways.[32] The first report of the Department of Agriculture in 1862 indicated that American leadership over eastern Europe in the British grain market resulted from American technical progress, especially in agricultural machinery and transportation facilities. The statistician of the department stressed the relative superiority of the transportation system between American grain fields and British ports.[33]

Lincoln himself, speaking to the Congressmen of the West in his annual message of December 1862, stressed the economic necessity of the interior for access to the markets of the world. The West had no seacoast and touched no ocean anywhere, he began. "As part of one nation, its people now find, and may forever find, their way to Europe by New York, to South America and Africa by New Orleans, and to Asia by San Francisco; but separate our country into two nations, as designed by the present rebellion, and every man of this great interior region is thereby cut off from some one or more of these outlets. . . ." Lincoln concluded his appeal for national unity by reminding his listeners that those "outlets east, west and south are indispensable to the well-being of the people inhabiting and to inhabit this vast interior region."[34]

The wartime wave of prosperity did not completely submerge the interest in transportation problems. The strain upon carrying facilities was felt everywhere in the West, and indirectly in the East as well. Virtually every group concerned with the problem joined in the demand for better and cheaper transportation as a way to strengthen the war effort and increase agricultural exports. Chicago, the largest interior market in the country, acutely felt the shortage of facilities and took the lead in the wartime agitation for cheap transportation.[35]

Rapid improvement of the Erie Canal was the most important project urged by the Chicagoans. The New York State legislature favored such development—provided Congress paid for it. Samuel B. Ruggles, a representative of railroad and canal interests in New York, was appointed special commissioner by Gov. Edwin D. Morgan in April 1862. During a large part of two sessions of Congress, Ruggles tried to win approval for government action to enlarge the facilities of the Erie Canal for reasons of national defense. Canals built in Canada, he argued in a long memorial to President Lincoln, made it possible for the British to admit into the Great Lakes warships of greater size than those the United States could send through the Erie Canal. Furthermore, he pointed to the ability of the United States to "feed the world," and used elaborate statistics to show the commercial advantages to the Union of an enlarged canal.[36] Congress at first seemed favorably disposed to the project; however, the demand for aid to the canals in Illinois, and the difficulty of justifying large expenditures for somewhat dubious defense purposes, killed the plan after a long and stubborn House fight that ended in February 1863.[39]

To bring New York to terms, Chicago proceeded to rally the West behind demands for the improvement of Canadian waterways as an alternative route. William H. Osborn, president of the Illinois Central Railroad during the Civil War, recognized the inadequacy of the existing transportation facilities to eastern and foreign markets. That awareness was not surprising, for Chicago was the most important terminal of the Illinois Central. Osborn felt that the discontent among farmers in the West was closely tied to the question of high freight rates, and he scored the excessive tolls charged by the Erie Canal and trunk-line managers. "The West cannot consent to be held by the throat any longer to enrich Albany and Buffalo.

. . ." The people of Illinois, Osborn protested, "are bound to have an outlet to the sea; this leaning toward Canada is a natural consequence of the apathy and indifference manifested by the State of New York." Osborn aroused the Illinois State Agricultural Society, which took a strong stand in behalf of the enlargement of the Erie Canal. Through his access to influential farm journals such as *The Rural New Yorker* and the *Prairie Farmer,* Osborn focused wide attention on the problem.[34] By the spring of 1863 the country was aroused, and ninety-eight members of Congress issued a "call" for a large "National Ship Canal" convention to meet in the Windy City.

The abortive Chicago convention of 1863 marked a formal recognition of the importance of adequate internal transportation facilities to the goal of American commercial strength abroad. A delegate from the Chicago Board of Trade expressed a hope that the proposed enlargement of the Erie and Illinois-Michigan canals would not only join the Lakes with the Atlantic and the Mississippi but that it would "form part of a great highway from the Atlantic to the Pacific, by means of which the wealth of Asia, on the one hand, and of Europe, on the other, may be grasped and made to pass through the bay of New York and the Golden Gate of San Francisco, thus encircling the whole earth, and bringing all nations to pay tribute, and bow before the sceptre of our commerce."

Samuel Ruggles appeared before the delegates undeterred by the failure of his behind-the-scenes efforts in Congress earlier in the year. The foreign exchange earned by the export of western food products would more than pay for the canals. *"American Food,"* he emphasized, "has now become the very substratum, the vital, vivifying principle of *American Commerce.*" By cheapening the transit of food to the seaboard, Ruggles concluded, the West could carry out its destiny of feeding not only the new world but overcrowded Europe as well.[40] One sympathetic railroad man suggested that even with the aid of all existing canals and railroads, "a bushel of wheat in the Northwest is only worth half its value in Liverpool." The question of cheap transportation between the grain-growing regions of the interior and eastern and foreign markets, he noted prophetically, "must for years, if not generations, to come, become the most engrossing topic of public concern."[41]

Many rival geographic interests were represented in the convention. They urged a ship-canal around Niagara Falls (and around the rapids of the Mississippi), the improvement of the St. Clair Flats and of the Fox, Wisconsin, and Hudson rivers, a canal between Lakes Cayuga and Ontario, and the improvement of all the Ohio canals. These plans were allowed to be presented in order to placate the various localities, but the Chicago and New York delegates prevailed. The final resolution called upon the national government to improve Illinois canals, construct a ship-canal around Niagara, and pressure Canada to improve the St. Lawrence Waterway. The drive for cheap transportation during the war, however, was blunted by the continued rise in commodity prices at a much greater rate than the increase in freight costs. Despite the presence of fourteen senators and eight representatives at the Chicago convention, Congress paid no heed to its resolutions.[42] In fact, Congress made only nine minor appropriations for internal improvements—excepting the land grants for the Union Pacific and Northern Pacific—during the war years.[43]

The Intensification of the Transportation Crisis

The "cheap transportation movement" in the West, begun in the early years of the Civil War, revived again in disparate locations during the brief economic recession of 1865–1866, and reached its height in the whole region with the approach of the Panic of 1873 and the massive depression which followed. The impetus behind the movement first centered on boards of trade and chambers of commerce, but rapidly passed to the farmers who organized into Granges after 1869. Spokesmen for these groups, including governors and Congressmen, repeatedly pointed to the need for cheap transportation if the United States was to achieve a strong market position abroad and a prosperous economy at home. Not all who employed these arguments were engaged in the export business. Their motives were largely self-interested and specific demands were almost as diverse as their number. But as the report of the Senate Committee on Transportation to the Seaboard (the Windom Report of 1874) makes abundantly clear, the common political and ideological ground of the cheap transportation movement, especially in the West, was its appeal to economic nationalism.

The close of the war brought a sharp fall in commodity prices and an increased volume of produce seeking markets. That renewed the demand for cheap transportation in the West.[44] Some 500 delegates, representing forty-five commercial organizations from the Great Lakes region and Canada, met in Detroit in May 1865 to demand cheaper transportation to the seaboard. Joseph Aspinwall, president of the Detroit Board of Trade and keynote speaker at the convention, went to the heart of the western problem. "The West has long felt the exorbitant transfer charges and tax levied by the state of New York upon its passing through the Erie Canal, which is assessed regardless of the demand or value of the property or place of destination." These charges absorbed all the profit.[45]

Looming over the proceedings of the convention was the impending abrogation of the Reciprocity Treaty of 1854 with Canada that guaranteed American commerce the free navigation of the St. Lawrence River. Debate on that issue polarized around the positions taken by James B. Taylor of Minnesota and Consul Potter of Montreal. Taylor, who later became the strongest advocate of Canadian annexation in the country, argued in 1865 that a renegotiated reciprocity treaty was absolutely necessary to the solution of the greatest problem of the West—cheap transportation to eastern and foreign markets. Taylor wanted the St. Lawrence and Great Lakes route improved so that vessels of 1,500 tons could pass from the Atlantic to the interior without breaking bulk. New York was the only seaport for western produce, and Taylor recognized that the monopoly would be broken if the Canadian canals were deepened and the navigation of the St. Lawrence improved. Consul Potter, on the other hand, spoke of the greater benefits of reciprocity to Canada than to the United States. Without the treaty, Potter claimed, Canada's economy would be so disrupted that its government would apply for admission to the United States within two years. Apparently most of the delegates agreed with Consul Potter's view, and a compromise resolution was passed simply calling for a ship-canal around Niagara Falls on the American side.[46]

The question of the free navigation of the St. Lawrence had been a key point in earlier reciprocity discussions. Rep. Isaac N. Arnold of Illinois charged, in 1864, that the West had been taxed for years by the high tolls on the Erie Canal, and he favored renewal of the reciprocity treaty primarily for the free navigation of the St. Lawrence. But the West was never united on the question. The powerful lumber interests in Wisconsin, for example, favored a policy of protection against Canadian competition. So did many wheat farmers. Eastern Congressmen who led the forces opposed to the renewal of reciprocity charged Canada with violating the 1854 Treaty for the avowed purpose of diverting American trade from routes within the United States by means of special rates. Thus, division in the West between those who favored reciprocity, protection, or annexation, and the opposition of the East, combined to allow the Reciprocity Treaty to expire in

1866.[47] The cry in the West for cheap transportation after 1869, however, revived the issue of the free navigation of the St. Lawrence and the demands for a new commercial arrangement with Canada.

Interest in transportation problems after the war was not confined to the Great Lakes region. The organization of an extraordinary alliance between the Mississippi River steamboats and the railroads connecting upper river points aroused opposition that reached its climax in the so-called antimonopoly revolt of 1865–1866.[48] An Antimonopoly Convention held in St. Paul charged the river packets and the railroads of Wisconsin and Illinois with attempting to monopolize the wheat trade of the area. Three proposals were made to solve the problem. Some river-town businessmen proposed a rival packet company. Others favored state railroad regulations to fix just and reasonable rates. Still others suggested the use of alternative routes to the seaboard, especially the encouragement of shipping down the river to New Orleans. "One of the other remedies for the relief of the people in the cost of transportation," argued Warren Bristol of Red Wing, Minnesota, "would be in diverting commerce of the State to other and competing centers of trade in the valley of the Mississippi River, and that to this end every influence ought to be brought to bear in favor of the removal by the government of all obstructions to the navigation of the river."[49] The committee to study the cost of transportation to New York from St. Paul via New Orleans thought the route feasible, and the convention prepared a memorial to Congress on the necessity for the improvement of the Mississippi.[50]

Following the lead of the Antimonopoly Convention in St. Paul, 500 delegates from Iowa and Illinois assembled at the Hall of the Produce Exchange in Dubuque, Iowa, for a River Improvement Convention. Gov. William M. Stone of Iowa opened the proceedings with an attack on the railroad monopolies and demanded the national government repair the

Mississippi as a modest repayment for the help of the Northwest in defeating the Confederacy. State Sen. D. P. Stubb
played on the sentiment of reconciliation. Improvements on
the Mississippi would stimulate commerce between the West
and South and thus help to heal the wounds of war. He predicted a growing population of producers in the Northwest
who would use the Mississippi as a channel leading to the
"markets of the world."[51]

Phillip Robb, secretary of the Produce Exchange, provided
the most thorough analysis of the importance of internal improvements to the West. He noted the feeling of great depression everywhere in the upper Valley as a result of the combination of falling prices and constant transportation costs. "In
the midst of what ought to be unbounded prosperity, we are
staggering under a weight of oppression that is crushing the
very spirit out of our people." The war had brought unparal-
leled prices for farm commodities, and the high transport costs
could be met. But one year after the end of the war, prices
for corn, oats, pork, and wheat had fallen an average of 42
percent while the cost of transportation remained the same.
In anger, some people argued that the West ought to turn its
attention to manufacturing.

Robb opposed that idea. Nature had designed the Mississippi Valley "as the granary of the world," he said. "Relief
from our present condition is not to be found in a change of
pursuits but in a change in the means and routes of transportation." If the obstructions on the Mississippi at Rock
Island and Keokuk were removed, Robb predicted, the producers in the Northwest could market their surplus grain in
Liverpool, successfully competing with European farmers on
their own soil. They could "eventually control the price of
breadstuffs in the very center of the world's trade. The only
obstacle that prevents the western producer from underselling
and, by successful competition, driving foreign producers from
their own markets, is the want of cheap transportation." Robb

had no misconceptions about the formidable forces that would be arrayed against the improvement of the Mississippi. Chicago, Buffalo, the Erie Canal, and trunk-line railroad interests would combine against the project. But even if the threat of the improvement of the Mississippi only forced the completion of the Niagara ship-canal project, the object of cheap transportation to the seaboard would be advanced.[52]

Improvement of the upper Mississippi had no greater advocates than the merchants of St. Louis after the Civil War. It was clear to them that trade and enterprise were deserting St. Louis for Chicago. Though St. Louis realized the importance of building a network of railroads leading to the city and of bridging the Mississippi in order to combat its chief rival, the value of the river system was not deprecated. By establishing facilities for the direct export of western products to South America and Europe via New Orleans, St. Louis merchants hoped to recapture and hold the grain trade of the upper Valley. The antebellum question of whether shipments ought to go north and south or east and west was once again at issue; in great measure it was defined as an economic duel between water transportation on the Mississippi and the railroad interests of Chicago.[53]

Taking advantage of a postwar wave of resentment against the malpractices of a livestock ring in Chicago and the monopolistic practices of railroads serving Chicago, St. Louis held the most important river improvement convention prior to the depression of the 1870s in February 1867. The keynote of the meeting was a determined effort to obtain federal money for the improvement of western waterways so that they might be used as reliable routes for cheap transportation. The future agricultural development of the entire Valley, it was asserted, was at stake.

After a review of the statistics indicating how railroad traffic was flourishing at the expense of river transportation, the report of the central committee of the convention contended that cheap transportation was a national necessity and could be accomplished only by the removal of obstacles to navigation in the Mississippi River. Furthermore, cheap transportation for the surpluses of the Mississippi Valley would allow the United States to monopolize the markets of the world. It is not the "question of the ability to produce," the report emphasized, reflecting the confidence of a year of prosperity. "But it is the question of facility and cheapness of transportation which must be solved before we can monopolize the markets of the world."[54]

One delegate reviewed the way that the Civil War had changed the channels of commerce so that New York had obtained control over trade that "rightfully" belonged to the West. One solution to this problem, he suggested, was direct trade with the West Indies and Latin America. Such trade would "not only place the control of the grocery business of the Northwest in our [St. Louis] hands but also greatly enlarge our exportations." The flour, lard, meat, and so on of the West, he concluded, was the "fruitful and main source of those commodities which South America requires."[55]

The return to prosperity in the summer of 1866 did dampen the impact of the St. Louis convention in Congress and throughout the West. Wheat prices soared to more than two dollars a bushel in 1866 and 1867; corn prices reached a peak of seventy-eight cents a bushel in 1867, the highest in the decade after the Civil War.[56] One important reason for the excellent relative economic position of the farmer in the years immediately following the war, as the *Commercial and Financial Chronicle* pointed out, was that poor crops in Europe insured a large demand for American breadstuffs.[57] Wheat exports, including flour, jumped from 12.5 million bushels in 1866 to 25 million in 1867, and to 30 million in 1868. So prosperous were the farmers that no interest was taken in the financial and currency questions that raged in other sectors of the economy.[58]

A sharp break in the price of grain in the winter of 1868–1869, combined with the rainy harvest of the next summer, marked the beginning of a severe and extended crisis throughout the West. Commissioner of Agriculture Horace Capron observed that the low prices for 1869 had "not been exceeded in the same quarters for years. The wheat farmer, with a full garner, is not joyous over his market return."[59] The next three years brought little relief. Prices of farm products remained low and only dairymen and cattle-fatteners had any money. The exceptionally cold winter of 1871–1872 killed much winter wheat, and with the return of warm weather hessian fly and cinch bug took their heavy toll.[60] "Poverty, if not actual bankruptcy, stares the farmer in the face," summed up the situation for more than one Illinois farmer in 1873.[61]

The farmers responded with anger and determination to find relief from their economic plight. Increasing numbers in the West joined the Patrons of Husbandry. Founded as a fraternal organization in 1867 by Oliver H. Kelley, the Grange developed within a few years as the most important political expression of farmers' self-conscious and articulate militancy. Their complaints against railroad abuses mounted, and the demand for alternate and cheap routes of transportation to the seaboard revived with new vigor. Western businessmen recognized both the need to respond to the continuing protest and the usefulness of an alliance with the farmers on the question of cheap transportation: they, too, were dependent on distant markets for the sale of their surpluses. James M. Richards, president of the Chicago Board of Trade, pulled together these strands of thought in a succinct remark of April 1869. "Too large a part of the value of [the farmers'] productions is consumed in the cost of getting them to a point where the exchanges are made. As is well known, the markets of England fix the price at which nearly all the production of our country are sold, whether for export or consumption in our own country."[62]

The downward slide of prices and the drive for cheap transportation were reflected immediately in the reciprocity negotiations with Canada in 1869. After the abrogation of the 1854 Treaty, representatives of the West continued their agitation to obtain the privilege of using the St. Lawrence Waterway. As the volume of surplus produce increased after the Civil War and the demand of the foreign market grew, the attractiveness of the Canadian route increased correspondingly.[63] The British minister in the United States advised the Foreign Office early in 1867 that if Canada did not meet the demands of the Northwest for "greater facilities for the transit of produce from the Lake region through the St. Lawrence to the Atlantic, the desire of the United States to drive their British rivals off this continent will be powerfully reinforced by the material interests of the Northwest which will be enlisted in favor of conquest or annexation."[64]

At the request of the Canadian government, reciprocity negotiations were renewed in November 1868. Commissioner of Agriculture Horace Capron claimed that the farmers in the country would vigorously protest the renewal of the 1854 Treaty or any "arrangement admitting untaxed and low-priced Canadian production custom free. . . ."[65] Surveying opinion in the Northwest for Secretary of the Treasury Hugh McColluch, James Taylor outlined the strategy of the Republican leadership in favor of a new commercial arrangement with Canada. He supported the judgment that farmers were opposed to any measure that would increase competition from Canada, although he appreciated the importance of agricultural exports and cheap transportation to the West. The Northwest would assent to a treaty that offered a quid pro quo, he asserted. "The free navigation of the St. Lawrence *as it is,* will not satisfy the Western people. Of that, we are reasonably sure now. Let Canada put $6 million into the enlargement of the Welland and St. Lawrence Canals and the way will be clear to a new arrangement."[66]

The inauguration of the Grant administration in March 1869 created a new opportunity for the advocates of reciprocity with Canada. The House recommended that the President initiate negotiations with England regarding commerce, the fisheries, and the navigation of the St. Lawrence. To sound out the prospects of a treaty, during the summer Secretary of State Hamilton Fish conferred with Sir John Rose, the British minister to Washington, and the two men drew up an informal and confidential paper on the terms of a possible settlement. But Fish informed Rose that nothing could be done on the matter until Congress reconvened in December.[67]

Grant's annual message to Congress put a damper on attempts to renegotiate reciprocity. His contention was that reciprocity would actually protect the Canadian farmer, but he did concede that some arrangement for the regulation of commercial intercourse between the countries was desirable.[68] His real aim appeared to be the securing of concessions on the St. Lawrence canals and the fisheries without serious American concessions in return.[68] The *Commercial and Financial Chronicle* agreed with Grant that the transportation routes of both countries must remain free. "One great obstacle in the way of our more rapid commercial development," began the editors of the *Chronicle*, "is the enormous cost of transportation from the West to the seaboard. The fullest competition between the railroads and canals of both countries is the best possible means by which to obtain control of the European markets as an outlet for our surplus products."[69]

Apprehensive about the reluctance of the administration to enter into an agreement with Canada, a seven-man delegation of western Congressmen visited Secretary of State Hamilton Fish on 21 December 1869. They asked to be informed on the state of negotiations, and on what had happened during the summer. The burden of Fish's reply was that recent elections in New Brunswick had returned a substantial majority opposed to confederation, and that annexationists there were gaining strength.[70] Apparently Fish intended to continue the waiting game of annexation through economic coercion which had proven unsuccessful since 1866.

To counter Fish's view, the western Congressmen prepared a lengthy memorandum dated 28 January 1870 that provides a good insight into the cheap transportation struggle and its relation to economic nationalism. Of vital importance was some commercial arrangement by which "the distress at the West, arising from a lack of cheap transportation, may be relieved." With the free use of the St. Lawrence and the enlargement of its canals, direct trade between lake ports and Europe could be established. Freight rates on wheat, for example, would then be no higher from the interior ports than from the Atlantic seaboard. "The price of export wheat being determined by the Liverpool market, the American producers would thus receive the full price of their wheat, in Liverpool, less the water freight. Or, in other words if we now possessed the means of direct transportation, even at existing rates, our farmers would save the whole cost of the present inland freight from the Lakes to tidewater."[71]

As for the reputed annexationist talk in Canada, the westerners thought it the "veriest will-o'-the-wisp" which a change in the tariff could wipe out at once. Meanwhile, western farmers would suffer along with business interests. The delegation concluded that only the freedom of the St. Lawrence, from its source to the sea, would secure the revival of prosperity for farmers and merchants.[72]

By the fall of 1870, Secretary Fish had abandoned the chimera of the annexation of Canada. In a sudden change of attitude, he proposed to the British minister a settlement of all outstanding issues between the United States, Canada, and Great Britain, including the free navigation of the St. Lawrence and the enlargement of its canals.[73] President Grant, who but a year before had been an ardent annexationist, told the Congress in December 1870 that "liberal regulations" were needed to protect American commerce on the St. Lawrence. "The whole nation is interested in securing cheap transportation from the agricultural States of the West to the Atlantic Seaboard. . . . It is hoped that the Government of Great Britain will see the justice of abandoning the narrow and inconsistent claim to which her Canadian Provinces have urged her adherence."[74] A Joint High Commission of American and British members then began negotiations for a settlement of the disputes on 27 February 1871. Those talks resulted in the Washington Treaty of 1871. The St. Lawrence question played only a subordinate role in the discussions. The river was thrown open in perpetuity to the United States; the same principle was applied in Canada's favor to rivers which flowed through Alaska to the sea.[75] Since no provisions for the improvement of the canals on the St. Lawrence was made part of the treaty itself, the campaign of the western spokesmen for cheaper transportation was not entirely successful. But the effort did heighten the concern of the Grant administration with the transportation issue and the need for overseas markets.

The worsening agricultural depression produced many other manifestations of the agitation for cheap transportation in the West. A flood of resolutions and memorials descended upon Congress from state legislatures, commercial organizations, the Grangers, and other farmers' groups for various projects. In Minnesota, Iowa, and Wisconsin, demands for cheaper routes to the seaboard centered on the Fox-Wisconsin river project. "The great want of the West, with its bulky productions and heavy freights, is cheap transportation," Gov. Horace Austin told the Minnesota legislature in January 1870, "and this necessity must be supplied or the expense of marketing our crops will consume our profits. . . ."[76] The Fox-Wisconsin river route, he felt, was more important to Minnesota than to Wisconsin. Later in the year, Austin joined the governors of Wisconsin and Iowa on a trip to Washington to plead for the government purchase of the canal connecting the two rivers.[77]

The three governors also toured the East to stir up interest there in the waterway. One of the gambits used by the West to gain eastern support was the promise to assist in securing appropriations for the Niagara ship-canal on the American side of the Niagara River. The Iowa legislature memorialized the Congress for the Niagara Canal early in 1872, insisting that the entire Mississippi Valley demanded facilities for reaching eastern and European markets. Rates of transportation can be so reduced, the memorial argued, that "the cereals and other agricultural products of the western states can at once command the provision markets of Western Europe, from which they are now excluded in consequence of the excessive cost of transportation thither."[78] The legislature of Kansas made a similar demand for new and competing lines "to the markets of the world," while the Nebraska legislature argued that railroads, though necessary, could never cheapen the cost of transportation for heavy commodities like wheat for entry into the world marketplace.[79]

In Illinois, Missouri, Ohio, and Iowa, much of the activity for cheap transportation focused on the improvement of the Mississippi River. At a convention in Louisville in 1869, for example, delegates from the lower West argued that the immense bulk of commodities far exceeded the carrying capacity of the nation's railroads, and that as new territories opened up the situation would grow worse. The only solution for the food producer of the Mississippi Valley was the improvement of water routes, especially the Mississippi River.[80] At a commercial convention the next year in Cincinnati, Congressman George H. Pendleton of Ohio told his listeners that the great Mississippi Valley would not "submit to isolation." Its people would require free, uninterrupted, and easy communication to the Gulf of Mexico by the Mississippi River.[81] Perhaps the strongest demands for the improvement of the Mississippi came from western Democrats who sought to restore a community of interest between the West and South. Henry Clay Dean of Iowa expressed, in somewhat extravagant language, a popular sentiment when he wrote that after "destroying our great highway to the markets of the world through the Mississippi, New England drove us into her market to be robbed by her carriers on the way. . . . The East now holds the West in her hand with a deadly grasp. . . . New England owns the railroads, telegraphs and every other means of transportation."[82]

By the end of 1872, the issues of cheap transportation and foreign markets provoked two major responses from the Grant administration. First, Secretary of the Treasury George S. Boutwell, in his annual report, called for increased appropriations for internal improvements. His analysis of the issue in terms of American overseas market expansion is striking. "The contest for final peaceful supremacy in the affairs of the world," Boutwell stated, was tied to the ability to maintain specie payments and the condition of foreign trade. "Every measure which increases or improves the channels of transportation between the seaboard and the cotton- and grain-growing regions of the country, or lessens the cost of freight, adds something to our capacity to compete successfully in the markets of the world."[83] Second, President Grant called to the attention of the Forty-second Congress the "various enterprises for the more certain and cheaper transportation of the constantly increasing Western and Southern products to the Atlantic seaboard," and then recommended a special committee to gather information on the subject.[84] That push led to the creation of the Senate Select Committee on Transportation Routes to the Seaboard, appointed in April 1873 with the energetic Senator William Windom of Minnesota for its chairman. The Windom Committee toured the country and gathered testimony from merchants, farmers, manufacturers, and railroad men. As it did, a financial panic and business depression staggered the nation. The Windom Report, submitted to Congress in the spring of 1874, indicates forcefully that the agitation for cheap transportation and increased foreign markets was intensified and heightened by that crisis.[85]

Reflecting over a decade of convention resolutions, political speeches, and congressional debate, the Windom Report dealt with the problem of cheap transportation in its international context. Grain production in the West had, since at least 1860, exceeded the local demand. As a result, the British market had been used to absorb the surplus. But the rising competition of the Russians, the result in good measure of internal improvements that reduced transportation charges from the Russian interior to the seaboard, made the continuation of the trade "a very uncertain business." One possible solution to the problem was to find a southern market for the surplus grain by improving transportation between the West and South. Not only would the West thereby be liberated from the fluctuations of the British market, but southern planters would be able to devote their lands to increased production of cotton. Cotton exports would be increased and the recent gains by other cotton-supplying nations would be offset.[86]

Though that alternative appeared to be the most attractive, the Windom Report quietly laid it aside. Instead, the program for internal improvements was presented as a means of making it possible to compete with the Russians in the British market. When the Russians adopt the American grain elevator system to complement their railroad network, they will be able to "drive us from the markets of the world." And when that happens, Russia will "become an active competitor in Boston and Portland, if cheaper means of internal transport be not provided." Every cent added to the cost of transportation from the West and South to the seaboard was in effect protection to the cotton planter of India and the wheat grower of Russia. "If we would assure our imperiled position in the markets of the world," concluded the Windom Committee, "reinstate our credit abroad, restore confidence and prosperity at home, and provide for a return to specie payment, let us develop our unequaled resources and stimulate our industries by a judicious system of internal improvements."[87]

Public reaction to the Windom Report varied widely. The Chicago *Tribune* did not think the proposed improvements would benefit the Northwest, and argued that the whole scheme was visionary and too expensive. The St. Paul *Press* concluded, on the other hand, that the water routes, if improved, would "emancipate the country from the chains of the railroad monopoly."[88] The *Nation* applauded the Windom Committee for exploding the illusion that transportation could be made cheap by government regulation.[89] Criticizing the report for failing to mention the St. Lawrence route to the seaboard, the *Railroad Gazette* suggested that improvements in the Canadian canals would make the water routes in the United States less than competitive.[90] The National Board of Trade endorsed the report, however, and recommended starting the improvements immediately.[91]

Perhaps the most significant comment on the Windom Committee came from Ignatius Donnelly, the fiery Grange leader from Windom's home state of Minnesota. A vigorous expansionist, Donnelly supported the proposals for improved waterways. But he did not see what Senator Windom could do to help the Northwest, "considering that he cares nothing for the farmers, and has been supported by the railroads ever since he came to have any property."[92] Donnelly clearly suspected the political motive behind the Windom Committee, for it was in fact a major attempt by the Republican party to stem the widescale defection of western farmers from its ranks.

Dissatisfaction with the Republican party in the West had grown with the harsh economic conditions of the early 1870s. Farmers joined the Patrons of Husbandry to remedy the ills they believed beset them. Although they denied participation in partisan politics, the Grangers revived the Democratic party in the West and helped organize third parties. That was necessary because the party of Lincoln appeared to them to be controlled by railroad interests at every level of government. Moreover, the Republicans failed to provide sufficient appropriations for internal improvements that would ease transportation costs. The Grangers sent new Congressmen to Washington, and for the first time since the Civil War, the Republicans lost control of the House of Representatives in the elections of 1874. Agitation by the Grangers—against railroad practices and for cheap transportation—attained its greatest intensity during the early 1870s in the upper Mississippi Valley. And it had important effects upon political developments elsewhere throughout the nation.

NOTES

1. Robert G. Albion, "The 'Communication Revolution,'" *American Historical Review*, XXXVII (July 1932), 718–720.

2. Lee Benson, "The Historical Background of Turner's Frontier Essay," *Agricultural History*, XXV (April 1951), 59–82.

3. Edward L. Pross, "A History of Rivers and Harbors Appropriations Bills 1866–1930" (Ph.D. dissertation, University of Ohio, 1938), p. 43.

4. Kirk H. Porter and Donald B. Johnson, comps., *National Party Platforms 1840–1964* (Urbana: University of Illinois Press, 1966), pp. 31–33.

5. Roy F. Nichols, *The Disruption of American Democracy* (New York: Macmillan Co., 1948), pp. 29–31. Henry Nash Smith, *Virgin Land* (New York: Random House, 1957), p. 168.

6. Pross, "Rivers and Harbors Appropriations Bills," p. 39. Porter and Johnson, *National Party Platforms*, p. 33.

7. Frederic Bancroft, *The Life of William H. Seward* (New York: Harper & Brothers, 1900), I, 546.

8. George E. Baker, ed., *The Works of William H. Seward* (Boston: Houghton, Mifflin and Company, 1886), IV, 319.

9. Walter LaFeber, *The New Empire: An Interpretation of American Expansion 1860–1898* (Ithaca: Cornell University Press, 1963), p. 27. William A. Williams, *The Contours of American History* (Chicago: Quadrangle Books, 1961), pp. 317–319. Walter G. Sharrow, "William Henry

Seward and the Basis for American Empire, 1850–1860," *Pacific Historical Review*, XXXVI (April 1967), 325–342.

10. Baker, ed., *The Works of William H. Seward*, III, 657.

11. Ibid., p. 425.

12. Bancroft, *The Life of William H. Seward*, II, 58.

13. LaFeber, *The New Empire*, p. 30. Sharrow, "William Henry Seward and the Basis for American Empire," p. 339.

14. Baker, ed., *The Works of William H. Seward*, V, 571.

15. Ibid., IV, 331.

16. Smith, *Virgin Land*, p. 31.

17. Smith places this transition in 1898 with the capture of the Philippines; however, James J. Hill revived the idea as early as 1886. See Chapter 8.

18. William H. Seward, *Life and Public Services of John Quincy Adams* (Auburn: Derby, Miller and Company, 1851), pp. 206–208.

19. Bancroft, *The Life of William H. Seward*, II, 158.

20. Baker, ed., *The Works of William H. Seward*, IV, 686–688.

21. Ibid., pp. 122–123.

22. Morton Rothstein, "America in the International Rivalry for the British Wheat Market, 1860–1914," *Mississippi Valley Historical Review*, XLVII (December 1960), 401–418.

23. Henry C. Hubbart, *The Older Middle West, 1840–1880* (New York: D. Appleton-Century, 1936), pp. 158–159.

24. Frank L. Klement, *The Copperheads in the Middle West* (Chicago: University of Chicago Press, 1960), pp. 3–10.

25. Emerson D. Fite, "The Agricultural Development of the West in the Civil War," *Quarterly Journal of Economics*, XX (1906), 269.

26. Klement, *The Copperheads*, p. 11. Hubbart, *The Older Middle West*, p. 191.

27. James G. Randall and David Donald, *The Civil War and Reconstruction* (Boston: D. C. Heath & Co., 1961), pp. 458, 476. Hubbart, *The Older Middle West*, pp. 188–189.

28. *American Railroad Journal*, 5 and 12 October 1861. Alfred D. Chandler, Jr., *Henry Varnum Poor* (Cambridge: Harvard University Press, 1956), pp. 180–204.

29. Quoted in Henrietta M. Larson, *The Wheat Market and the Farmer in Minnesota, 1858–1900* (New York: Columbia University Press, 1926), p. 26 n 2.

30. Besse L. Pierce, *A History of Chicago: From Town to City, 1848–1871* (New York: Alfred Knopf, 1940), pp. 246–301.

31. U.S., Department of Commerce, Bureau of Statistics, *Historical Statistics of the United States, Colonial Times to 1957* (Washington: Government Printing Office [hereafter cited as GPO], 1960), p. 547.

32. U.S., Department of Agriculture, *Report of the Commissioner of Agriculture for the Year 1862* (Washington: GPO, 1863), p. 425.

33. Ibid., pp. 548–550.

34. James D. Richardson, ed., *Messages and Papers of the Presidents, 1789–1897* (Washington: GPO, 1898), VI, 135.

35. Lee Benson, *Merchants, Farmers, & Railroads: Railroad Regulation and New York Politics, 1850–1887* (Cambridge: Harvard University Press, 1955), pp. 17–18.

36. D. G. Brinton Thompson, *Ruggles of New York: A Life of Samuel B. Ruggles* (New York: Columbia University Press, 1946), p. 54.

37. Paul W. Gates, *Agriculture and the Civil War* (New York: Alfred Knopf, 1965), p. 350.

38. Ibid., p. 351.

39. *Proceedings of the National Ship Canal Convention,* held in Chicago 2, 3 June 1863 (Chicago: n. p., 1863).

40. Ibid.

41. Laura Alfred Poor, ed., *Life and Writings of John Alfred Poor* (New York: G. P. Putnam's Sons, 1892), pp. 211–217.

42. Emerson D. Fite, *Social and Industrial Conditions in the North During the Civil War* (New York: Frederick Ungar Publishing Co., 1963), p. 51. For the opposition of Boston, Philadelphia, and Baltimore merchants to the Chicago Convention, see George R. Woolfolk, *The Cotton Regency, the Northern Merchants and Reconstruction* (New York: Bookman Associates, 1958), pp. 120–122.

43. Pross, "Rivers and Harbors Appropriations Bills," p. 41.

44. Rendig Fels, *American Business Cycles* (Chapel Hill: University of North Carolina Press, 1959), pp. 92–96.

45. *Proceedings of the Commercial Convention,* held in Detroit, 11–14 July 1865 (Detroit, 1865), p. 8.

46. Ibid., pp. 25–28. For a fuller account of Taylor's position, see Alvin C. Gluek, Jr., *Minnesota and the Manifest Destiny of the Canadian Northwest* (Toronto: University of Toronto Press, 1965), p. 200.

47. J. Laughlin and A. Willis, *Reciprocity* (New York: 1903), pp. 51–58.

48. Frederick Merk, *Economic History of Wisconsin During the Civil War* (Madison: The Society Press, 1916), pp. 322–327.

49. Milwaukee *Sentinel,* 13 February 1866.

50. Ibid., 16 February 1866.

51. *Proceedings of the Mississippi River Improvement Convention,* held at Dubuque, Iowa, 14 and 15 February 1866.

52. Ibid.

53. Wyatt W. Belcher, *The Economic Rivalry Between St. Louis and Chicago, 1850–1880* (New York: Columbia University Press, 1947), p. 171. See also William E. Parrish, *Missouri Under Radical Rule 1865–1870* (Columbia: University of Missouri Press, 1965), pp. 189–191.

54. *Proceedings of the River Improvement Convention,* held in St. Louis, 12 and 13 February 1867 (St. Louis: 1867).

55. Ibid.

56. U.S., Department of Commerce, Bureau of Statistics, *Historical Statistics of the United States, Colonial Times to 1957,* p. 297.

57. *Commercial and Financial Chronicle,* 10 August 1867, 12 October 1867.

58. Robert P. Sharkey, *Money, Class, and Party: An Economic Study of the Civil War and Reconstruction* (Baltimore: Johns Hopkins University Press, 1959), pp. 135–140.

59. Department of Agriculture, *Report of the Commissioner of Agriculture for the Year 1869* (Washington: GPO, 1870), p. 5.

60. William T. Hutchinson, *Cyrus Hall McCormick* (New York: D. Appleton-Century Company, 1935), II, 466–467. Hutchinson gives an excellent description of the effects of the depression in various localities throughout the West.

61. Transactions of the Department of Agriculture of Illinois, 1873. *Proceedings of Farmers' Convention,* Bloomington, 15 and 16 January 1873, p. 227.

62. *Country Gentleman,* 22 April 1869.

63. William R. Willoughby, *The St. Lawrence Waterway* (Madison: University of Wisconsin Press, 1961), p. 45.

64. Quoted in Lester B. Shippee, *Canadian-American Relations 1849–1874* (New Haven: Yale University Press, 1939), p. 303.

65. Department of Agriculture, *Report of the Commissioner of Agriculture for the Year 1869,* p. 7.

66. James W. Taylor to Hugh McColluch, 13 November 1868, James W. Taylor MSS, Minnesota Historical Society, St. Paul, Minnesota.

67. Shippee, *Canadian-American Relations,* pp. 309–312.

68. Richardson, ed., *Messages and Papers of the Presidents,* IX, 3988–3989. Edgar W. McInnis, *The Unguarded Frontier: A History of American-Canadian Relations* (Garden City: Doubleday, Doran & Co., 1942), p. 262.

69. *Commercial and Financial Chronicle,* 20 November 1869.

70. Shippee, *Canadian-American Relations,* p. 315.

71. James A. Garfield to Hamilton Fish, 28 January 1870, Hamilton Fish MSS, Library of Congress.

72. Allan Nevins, *Hamilton Fish: The Inner History of the Grant Administration* (New York: Frederick Ungar Publishing Co., 1957), I, 423–428.

73. Ibid.

74. Richardson, ed., *Messages and Papers of the Presidents,* VII, 106.

75. Nevins, *Hamilton Fish,* II, 479–480.

76. Executive Documents of the State of Minnesota for the Year 1869, *Annual Message of Governor Austin to the Legislature of Minnesota* (Saint Paul: Press Printing Company, 1870), p. 16.

77. Richard N. Current, *Pine Logs and Politics: A Life of Philetus Sawyer, 1816–1900* (Madison: The State Historical Society of Wisconsin, 1950), p. 65.

78. U.S., Congress, House, Miscellaneous Documents, *Memorial and Resolution of Iowa Legislature on the Niagara Ship Canal, 4 April 1872,* 42d Cong., 2d sess., no. 124.

79. U.S., Congress, Senate, Miscellaneous Documents, *Resolution of Legislature of Kansas,* 42d Cong., 2d sess., no. 51. Ibid., *Resolution of Legislature of Nebraska,* 42d Cong., 2d sess., no. 55.

80. Reports and Resolutions, New Orleans, Keokuk, and Louisville Conventions, *Cheap Transportation a Public Necessity* (Dubuque: Daily Herald, 1869).

81. Baltimore *Gazette,* 5 October 1870.

82. Quoted in Hubbart, *The Older Middle West,* p. 241.

83. Secretary of the Treasury, *Annual Report for 1872* (Washington: GPO, 1873), pp. xix–xxiii.

84. Richardson, ed., *Messages and Papers of the Presidents,* IX, 4149.

85. U.S., Congress, Senate, *Report of the Select Committee on Transportation Routes to the Seaboard,* 43d Cong., 1st sess., no. 307, 2 vols. (Washington: GPO, 1874). (Hereafter cited as *Windom Committee Report.)*

86. *Windom Committee Report,* I, 38–45.

87. Ibid., 251–252.

88. Quoted in George A. Wright, "William Windom 1827–1890" (Master's thesis, University of Wisconsin, 1911), p. 49.

89. *Nation,* 7 May 1874.

90. *Railroad Gazette,* 16 May 1874.

91. *Congressional Record,* 43d Cong., 1st sess., p. 4618 (1874). From a statement by Representative Crocker of Massachusetts.

92. Saint Paul *Weekly Press,* 3 July 1873.

2

Railways, Waterways, and the Grange

THE GRANGER movement of the 1870s has generally been associated with farmer grievances against the railroads. And it is clear that railroad men did corrupt legislatures, disregard customers and shippers, abuse legal privilege, discriminate between locales, and often charge exorbitant rates. The public, however, gave little thought to the control of railways prior to 1870. Up to that time the extension of the railroad system was looked upon as a blessing; competition, it was assumed, would curtail those abuses. But, during the period of rapid railroad construction that followed the Civil War, it became evident that competition failed to curb the power of railroad corporations. Consolidations and rate agreements, in part made necessary by competition, aroused the antagonism of farmers and generated demands for government regulation.[1]

Farmers in the upper Mississippi Valley focused attention on the railroads and the need for government regulation. The feeling was quite general that the abuses of the railroad system resulted from the fact that the railroads were owned and controlled by men who lived in the East or abroad. "We today are sold, soul and body, in bonds to Europe, and if not there to our cities," lamented an Illinois farmer in 1873.[2] A few individuals on Wall Street were pictured as feudal lords enjoying almost total control of the railroad system of the country. Cartoons, offering in vehemence what they lacked in humor, ridiculed and damned eastern railroad presidents huddled over a table fixing rate schedules or consolidating competing roads.[3]

This anger and opposition was based on more than the collective need for a scapegoat, as was demonstrated and acknowledged by Charles Francis Adams, Jr., an astute and urbane easterner who was also a severe Granger critic. Many people who have read the attacks leveled at the Grange by Adams in the *North American Review* during 1875 have overlooked his admission that there were realistic causes for its growth. Adams did not believe (as did many easterners) that the movement was baseless, or, still worse, communistic. He argued that the protest could be traced to the "improvident bargain" that the West, in its eagerness for railroads, had made with the East. The West had given "for her longed-for-railroads all that she had, all that anyone asked; and now that she had them she began to shrewdly suspect that her bargain had after all been somewhat of the hardest. It was indeed a case of absentee ownership, with all that those words imply." Not content to leave it to the readers to draw their own conclusions about absentee ownership, Adams made an explicit comparison between the servants of the East India Company in India and railroad officials in the American West. Both groups exploited the local population in order to meet the incessant demand for dividends of stockholders in England or the East.[4]

To break the colonial grip that eastern and foreign capital imposed upon them through the railroad system, the Grange leaders evolved four broad strategies to attain economic independence. The first approach came to be known as the condensation theory because it was based on having the farmers reduce the weight, and thus enhance the value, of all their products by "selling less in the bushel and more on the hoof and in fleece, less in lint and more in warp and woof. . . ."[5] The ratio of transportation costs to the value of the products would thereby be greatly decreased. The panacea for the ills bred by excessive dependence on railroads was to be found in tanneries, oil mills, paper mills, woolen mills, meatpacking and curing houses, cheese and butter factories, candle factories, and a multitude of other secondary industries.

This systematic diversification of livestock and cereal operations would, so the Grangers hoped, provide another assist in their battle with transportation agencies.[6] If the farmer produced his own cereals, raised his own timber, manufactured his own butter, and grew his own vegetables, then he would meet the needs of his family independent of railroads or navigable waterways. Diversified farming would also make the farmer less vulnerable to the fluctuations of the market and to the variations of the weather.

A third strategy called for the establishment of enterprises in addition to those connected with processing, in order to create a home market. Plowshops, reaper factories, and iron foundries would draw laborers from the farming community into urban areas where they would have to be fed, clothed, and housed. Those who remained on the farm would find an important local market for their surplus products without having to pay to send them long distances (and through the hands of numerous middlemen).[7]

But most Grangers in the West recognized that agriculture would dominate their region in the foreseeable future, and that there would continue to be large surpluses. Easterners and foreigners would continue to do the manufacturing while the farmers of the West fed them and furnished them with raw materials. Cheap and abundant facilities for transportation were, therefore, absolutely necessary if the farmers were to obtain an equitable share of the profits of their labor. "We

shall . . . advocate for every state in every practicable way,"
the Grangers proclaimed in their Declaration of Purposes,
"all facilities for transporting cheaply to the seaboard, or between producers and consumers, all the productions of our
country."[8]

As he analyzed these strategies for economic independence,
the farmer in the West confronted an historic predicament.
His region failed to develop at a rate sufficient to absorb the
enlarged production made possible by increased inputs of labor and capital on virgin soils. Despite favorable trends in the
diversification of agriculture, in the growth of secondary industries, and in the development of urban-industrial centers,
the western farmer remained dependent upon distant markets
and upon a system of intermediaries in transportation and
wholesaling. Indeed, his reliance on the market actually increased. "I am simply a tenant on my own farm," contended
one Iowa farmer in 1873. "I am not consulted as to the share
of my crop which transportation companies may require to
lay the surplus in a market."[9] The conclusion was inevitable
that only improved transportation would bring the primary
farmer closer to his market and at the same time facilitate
the growth of more diversified activity in his region.[10]

In an article recommended to the general body of the
Grange, William Grosvenor offered an over-simplified, but
readily understandable, summary of the problem. "As far as
the price of crops is controlled by distant markets all the
profits and even the very existence of agriculture depend upon
the rate charged for transporting its products."[11] For the
farmers of the West, the rates charged for transportation
meant primarily the rates charged by railroads. There were
two interrelated aspects to the problem. First, the unjust discrimination in the arrangement of the rates; second, the general high cost of transportation to market. For the problems of
discrimination, farmers sought solutions in rate-law reforms.
To obtain cheap transportation, they advocated canal and

river improvements, government-built railroads, and low-cost narrow-gauge lines.

In the West, where the Grangers were numerous and politically organized, state regulatory laws offered a practical way to assert popular authority over tyrannical railroad companies owned by eastern and foreign stock and bond holders. High local rates, rate discriminations, and other arbitary railroad practices then would end. William C. Flagg, president of the Illinois State Farmers' Association, provided a common rationale for the advocates of state regulation of railroads. He pointed out that John Stuart Mill opposed private control of natural monopolies such as roads, canals, and railroads. They were part of the very structure of the marketplace, and therefore had to serve all people equitably.[12] The authors of the Illinois Constitution captured the prevailing sentiment for regulation in a single phrase: "Railways . . . are hereby declared public highways."[13]

Fully aware of their dependence on distant markets to absorb surplus production, the Grangers also advocated national measures to meet the transportation problem. "Illinois [railroad] commissioners will want cheap freights to the seaboard; but they are powerless," complained William Flagg. "Indiana, Ohio, and New York, at least, are in the way. National legislation or regulation is needed."[14] Thus, many Grangers joined Flagg in a vigorous campaign for national regulation of the railroads on the same order as state regulation. The movement climaxed with the House passage of the McCrary bill in 1874. The most significant feature of that bill, in contrast to later federal railroad bills, reflected the agitation for cheap transportation for through traffic from the interior to the seaboard. The bill provided for a nine-man board of commissioners, to be appointed by the President, which would establish maximum rates on all interstate railroads. The McCrary bill, however, did not survive the opposition of entrenched Senate conservatives.[15]

Most Grangers hoped to achieve the objective of national railroad regulation and cheap transportation through a successful campaign for increased internal improvements appropriations. It was widely believed that the causes of high through rates were insufficient facilities and lack of competition. To regulate the railroad system nationally, therefore, the Grangers demanded Congress improve rivers and harbors, build canals, open the St. Lawrence route, and construct trunk-line railroads. Such a program would serve the farmer a double purpose. The vast economic and political power of the major railroads would be weakened, and cheap transportation would be provided to the markets of the world.

Historians of the Granger movement have tended to concentrate upon and emphasize the problem of rate discriminations, thereby slighting the efforts to lower general transportation costs.[16] Several reasons may be suggested to account for this trend. The agitation against rate discrimination seemed to originate primarily from the farmers, and appeared to have been strongest in those states where the Grangers were most numerous. It also resulted in legislation bearing the Granger name. The demand for cheap transportation, on the other hand, was clearly not made by farmers alone. Neither was it embodied in any legislative act, nor did it originate or arise solely in Granger states.

A recent study of the state railroad laws of the 1870s in the upper Mississippi Valley by George Miller challenges the view that the legislation was produced by Granger agitation. He argues that the so-called Granger laws were prepared by lawyers for merchants and shippers who used the Granger revolt to broaden the political base of protest against railroad practices. The farmer was not excluded from the rate reform struggle, but political action centered around local connecting points and boards of trade. Farmers, as a single united class, Miller argues, were "primarily" concerned with cheap transportation to the seaboard, not rate reform laws.[17]

Miller has pointed the way toward an important reevaluation of the Granger contribution to the cheap transportation movement. So long as farmers produced a surplus at failing prices, the need for cheap transportation to distant markets was a principal concern and an urgent necessity. The careers of Joseph H. Osborn of Wisconsin and Col. W. B. Smedley of Iowa chart the course of the Granger cheap transportation movement and its ties to state regulation and the demands for expanded overseas markets.

Osborn's Struggle with the Railroads

Joseph Osborn was one of the most astute and influential leaders of the Patrons of Husbandry. Educated in mathematics and civil engineering in New York, Osborn settled in Oshkosh, Wisconsin, in 1844 to engage in teaching and Indian trading. He later became a gentleman farmer. Intelligent, articulate, and business-minded, Osborn served not only as leader of the Grange movement for cheap transportation, but as purchasing agent and member of the Executive Committee of the Wisconsin State Grange, state railroad commissioner, member of the National Grange Committee on Cooperation, and Worthy Master of the Wisconsin State Grange.[18]

Osborn's interest in transportation problems is symbolized by his membership in the Grange-inspired Reform party, which made restrictive railroad legislation the main plank of its platform. By fusing with the Democrats, the Reformers won the November 1873 state election. They secured control of the Assembly and placed William R. Taylor, a prominent Granger, in the governor's chair.[19] As a member of the Executive Committee of the state Grange, Osborn hoped to exert great influence on the governor's political program. "I regard it as a foregone conclusion of the American people that the political power of RR Corporations is to be broken" he wrote the governor-elect, "and again that it is equally certain that the financial policy of RR's is to be made answerable to law."[20] Osborn wanted bold and aggressive moves against the railroads to satisfy the Grangers and to induce others to rally to the banner of the Reform party.

That expectation about the political effects of a strong railroad bill was a manifestation of a deep and basic commitment made by Osborn and other Grangers to the practice of representative government and the maintenance of an equitable marketplace structure. When he wrote to Taylor, Osborn made no mention of any particular bill and evidenced no understanding of the practical difficulties of administering a railroad law. Those were secondary matters. Other questions than those strictly relating to transportation were involved in the consideration of government regulation of railroads. The very organization of society was at stake, he explained to F. B. Thurber of the National Cheap Transportation Association: "We are gravitating towards a crisis having for its animating spirit the demand for new relations between capital and labor. [There is] a sense of oppression among the masses, a sense of injustice. . . ." and nothing had brought this about more than the attitude of railroad managers. The railroads, Osborn concluded, "must be brought in harmony with the aspirations of the great producing class."[21]

Passed by the legislature in March 1874, the Wisconsin Railway Law (usually known as the Potter Law) gained a reputation as being the most radical of all Granger laws. The editors of the *Nation* spoke for many easterners when they condemned the Potter Law as "spoilation as flagrant as any ever proposed by Karl Marx."[22] Maximum rates were set considerably below the existing level, and a three-man commission appointed by the governor was established to enforce the law. The executive body of the state Grange met with Gov-

ernor Taylor on 17 March 1874 and, joined by a committee
chosen by the Patrons who had been members of the legislature, recommended Joseph Osborn for railroad commissioner.
One month later he assumed his duties as chairman of the
Wisconsin State Railroad Commission in charge of administering the Potter Law.[23]

Osborn found his task extraordinarily difficult. The two
largest railroads in the state, the Chicago, Milwaukee, & St.
Paul and Chicago & Northwestern, denounced the Potter
Law as confiscatory and advised Governor Taylor that they
would not obey its provisions until it was tested in the courts.
Other groups demanded rigid and strict enforcement of the
law, which Osborn knew to be imperfect and, in certain aspects, impractical.[24] But his commitment to the principle of
the power of the state over private corporations helped sustain
Osborn under these conflicting pressures.

The opponents' main argument was that no outside capital
would be invested in Wisconsin railroads until the law was
repealed. Osborn considered this a subtle, corrupt, and dangerous tactic, used by eastern railroad interests and their allies
to retain their power in the state. When one of his assistants,
who was gathering information on the theory and practice of
railroad regulation, suggested that Wisconsin might have
gone too far by giving the impression that railway investments
in America were unsafe, Osborn took offense. "The control of
the roads by legislative enactment is a foregone conclusion,
but control does not mean confiscation and it is a gross *per-
version* of the *intent* of Western people to endeavor to fasten
upon them the odious [*sic*] of adopting any legislation which
contemplates injustice to railway companies."[25] The Grangers
of Wisconsin, he added, understood the importance of railroads to their prosperity and did not intend to block further
investments. It was the "aggressive power of organized capital," as Osborn phrased it in the midst of the court fight between the railroads and the state, that had to be curbed.

On 15 September 1874, Chief Justice Edward G. Ryan of the Wisconsin Supreme Court declared the Potter Law valid. The presidents of the St. Paul and Northwestern companies then publicly agreed to honor the court decision. Governor Taylor, Osborn, and other Grangers were understandably enthusiastic over what they considered the vindication of a great principle. "The open defiance of the laws—the power which assumed to be greater than the sovereignty of the people was met and rebuked by both the executive and judicial authorities."[26] The railroads felt differently, and directed their energies toward regaining control of the legislature.

In their campaign for the repeal of the Potter Law, the railroads had the assistance of numerous newspapers inside and outside the state. Time and again, these newspapers asserted that the railroad law had destroyed the credit of the state. Replying in the pages of the *Bulletin* of the Wisconsin State Grange, Osborn attempted to defend the Potter Law against its enemies. He declared that the law needed to be perfected, not repealed; that the railroads were using the law as a scapegoat for bad management; and that the falling off of railroad investment in the state was the inevitable result of the mania for railroad building in the early 1870s.[27]

But Osborn's arguments did not carry the battle. Governor Taylor, running on a platform demanding the continued regulation of the railroads by the state, was defeated in the October 1875 elections by the Republican candidate, who was expected to favor the repeal of the Potter Law. The Republicans also obtained a majority in both houses of the legislature. Early in the session of the new legislature the railroad forces introduced their bill. It was passed by large majorities in the Senate and House and became law in March 1876. The measure was "practically a total surrender of effective control of railroad rates by the state," and marked the end of Granger railroad legislation in Wisconsin.[28]

Osborn was, of course, deeply disappointed. Several of his

friends suggested that the differences between Democrats and Reformers, and the weakness of Governor Taylor under railroad pressures, undermined support for the law.[29] The more important factor was probably the decline in the numbers and the influence of the Wisconsin Grange. In order to reverse that trend, and to revitalize business cooperatives, Osborn returned to active participation in the affairs of state and national Granges in March 1876.[30]

Osborn's activities on behalf of the cheap transportation movement were an extension of the same principles behind his campaign for state regulation of railroads. If the farmers of the West were not to be crushed by a marketplace system increasingly biased in favor of railroads and other organized capital, the government would have to guarantee easy and cheap access to distant markets. State regulation of the railroads appeared politically sound to Osborn. But national regulation of the same kind, though desirable, seemed impractical. Instead, Osborn pushed for Congress to provide funds for the improvement of key waterways to the seaboard.[31]

Osborn was not alone. Almost as soon as they were organized, the state Granges of the Mississippi Valley and the Far West began to agitate for the construction of new canals, and for the improvement of river and lake channels. Though many small proposals were favored as local projects, the scheme that received the most general approval of the Grangers was a continuous navigable water-route from the Lakes to the Gulf via the Fox and Wisconsin rivers and the Mississippi River.[32]

By 1873, Grange leaders recognized that their potential political power, if well-directed and organized, could be used to secure federal appropriations for the internal improvement project. Prompted by the Missouri State Grange, the Executive Committee of the Iowa Grange issued a call for a meeting at Keokuk, Iowa, on 16 October 1873. Osborn and other executives of the various Mississippi Valley Granges received the following invitation: "You are earnestly requested to be present as business of great importance to our Order will be presented for consideration viz; the subject of Cheap Transportation—the improvement of the Mississippi River, the natural outlet of this region to the European markets; and other matters of interest."[33] As the wording of this call indicates, the Granger drive for cheap transportation was predicated upon the need for alternative routes to foreign markets.

Osborn and John Cochrane, Worthy Master of the Wisconsin Grange, were appointed to the five-man transportation committee of the Keokuk Convention. The committee report outlined the political strategy proposed for the Granger fight for improved water transportation. First, each state executive committee was charged with corresponding with their Congressmen about the speedy improvement of the mouth of the Mississippi River, the channel of the river where the government had already commenced work, and the improvement of the Fox and Wisconsin rivers. This correspondence would be sent to a central committee (to be appointed by the convention), which in turn would circulate a shortened version to all state and subordinate Granges in the country. By holding Representatives and Senators strictly accountable for their votes on given improvement bills, the Grangers could then "take such measures as will in no uncertain terms, manifest the determination of the Order to insist upon prompt and decisive action by our National legislature. . . ."[34]

The report of the transportation committee prompted a discussion that revealed the difficulties of organizing effective political action for specific improvements. The delegate from Indiana thought that a demand should be made for a double-track freight railroad, built and operated by the government, which would run from the Mississippi River to the Atlantic seaboard. That system would furnish proper and speedy transport for livestock. In response, one delegate suggested that the opening of the Mississippi, by relieving the trunk railroads from carrying so much grain, would allow more facilities for transporting livestock. Osborn's reply probably carried more weight. By concentrating on one set of demands and securing them, Osborn argued, "other good will follow."[35]

When the report was adopted, the convention turned to nominating members for the central committee. Osborn was nominated for the chairmanship. Feeling that the responsibility belonged to those who had called the meeting, Osborn declined in favor of E. R. Shankland of Iowa. The convention refused to accept his withdrawal, however, and with great reluctance Osborn took command of the Grangers' cheap transportation movement.[36]

The most significant aspect of the strategy outlined in the Keokuk meeting, at least for Osborn, was the idea of holding Congressmen to "STRICT, REAL, and ACTUAL" accountability. The capitalization of the phrase was indication of the fear and suspicion that Grangers, including Osborn, felt toward national politicians. He once conceded that he had lost all faith in the sincerity of assurances from Congressmen "unless prompted by a healthy fear of public indignation."[37]

Politics in Oshkosh justified that feeling. Located on Lake Winnebago along the line of the Fox and Wisconsin rivers, the people of Oshkosh held a common vision of their city as a great inland seaport. With a ship canal connecting the Fox and Wisconsin rivers (separated by only one mile), and the improvements of those rivers, cargo vessels could steam all the way from the Gulf of Mexico to the Atlantic seaboard, stopping at the port of Oshkosh on the way.[38] Such was the dream. But money was required, and the support of one man was needed. That man was Philetus Sawyer, Republican Representative from Winnebago County and a resident of Oshkosh. Sawyer was the leading member of the House Commerce Committee. From his first speech on the floor of the House in 1867 until the end of his congressional career, Sawyer appeared to be the very embodiment of the West's drive for internal improvements, water and rail.[39] But to readers of the Democratic Oshkosh *Times* (including Osborn), the intensity of his interest in and commitment to the Fox-Wisconsin river project was suspect.[40]

When Sawyer returned to Oshkosh in 1870 to campaign for his second term, the *Times* denied that Sawyer truly favored the improvements. The paper argued that Sawyer was the candidate of the Chicago & Northwestern Railroad which ran through Oshkosh and competed with the river route from there to Lake Michigan, and asserted he had been renominated because the Northwestern "directed by Chicago interests, dictated it; an interest in direct opposition to, and which has in fact killed the River Improvement."[41] Sawyer had succeeded in transferring the faltering canal and river improvements from the state to the federal government in 1872, but the *Times* insisted that he had done only what all Wisconsin Congressmen were compelled to do by public pressure. "His most barefaced attempt at a fraudulent reputation" contended the *Times*, "is in relation to the Fox and Wisconsin Improvement."[42]

Sawyer's failure to censure two colleagues in the Credit Mobilier Scandal in March 1873 no doubt confirmed the suspicions of discontented Winnebago County farmers that special interests prevailed over the general welfare in the halls of Congress. Osborn was one such farmer who knew Sawyer's ways, and it is not surprising that, as leader of the Granger cheap transportation moveemnt, he based his strategy upon the strict accountability of Congressmen to the demands for the implementation of the great waterway scheme.

A few weeks after the adjournment of the Keokuk Convention, Osborn set in motion the wheels of the Granger movement for cheap transportation to the seaboard. Every Wisconsin Senator and Representative received a circular letter from the Executive Committee of the state Grange demanding a reply as to his position on the improvement of the Fox,

Wisconsin, and Mississippi rivers. He asked Governor-elect
Taylor, who had often indicated his support for the Fox-
Wisconsin improvement, to mention the Keokuk resolutions
in his inaugural address.[43] Not only did a delay in the improvements provide an indirect subsidy to the railroads, but
the speedy completion of the project "would so stimulate the
competitive enterprise of the great eastern cities, as to ensure
the construction of increased railroad facilities." Osborn also
expressed the hope that the cause would be adopted by the
governors of other states, and so extend the influence on the
Congress.

Osborn then asked the leading Grangers of other states to
follow Wisconsin's lead on the Keokuk resolve. Osborn hinted
to D. Wyatt Aiken, a South Carolina member of the National
Executive, of the possibilities of an alliance between western
and southern Grange members on the issue. Knowing of
Aiken's public interest in the opening of the mouth of the
Mississippi, Osborn expected full cooperation. "I now propose
to send a form of petition to Congress to every Grange in the
U.S.," he explained to Aiken, "with request to have them
signed as numerously as possible and then pass them to their
respective members of Congress. The project ought to be
pushed through on its own merits and not omnibussed up
with all sorts of projects." If it should be delayed in committee, then, at a signal given by Osborn, "each Executive Committee of every State would forward to their respective Senators and Representatives a respectful application to *report
progress. . . .*"[44] In view of the results of the 1873 elections,
Osborn felt that Congress could not underestimate the determination of the Grangers to have improved waterways to the
seaboard.

Osborn hoped to receive the most help from the Iowa
Grange. Not only did Iowa farmers, because of their geograph-
ical location, stand to benefit most from the improvements
called for in the petitions, but the Iowa organization was the

largest and best organized in the country.[45] "When it becomes known that other states besides Wisconsin have addressed the Senators and Representatives on the transportation subject," Osborn wrote Shankland, "it will be seen at once to be a *concentrated* movement, that there was *combination* and consequently *power* and . . . influence."[46]

The Grangers were also prepared to work with the National Cheap Transportation Association, although dominated by New York merchants, in order to exert more political pressure upon Congress. Osborn carried on a regular correspondence with R. H. Ferguson and F. B. Thurber, respectively secretary and president of the association, from 1872 to 1875.[47] When invited by Ferguson to the Washington, D. C., meeting of January 1874, Osborn wrote Shankland that he would not be able to attend because of the state Grange meeting being held at the same time. But he did recommend that someone from the Grange attend. "Judging from the circular sent me . . . the programme is more comprehensive than ours, it includes the RR question as well as water communication—but it will doubtless act as an aid to our project as arranged at Keokuk." Osborn felt that the direction of the Cheap Transportation Association was the same as the Grange's, but added that it lacked "that power to *enforce* which is possessed by our organization if it will only act as a unit."[48]

At the outset, in December 1873, Osborn had high hopes that his effort would succeed. Senators Timothy O. Howe and Matthew H. Carpenter of Wisconsin had responded favorably to the demand for assurances on internal improvement bills. The forthcoming meeting of the Iowa Grange would certainly endorse the plan, and an alliance with the Cheap Transportation Association would provide additional strength. "Everything looks favorable for a general demand for something to be done," Osborn concluded, "the masses of the people are in no temper to be refused."[49] By the end of the month, however, Osborn's mood had changed very considerably.

The first disappointment was the failure of the Iowa Grange to endorse the Keokuk resolution. Worthy Master Smedley opposed any one plan to meet the growing need of the West for cheap transportation. He did favor improvements on the Mississippi and Fox and Wisconsin rivers. But he emphasized the importance of a double-track railroad built by the government as an alternative route to the seaboard.[50] That proposal enjoyed wide support from Grangers in Indiana, Illinois, Kansas, Missouri, and South Carolina as well as Iowa, especially after the trunk-line pools threatened to raise through rates.[51]

Shortly after the Iowa meeting, Osborn received a call from the secretary of the Minnesota Grange. It had also taken independent action so far as the Keokuk recommendations were concerned.[52] Though Osborn received many letters approving the course determined at Keokuk, the harsh reality was that no state, except Wisconsin, had cooperated in obtaining assurances from their Senators and Congressmen by the opening weeks of 1874. Osborn felt that such independent action by the state Granges made it impossible to carry out the real spirit of the Keokuk resolution. The internal organization of the state Granges and the naiveté of Grange leadership were responsible for the situation.

"Our organization even in the 'upper houses' has very little sense of the power of combination," Osborn lamented. "There seems to be no appreciation of the power of the Order to affect important results in our national legislature and yet what tremendous dormant power we really possess in that direction. . . ." By not cooperating on the Keokuk plan, Osborn felt, nine-tenths of Granger power had been thrown away. Despite his frustration and disappointment, however, Osborn resolved to continue the effort. If the Grangers were to win a victory, they would have to continue to "manifest a lively determination to keep 'pushing things.'"[53]

The Wisconsin Grange encouraged Osborn. Worthy Master

Cochrane referred to the Keokuk resolution as the embodiment of the "relations existing between the people at large, their material interest, and their representation in Congress," and then presented the favorable replies of Senators Howe and Carpenter and Rep. Jeremiah Rusk to the demands for completion of internal improvements. But no reply had been received from other Wisconsin Congressmen. "There is but one conclusion to be arrived at from this want of attention to our request," Cochrane said, pointing out the vital importance of cheap transportation to the farmers of Wisconsin, "that so far as regards the people themselves and their representatives, the connection is broken from the date of election." The people of Wisconsin would now have to join battle with "creatures of their own creation" in order to solve the great question of cheap transportation.[54] Even the New York *Herald* applauded the effectiveness of the Wisconsin Grange in revealing the insincerity of the promises made by Congressmen.[55]

Following the state Grange meeting, Osborn began the wide circulation of a petition demanding congressional action on the great waterway project. The Chicago *Times* followed Osborn's work in Wisconsin and adjoining states, and noted that Louisiana was "taking up the cry and is strong in urging the consummation of these projects." The campaign was "being felt in Congress," concluded the *Times* correspondent.[56] Petitions to Congress were necessary, but Osborn needed an endorsement from the National Grange to provide additional leverage in securing appropriations from the Congress. Two days before the National Grange meeting in St. Louis in February 1874, Osborn met with the members of the Central Committee formed at the Keokuk Convention.[57] Though there is no record of their discussions, plans were undoubtedly made to win a resolution favoring the plan for the Mississippi, Fox, and Wisconsin rivers. Osborn was only partially successful. The "Declaration of Purposes" adopted by the National

Grange advocated the improvement of facilities for cheap transportation in every practicable way, but the only specific project that was generally approved by the Grange was one calling for the Mississippi to be made navigable with a permanent outlet to the Gulf.[58]

The failure of the National Grange to endorse the Fox-Wisconsin river project marked the end of the Central Committee established at Keokuk and the passing of the leadership of the Granger cheap transportation movement from Osborn to the National Grange's Committee on Transportation and Cooperation headed by Col. W. B. Smedley, Worthy Master of the Iowa State Grange. Osborn continued to manifest a keen interest in the cheap transportation movement, but his major efforts after February 1874 centered on the state regulation of railroads and on business cooperation.[59]

Smedley's Work for Free and Open Highways

Smedley led the final phase of the Granger cheap transportation movement, and under his direction the international significance of the movement became explicit and paramount. Smedley was born in New York in 1825. He moved to Iowa after serving in the Union Army and settled in Cresco, Howard County, as a fruit farmer. He was elected Worthy Master of the Iowa State Grange in 1873 to succeed Dudley Adams, newly elected Master of the National Grange, and served for two years.[60] Like Osborn, Smedley was a vigorous advocate of Granger business cooperatives. Smedley believed that the success of Iowa cooperatives, and of the farmers generally, hinged upon cheap transportation to market.

A state railroad law was the first step in solving the transportation problem. The failure of the state Assembly to pass a regulatory bill in February 1873, despite the presence of

1,200 Grangers meeting in Des Moines, provoked bitter resentment. During the summer a group of Grangers organized the Anti-Monopoly party, and made government control of railroads the main plank of their platform. They nominated a candidate for governor and a full slate of candidates for the legislature. Shortly after the Anti-Monopoly party convention, the Republican party renominated Gov. Cyrus C. Carpenter, a prominent Granger and vigorous advocate of state regulation. In the November elections Carpenter retained the governorship, but 50 percent of the lower house were Anti-Monopolists and 70 percent were Grangers. A regulatory law, therefore, appeared to be a certainty at the 1874 session of the Iowa state legislature.[61]

With a Granger in the governor's mansion, a majority of Grangers controlling the legislature, and the Iowa Grange at the peak of its strength, Worthy Master Smedley spoke with considerable authority at the fourth session of the state Grange in December 1873. He knew the complexity of railroad regulation and he did not offer a specific, detailed proposal for regulation. "One point must, however, be borne in mind," Smedley began, "the ratio of present production in our State which must find a market abroad, to what it will be in the future is but small."[62] With a just system of transportation, Smedley predicted, Iowa farm production would double within ten years. The states along the Mississippi River, Smedley insisted, "need and must have the mouth of the river so improved that vessels of heavy drought can pass the bar and load at any point." By diverting a portion of western products, a navigable Mississippi would give the farmer a choice of markets.

Improvement of the Mississippi would be of no value whatever if Chicago railroads continued to discriminate against the Iowa river towns, Smedley believed. Such discrimination was one of the greatest evils of the railroad system in Iowa, and he presented a table of rates to document his argument.

On the Rock Island Line, for example, the farmer had to pay
sixty-six cents to ship a bushel of wheat from Des Moines, in
the center of the state, to Davenport on the river (a distance
of 168 miles). It cost only nine cents more to send the same
bushel of wheat to Chicago, a distance of 351 miles. Given
such rates, no wheat would ever stop at Davenport for shipment on the Mississippi.[63]

Other internal improvements were also necessary to insure
the prosperity of the Iowa farmer, Smedley asserted. A Niagara ship-canal would provide a through water route to the
seaboard (with low rates) during the spring and summer,
and a double-track freight railroad from some point on the
Missouri River to the Atlantic coast would prevent trunk
lines from raising freight rates during the closed period of
navigation on the Lakes and Erie Canal. Smedley revealed
the intensity of feeling against the control of Congress by
eastern interests when he remarked that the cost to the government of these internal improvements would be a "pit-
tance compared to the assistance which Eastern manufacturers
derive from protective tariffs."[64]

The report on transportation delivered by Smedley was
adopted at the conclusion of the Iowa Grange meeting as the
general sense of the body of delegates, and sent as a memorial
to the state and national legislatures. To push the matter at
the state level, a committee of twelve Grangers was chosen
to memorialize the legislature on specific regulatory proposals.
Smedley was not a member of the committee, but he approved
its report and considered it a reflection of his own views.[65]
Headed by John J. Scott, president of the Iowa State Agricultural Society, the Granger Committee met with Hon. John Q.
Tufts of the House Committee on Railways in Des Moines
early in February 1874.

Scott tried to impress Tufts with the point that the Grangers were not initiating a war against the railroads. The Order
wanted a bill that was fair to the people as well as to the

railroads and, at the same time, a law that would "tend to such extension of reaching the markets of the world as seems to be demanded in the present and must become a necessity at no distant day." Scott admitted that the task of reconciling the interests of the people and the railroads, in a law that would extend markets, would not be easy. When asked by Tufts to provide a trial bill to accomplish those objectives, Scott declined to try.[66]

The failure of the Iowa Grangers to offer anything beyond the most general recommendations for a railroad law opened the way for the passage of a maximum rate law drawn to meet the interests of Mississippi River town merchants.[67] The Anti-Monopolists in the legislature were pledged to secure a strong railroad bill, and the maximum rate schedule appeared to satisfy that objective. The Granger Committee, however, opposed the bill on the grounds that it merely shifted a portion of the rate paid by one product, or for one distance, to others, in no way solving the problem of cheap transportation. Nevertheless, they felt obliged to support the law once it passed. Smedley felt the law had been designed in good faith, and objected most to the weakness of the enforcement clauses. When the Chicago, Burlington & Quincy refused to obey the law, Smedley wrote to Railroad Commissioner Osborn for his experience in enforcing the Potter Law. "We propose to fight the matter to the bitter end," Smedley said, referring to the court suits against the CB&Q, "and determine whether capital or the people shall rule."[68]

That the transportation problem extended well beyond the boundaries of Iowa was clear to Smedley, Governor Carpenter, and other Grange leaders. For example, in his well-known speech before the State Agricultural Society, Carpenter argued that if the power of Iowa to regulate railroad rates was acknowledged, "still it will not carry the power to regulate transportation in the length and breadth to protect the people. Railroads are now not only *national* but *international*.

The great lines extend not only through a state but across states."[69] When Carpenter received an invitation to send a delegate to the Washington, D. C., meeting of the American Cheap Transportation Association in January 1874, he understandably chose Worthy Master Smedley, who held views similar to his own.[70]

At the meeting, Smedley heard the leading theorists of the time expound on the transportation question, and their influence on Smedley is apparent in his subsequent speeches. A year later, Smedley became a vice-president of the American Board of Trade and Transportation, the organization that succeeded the American Cheap Transportation Association.[71] By the opening of the St. Louis meeting of the National Grange in February 1874, Smedley was preeminently qualified to lead the cheap transportation movement. He was well informed on the subject, an articulate speaker, Worthy Master of the largest Grange in the country, and in touch with other like-minded organizations. His report from the Committee on Transportation and Cooperation is one of the key documents of the Granger cheap transportation movement.

The report opened with the flat assertion that facilities for transportation were wholly inadequate, and that freight costs were so excessive as to be onerous. Three steps by the federal government would relieve the situation. First, the channel of the Mississippi River must be made navigable and a permanent outlet at the Gulf secured. Second, Congress must regulate internal commerce so as to bring freight rates into a reasonable relationship to the actual costs of transportation. Finally, the government must pass legislation "to restore our foreign commerce to its former condition of efficiency"; that would raise the general level of prices and lower the burden of freight charges on the producer.[72]

The link made by Smedley between internal improvements and an expanded foreign trade was the central theme of the Windom Report published in 1874. Smedley read the final report closely. To his mind, the facts and ideas it presented should be "brought home to the thought and understanding of any farmer."[73] He quoted it extensively in his speeches and made its arguments his own.

For example, Smedley used the conclusions of the Windom Report at the fifth session of the Iowa State Grange in December 1874. He enumerated the amount and value of wheat, corn, and other Iowa farm products in excess of the local demand, and estimated the cost of shipping those surpluses to Liverpool at $72 million. Of the cost per bushel to ship wheat to Liverpool, nearly half was paid as freight between the Iowa farm and the Chicago market. Unless the internal freight charges on export commodities were radically reduced, Smedley predicted, the United States would be shut out of the markets of the world. Russian exports of wheat, from 1868 to 1872, had increased 70 million bushels, while those of the United States for the same period decreased 11 million bushels. "When we understand that Russia has just begun to adopt the handling of grain by elevator," Smedley warned, "and that the cost of their freight is diminished, while our grain fields are receding . . . from the seaboard, the prediction is not so visionary that when Russia has driven us from the markets of Europe, she will become our active competitor in the markets of Portland and Boston, unless cheaper means of transportation are provided."[74] Without mentioning the Windom Report by name, Smedley had incorporated its principal arguments into his own thought.

The National Grange meeting in Charleston, South Carolina, during February 1875 developed into a debate over the alternatives posed in the Windom Report: developing the southern market, or stressing the foreign market. Many southern speakers paid tribute to the unity of the agricultural classes of the South and West, stressed the possibilities of direct trade between western food producers and southern consumers, and emphasized the importance of having the

West redirect its export trade through southern ports.[75] Speaking as chairman of the Grangers' Transportation Committee, Smedley delivered the western reply.

Increased commercial cooperation between the West and the South was important, he admitted, and pointed out that Iowa Grange cooperatives had successfully experimented with shipments of produce to Georgia and South Carolina. But Iowans had learned that such trade was limited by inadequate direct rail connections. No doubt delighting his southern listeners, Smedley then proposed a government-built railroad from the Missouri River to southeastern centers. But, he added, the Grangers would have to continue their exports until that was accomplished. In that connection, he pointed out, there were barriers to commerce, not from inadequate facilities but from the monopolistic pooling practices of the trunk-line railroads. In a ringing phrase Smedley summed up the direction of his work: "To break up these impediments and to make a free and open highway for our exports is the work, aim, and object of our Order."[76]

The resolutions adopted by the delegates show the impress of Smedley's hand. Congress should provide "cheap and rapid means of transportation between all sections of the country and to the markets of the world."[77] Specific recommendations were offered for a freight railroad from the Missouri River to tidewater, for the completion of the Texas & Pacific Railroad, and for the opening of the mouth of the Mississippi River. The completion of the Eads jetties would open the Mississippi to the commerce of the world and bring a measure of prosperity to the whole Mississippi Valley.

The sale abroad of a large portion of each year's crop had become an accepted dogma among the leadership of the National Grange who met in Charleston. Smedley spoke for many western farmers who would be happier if their surplus grain moved overseas without going through the middlemen, money lords, and railroad magnates of the East. The trunk-line pools, begun in 1874, crystallized these feelings. The *Bulletin* of the Wisconsin Grange, for example, warned of the "selfish greed of Eastern. railway mongers" whose "long skinny fingers [were] grasping at the splendid crop of the West."[78] Such fears naturally suggested a diversion of shipments and an economic realignment between the West and South, and the idea was especially strong within the states along the Mississippi River.

Although the sharp memories of the war, and conflicts over reconstruction, prevented the political unity of the Mississippi Valley, Grangers (and some merchants) did hope that New Orleans could become a key point in an alternate route for the export of farm commodities. These economic and political considerations were met by a comprehensive proposal for direct trade between Granger cooperatives in the Mississippi Valley and the English Cooperative Union. Though it never succeeded as a business venture, the Mississippi Valley Trading Company provides an illuminating chapter in the history of the Grange, and the recurrent attempts by many economic groups in the West and South to meet the power of the industrial East by redirecting the course of exports. After February 1875, the Granger cheap transportation movement emphasized improvement of the Mississippi River and Gulf ports, and was tied directly to the effort to organize the Mississippi Valley Trading Company.

NOTES

1. Solon J. Buck, *The Granger Movement 1870–1880* (Cambridge: Harvard University Press, 1913), pp. 9–15. Though written over fifty years ago, Buck's book remains the standard source for any study of the Grangers.

2. *Transactions of the Department of Agriculture of Illinois, 1873,* Farmers' Convention, Proceedings, Bloomington, 15 and 16 January 1873, p. 233.

3. For expressions of the sectional aspects of the railroad problem, see Illinois Railroad Commission, *Reports, 1874,* p. 17; E. W. Martin, *History of the Grange Movement or the Farmers' War Against Monopolies; . . . etc.* (Chicago: National Publishing Co., 1874), pp. 28–29; Robert E. Riegal, *The Story of the Western Railroads* (New York: Macmillan Company, 1926), pp. 129–145.

4. Charles Francis Adams, Jr., "The Granger Movement," *North American Review,* CXX (April 1875), 394–424. Buck contends that Adams's article was the most widely known on the railroad phase of the Granger movement.

5. National Grange, *Proceedings* (1874), p. 57. This is quoted from the Grangers' Declaration of Purposes.

6. Iowa State Agricultural Society *Annual Report of the Secretary for the Year 1872* (Des Moines, 1873), p. 199. From an address by Gov. C. C. Carpenter, a prominent Granger. Diversification had its widest hearing among southern Grangers. See, for example, National Grange, *Proceedings* (1875), p. 92. "The planters are struggling hard to relieve themselves from this vassalage brought upon them by the . . . suicidal policy of appropriating their lands and labor almost exclusively to cotton. . . . We are giving more attention to our food crops. . . ."

7. Ibid., p. 200.

8. National Grange, *Proceedings* (1874), p. 58.

9. Iowa State Agricultural Society, *Annual Report of the Secretary for the Year 1872,* p. 208.

10. Harvey S. Perloff et al., *Regions, Resources, and Economic Growth* (Lincoln: University of Nebraska Press, 1960), p. 115.

11. William M. Grosvenor, "The Railroads and the Farms," *Atlantic,* XXXII (November 1873), 591–610.

12. *Transactions of the Department of Agriculture of Illinois, 1873,* Farmers' Convention, Proceedings, 15 and 16 January 1873, p. 233.

13. Quoted in Buck, *The Granger Movement,* p. 129.

14. *Windom Committee Report,* I, 633.

15. Buck, *The Granger Movement,* pp. 225–226. See also Riegal, *The Story of the Western Railroads,* p. 295.

16. Buck, *The Granger Movement,* pp. 123–237. Though Buck carefully qualifies the role of the Grangers in the passage of state regulatory laws, over one-third of his book is taken up with a discussion of the problem, while the cheap transportation drive is treated in four pages. The reader is left, therefore, with the impression that the state regulatory movement was of overwhelming importance. A similar bias afflicts studies of the state Granges. See, for example, Charles W. Lea, "The Grange Movement in Wisconsin" (Master's thesis, University of Wisconsin, 1897), and Mildred Thorne, "The Grange in Iowa," *Iowa Journal of History,* XLVII (October 1949), 289–324.

17. George H. Miller, "The Granger Laws: A Study of the Origins of State Railway Control in the Upper Mississippi Valley" (Ph.D. dissertation, University of Michigan, 1951).

18. Publius V. Lawson, ed., *History of Winnebago County, Wisconsin* (Chicago 1908), pp. 1067–1071. Robert McCluggage, "Joseph H. Osborn, Grange Leader," *Wisconsin Magazine of History*, XXXV (Spring 1952), 178–184.

19. McCluggage, "Joseph H. Osborn, Grange Leader," p. 181.

20. Osborn to W. R. Taylor, 8 December 1873, Joseph H. Osborn MSS, State Historical Society of Wisconsin. (Hereafter cited as Osborn MSS.)

21. Osborn to F. B. Thurber, 19 October 1874, Osborn MSS.

22. *Nation*, 17 July 1873.

23. Robert T. Daland, "Enactment of the Potter Law," *Wisconsin Magazine of History*, XXXIII (September 1949), 45–54. Buck, *Granger Movement*, p. 183.

24. Wisconsin Railway Commission, *Reports*, 1874, p. 17.

25. F. B. Thurber to Joseph Osborn, 16 May 1874, Joseph Osborn to F. B. Thurber, 26 May 1874, Osborn MSS.

26. Wisconsin State Grange, *Bulletin* (September 1875). Quoted from an address by Worthy Master John Cochrane.

27. Ibid. (September, October, and November 1875).

28. Buck, *Granger Movement*, 193.

29. J. A. Sawin to Joseph Osborn, 20 July 1875, and J. A. Noonan to Joseph Osborn, 25 September 1875, Osborn MSS.

30. Wisconsin State Grange, *Proceedings* (1877), pp. 3–4. National Grange, *Proceedings* (1876), 13. Buck, *Granger Movement*, pp. 58–59.

31. Keokuk Convention, Proceedings, October 1873, Osborn MSS, Oshkosh Public Museum (microfilm in Wisconsin State Historical Society).

32. Buck, *Granger Movement*, p. 112.

33. Call for Keokuk Convention to members of the Executive Committee of the Patrons of Husbandry of the State of Wisconsin, Osborn MSS, n.d.

34. Keokuk Convention, Proceedings, October 1873, Osborn MSS.

35. Ibid.

36. Joseph Osborn to D. Wyatt Aiken, 22 November 1873, Osborn MSS.

37. Joseph Osborn to E. R. Shankland, 29 December 1873, Osborn MSS.

38. Robert McCluggage, "The Fox-Wisconsin Waterway 1936–1876: Land Speculation and Regional Rivalries: Politics and Private Enterprise" (Ph.D. dissertation, University of Wisconsin, 1954), pp. 317–374.

39. Richard N. Current, *Pinelogs and Politics: A Life of Philetus Sawyer, 1816–1900*, pp. 44–102.

40. [JWS] to Osborn, 26 February 1871, Osborn MSS.

41. Quoted in Current, *Pinelogs and Politics*, p. 69.

42. Oshkosh *Times*, 20 November 1872.

43. Joseph Osborn to W. R. Taylor, 22 November 1873, Osborn MSS. McCluggage, *The Fox-Wisconsin Waterway*, p. 337.

44. Keokuk Convention, Proceedings, October 1873, Osborn MSS.
45. Thorne, "The Grange in Iowa," p. 299. For comparative membership figures by state, see Buck, *The Granger Movement*, pp. 58–59.
46. Joseph Osborn to E. R. Shankland, 26 November 1873, Osborn MSS.
47. F. B. Thurber to Joseph Osborn, 16 May 1874, 20 September 1875, 24 November 1875, 14 October 1874; R. H. Ferguson to Joseph Osborn, 7 October 1872, 17 November 1875, Osborn MSS. For a discussion of the composition of the National Cheap Transportation Association, see Lee Benson, *Farmers, Merchants & Railroads*.
48. Joseph Osborn to E. R. Shankland, 6 December 1873, Osborn MSS.
49. Ibid.
50. Iowa State Grange, *Proceedings* (1873), p. 86.
51. William A. Williams, *The Roots of the Modern American Empire* (New York: Random House, 1969), p. 161.
52. Joseph Osborn to E. R. Shankland, 29 December 1873, Osborn MSS.
53. Ibid.
54. Wisconsin State Grange, *Proceedings* (1874), p. 35.
55. Quoted in Oshkosh *Times,* 5 February 1874.
56. Quoted in ibid., 28 January 1874.
57. Joseph Osborn to D. Wyatt Aiken, 22 November 1873, Osborn MSS.
58. National Grange, *Proceedings* (1874), pp. 78–79.
59. F. B. Thurber to J. H. Osborn, 24 November 1875, Osborn MSS. Thurber invited Osborn to the Cheap Transportation Association meeting in Chicago.
60. Thorne, "The Grange in Iowa," pp. 302–303.
61. Frederick E. Haynes, *Third Party Movements Since the Civil War with Special Reference to Iowa* (Iowa City: State Historical Society of Iowa, 1916), pp. 67–73.
62. Iowa State Grange, *Proceedings* (1874), p. 33.
63. Ibid., p. 34.
64. Ibid., p. 35.
65. Ibid., pp. 39–44.
66. Ibid., p. 40.
67. George H. Miller, "The Iowa Granger Law," *Mississippi Valley Historical Review,* XL (March 1954), 657–680.
68. A. B. Smedley to Joseph Osborn, 24 October 1874, Osborn MSS.
69. Iowa State Agricultural Society, *Annual Report of the Secretary for the Year 1872,* pp. 194–195.
70. Iowa, *Legislative Documents,* 1874, II, no. 30. Also contains Smedley's report of his trip to the Governor.
71. R. H. Ferguson to Joseph Osborn, 17 November 1875, Osborn MSS. Smedley's name is listed among the vice-presidents at the side of the page.
72. National Grange, *Proceedings* (1874), pp. 78–80.

73. Iowa State Grange, *Proceedings* (1874), p. 36.
74. Ibid., pp. 36–37.
75. National Grange, *Proceedings* (February 1875), pp. 110–116.
76. Ibid., p. 117.
77. Ibid., pp. 85–86.
78. Wisconsin State Grange, *Bulletin* (November 1875).

3

Agrarians and the Mississippi Valley Trading Company

THE NATIONAL Grange Executive Committee became actively involved in the affairs of the Mississippi Valley Trading Company (MVTCo) during the summer of 1875. The enterprise was apparently conceived by Dr. Thomas D. Worrall in 1873. An English-born medical doctor, Worrall came to America in 1853, was a member of the legislature of Colorado Territory in 1865, and then abruptly appeared as a carpetbag legislator in Louisiana during the early 1870s. Worrall saw the MVTCo as an instrument of what was termed "direct trade" between British cooperative societies and the Granger cooperatives of the Mississippi Valley.[1]

Direct trade was predicated on the belief that eastern middlemen and railroad executives skimmed off the profits of the agricultural export trade which rightfully belonged to the producers. Specifically, American trade with Great Britain suffered from three unnecessary tolls, according to Worrall: (1) commissions to merchants who purchased commodities for consignment abroad; (2) commissions to British merchants for goods sold in the United States; and (3) burdensome railroad freights between the Mississippi Valley and the Atlantic seaboard. Through the union of British and American cooperatives, which would ship and distribute through their own agents and on their own accounts, the retinue of middlemen would be eliminated. The solution to high rail charges involved redirecting trade from its east-west axis to a north-south axis along the Mississippi River, with the Gulf ports serving as the principal entrepôts.[2] It was a bold and imaginative plan that met with considerable enthusiasm on both sides of the Atlantic. Although its practicality was always in doubt, the effort indicates the well of resentment towards eastern domination of the interior and the lengths to which Grangers and others went to achieve commercial independence.

The success of the project in its initial stages was due almost entirely to the promotional skills of Worrall. Journeying to England late in 1873, Worrall spoke before chambers of commerce and cooperative societies. The group that was most interested in direct trade with the United States comprised the manufacturing cooperative societies loosely federated in the English Cooperative Union.[3] Developed under the auspices of the Christian Socialists, the Cooperative Union had a membership of 500,000, and was the official organization of the cooperative movement in England. Its leader, Edward Vansittart Neale, was one of the foremost apostles of the cooperative creed, and he and his colleagues received Worrall with warm enthusiasm.[4] At the opening of one of the most serious depressions of the century, direct trade with the Mississippi Valley appeared as a proposal that would open new markets for the surplus productions of the manufacturing cooperatives and provide jobs for the growing army of unemployed. Moreover, MVTCo might strengthen the ideological bonds of cooperation across the Atlantic.[5]

Under the plan presented by Worrall, MVTCo was to be divided into two sections, one British and the other American, each having a projected capital stock of £ 25,000, or $125,000. Not until the stock of both sections was fully subscribed, however, would transactions be made in the name of the company. Though willing to admit the importance of the scheme, the British cooperators "were disposed to be cautious about taking immediate steps to that end."[6] Not until greater assurances that the American section would be organized did they give their full support to Dr. Worrall.

Returning from England in the spring of 1874, Worrall began a vigorous campaign in the South to win approval from the Grangers for MVTCo. In an address before the New Orleans Grange, Worrall coupled his scheme for direct trade with an attack on protective tariffs. "When you send your grain, pork, flour, or cotton to England," he stated, "the [English] Government throws wide open its ports and bids you welcome; no duties are imposed, and no Custom House official obstructs your course. How is it with the British manufactures sent to our country? They are burdened with excessive tariffs, which frequently amount to more than the first cost of the article. . . . As these are the goods that the British people desire to exchange for our grain, produce, and staples, [we] sell to them one bushel of grain or one pound of staples when we should sell four if our ports were as free [as theirs]."[7] Not only did protection raise the cost of imported goods, but it drove away customers for the surpluses of the South and West.

At an Albany, Georgia, mass meeting of Grangers, Worrall sought the support of the leadership of the Direct Trade Union. Organized in June 1874 by the Georgia State Grange, the Direct Trade Union attracted wide attention throughout the South as its agents solicited business in Virginia, North Carolina, South Carolina, and Alabama, as well as in Georgia and Great Britain.[8] Worrall wanted the Direct Trade Union to unite with MVTCo because their purposes were identical. According to the secretary of the meeting, Worrall "depicted most truthfully . . . the dependent & poverty-stricken condition of the Southern States—their thralldom to the great cities & money power of the New England States," and presented his proposal for direct trade with the English Cooperative Union. MVTCo permitted the producers of the South and West, and the manufacturers of England, to be "brought in direct contact without the intervention (as now) of the middlemen of New York and other Northern cities."[9]

The Mississippi Valley Society

The principles of direct trade had wide application, in Worrall's view, because the grievances of the Grangers were not peculiar to them. Emphasis on the agrarian unrest of the 1870s has tended to obscure economic discontent among other groups that also resented the dominance of the East and sought to achieve a measure of commercial autonomy through direct trade with Europe. The appearance of the Mississippi Valley Society of London, with branches in Chicago, St. Louis, Mobile, and other large cities of the South and West, symbolizes this sentiment. Unlike MVTCo, the Mississippi Valley Society was "strictly non-trading."[10] Its general object was to serve as an international chamber of commerce; it promoted direct trade between the valley and Europe, emigration, and foreign capital investment in the resources of the South and West. Though there was no official connection between the Mississippi Valley Society and MVTCo, Worrall corresponded with its leaders, spoke in its behalf, and prepared a widely distributed pamphlet, "Direct Trade," for its use.[11] A closer look at the Mississippi Valley Society provides a major clue to the later conflict between Worrall and the Grangers, and their ultimate repudiation of his operation.

Sent to England in 1872 to advertise the resources of his home state of Missouri, William T. Cordner apparently was the first to suggest the Mississippi Valley Society. He thought such an association might dispel the prevailing ignorance of the potential wealth of the valley that was common among the leading businessmen of Europe. John Crossley, a prominent carpet manufacturer and member of Parliament; Richard Potter, chairman of the London directors of the Grand Trunk Railway of Canada; and James Reed, a highly regarded engineer for the British navy, were among the members of the parent society in London. In the United States, the Chicago branch of the society, endorsed by the powerful board of trade, included Cyrus McCormick of the McCormick Harvesting Machine Company; J. F. Armour of the meatpacking industry; and L. Z. Leiter, a wholesale merchant. The St. Louis branch listed James B. Eads, engineer and capitalist; Lewis V. Bogey, Senator from Missouri; and Mayor Joseph Brown as members. Generals P. T. Beauregard and J. B. Hood; Jefferson Davis; and J. H. Oglesby, president of the chamber of commerce, supported the New Orleans branch.[12]

The membership of the Mississippi Valley Society on both sides of the Atlantic was composed of wealthy and influential entrepreneurs and politicians. Many of them, such as McCormick and Armour, were considered enemies or opponents of the Grange on a variety of issues. Yet in its arguments for direct trade between the Mississippi Valley and European markets, and even in its capacity for practical results, the Mississippi Valley Society was strikingly similar to the Grangers' involvement in MVTCo. From time to time throughout the post-Civil War decades, farmers and other businessmen in the South and West felt their inferior colonial relationship with the eastern metropolis and acted in alliance to redress the balance. This convergence of interest and program, however, seldom developed into a common organizational form because of the strong class and other differences between the two groups.

To the New Orleans Chamber of Commerce, for example,

C. R. Griffing, general manager of the American branches, stressed the crippling effects of the bar at the mouth of the Mississippi and the harmful effects of a protective tariff that required the South and West to pay "commercial tribute" to the Northeast.[13] In a welcoming address to a meeting of the Mississippi Valley Society, McCormick described Chicago as the "international entrance" to the Mississippi Valley. He then explained that Chicago needed, for direct trade with Europe, the opening and completion of improvements on the St. Lawrence route and its connections with the Great Lakes. "Chicago and the northwest seek more direct commercial relations with Europe," McCormick wrote to the President of the Grand Trunk Railroad, "and whatever tends to facilitate intercommunication between the businessmen of the old world and our western states will have at all times the earnest support of our citizens."[14] In its more expansive moments, the Mississippi Valley Society, like MVTCo, projected a network of its own agencies and ships. Jefferson Davis went to London in 1874 to confer with the capitalists and shipbuilders of the parent society about the feasibility of establishing a steamship service between Europe and the southern seaboard. The intention was to utilize steel vessels of light enough draft to carry passengers and freight directly to the ports of the Mississippi Valley.[15]

Worrall Organizes MVTCo

This widespread sentiment for direct trade with Europe among all classes of the South and West explains the favorable response to Worrall in 1874. The New Orleans *Price-Current* observed that the MVTCo plan for a steamship line connecting Gulf ports with England would help import business and greatly reduce export freights. The New Orleans *Times* thought that Worrall had shown convincingly that the "Mississippi and Gulf route for Western produce shipment is de-

cidedly the cheapest to European markets." The Galveston
Daily Mercury praised Worrall upon his visit to the city. Direct trade would save the people of the South and West "the
excessive charges of middlemen in New York and the exorbitant freight charges from eastern ports to the Mississippi." The
Kansas City *Journal of Commerce* expressed a similar sentiment: "[No] difference can exist among the people of this portion of the West . . . on Direct Trade with Europe, and dis-
posing with the middlemen of New York and intermediate
cities."[16]

In addition to press notices, Worrall received several important letters of endorsement. General Beauregard com-
pactly integrated the central elements in the ideology which
suffused MVTCo. "Direct and Free Trade with Europe," he
wrote Worrall, "is the great desideratum to restore commercial prosperity to the States bordering on the Mississippi River.
. . . Long enough have they submitted to the exactions and
extortions of the North Eastern States." Noting the opposition
of eastern Congressmen to improvements on the Mississippi,
Beauregard insisted that the jetties at the mouth of the river
were "essential to the maintenance of Direct Trade between
the Valley and Europe. . . ."[17] The southern agent of the
Illinois Central Railroad promised Worrall that his road
would give through bills of lading on all shipments from
Liverpool to stations on its road. Jefferson Davis also approved
of Worrall's efforts.[18]

Armed with credentials from state Granges, the press, and
leading businessmen, Worrall returned to England late in
1874 to persuade the English to join MVTCo. The administra-
tive obstacles he confronted were formidable. Approval by
the sections of the Central Board of the Cooperative Union
(and endorsement by the societies which they represented), and
ratification by the whole body at the annual congress, were
necessary preliminaries to action. Worrall had carried the
battle, however, by 15 April 1875, and articles of incorporation

were prepared explaining the purpose and structure of the company, and the officers of the English section were chosen.[19] Worrall was ecstatic over being appointed managing director for the organization of the company in both countries. He felt assured of success.

The next task was to organize the American branch. The important objectives were explained in a circular letter to the officers and members of the national, state, and local Granges in the Mississippi Valley, by E. V. Neale, secretary of the Congressional Board of the English Cooperative Union. "The staples, grain, meat, tobacco, and other products raised in the Mississippi Valley are largely sold in England. The manufactured goods produced in Great Britain are largely sold in the Mississippi Valley. A much greater quantity of your products would be sold, at remunerative prices, in England, but for the extravagant charges of middlemen, and the unnecessary cost of railway transport on the American Continent. The same is true respecting the manufactured articles sent to you from this country. The 500,000 members of the Cooperative body in Great Britain, by means of the Mississippi Valley Trading Company, propose to meet the Patrons of Husbandry on direct trade lines, and by sending their own ships freighted with their own goods, to exchange these for the products raised by the Grangers on fair, equitable, and economical terms."[21] Neale suggested that the local, state, and national Granges endorse the scheme and deal with Worrall in connection with organizational questions.

To assist in the formation of the American section, as well as to encourage more subscriptions to the stock of the English section, a deputation of five members of MVTCo, including Neale and Worrall, left for the United States on 10 July 1875.[22] By the time the group arrived in New Orleans, the National Grange Executive Committee had endorsed and recommended MVTCo to the state and local Granges. Worrall then asked all Worthy Masters of the state Granges in the

Mississippi Valley to organize large meetings for the visiting English representatives.[23] Worthy Master John Cochrane of the Wisconsin State Grange, for one, thought the scheme "worth trying," and had Joseph Osborn draft a favorable reply.[24]

The English spokesmen first moved out to meet with southern Granges, regrouping in St. Louis to attend the quarterly meeting of the National Executive Committee. The result of their observations, inquiries, and discussions convinced them of the feasibility of international cooperation and direct trade. But the Englishmen did not find the Grangers as prepared to embark on the project as they had expected and hoped. With a general understanding that the American section of MVTCo would be organized as soon as possible, they left Managing Director Worrall the responsibility of bringing the matter to a conclusion.[25]

Worrall and the Grangers Part

The activities of Worrall during the next few months are difficult to trace. Apparently, he and three of his colleagues, without consulting the English directors, began the organization of the American Cooperative Union in Louisville, Kentucky. According to a tract written by Worrall, the American Cooperative Union was to serve as a wholesale establishment for MVTCo, and one-fifth of its stock would be contributed to MVTCo. Moreover, membership in the Cooperative Union was not restricted to Grangers; therefore, membership in MVTCo was opened to non-Grangers.[26]

The National Grange executives, most of whom were on the board of directors of the American branch of MVTCo, were violently and bitterly opposed to Worrall's new proposal. The ensuing struggle ended with the complete break of the Grangers from MVTCo. The Grangers contended that Wor-

rall and his associates, by permitting unrestricted membership
in MVTCo, had subverted the objective of international cooperation. The very middlemen the Grangers had hoped to
eliminate by direct trade were to be allowed to control
MVTCo.[27] An investigation during the summer of 1875 into
the faltering condition of the state Grange business agencies,
some of which operated on a commission basis through agents
who were not members of the Order, undoubtedly contributed
to Granger suspicions of Worrall's proposal. Thus, when the
matter was given careful consideration in October 1875, the
National Grange Executive decided against joining MVTCo
unless changes were made in the articles of association.[28]

The English directors of MVTCo were first alerted to the
rift between Worrall and the Grangers at the end of October
1875, and placed (in what they later described in an under-
statement) in a "peculiar position." Naturally, the first approach was to end the rift through mediation and compromise, because the success of MVTCo depended upon the
participation of the Grangers.[29] The secretary of MVTCo,
Joseph Smith of Manchester, fired off a sharp dispatch to Managing Director Worrall. Smith, incredulous, asked Worrall why
he was following a policy that would destroy the "noble design you have had the genius to frame."[30] Director Neale took
a more pragmatic tack with Worrall. He favored a "wider
basis for the Company," but he warned that "we must not
sacrifice the chance of obtaining [Grange] support by insisting
upon the doors of the Company being opened for all persons."
Neale suggested that assuring the Grangers a majority of the
stockholders' votes, and giving them the right to elect the
board of directors, would remove their objections to outside
participation. In any event, Neale strongly urged Worrall not
to air the dispute in public because the damage to MVTCo
would be irreparable.[31]

Worthy Master John T. Jones informed the head of the
English deputation to America that the Order, despite its dif-

ferences with Worrall, still anxiously desired to establish business relations with the cooperative societies of Great Britain.
He warned, however, that more attention had to be given to
the credit problem if the experiment was to be successful.
Speaking as an Arkansas planter of forty years' experience,
Jones explained how the New York merchants who loaned
capital to the southern planter also controlled the cotton
crop when ready for market. Direct trade "must be comparatively small . . . unless your capitalists will take the place
of New York in advancing for the growth of cotton two or
three seasons. . . ."[32] To arrange this, and to handle other
important matters, at its November 1875 Louisville meeting
the National Grange commissioned J. W. A. Wright, a California wheat grower, to negotiate new terms for the American
branch of MVTCo.[33]

The appointment of Wright as Grange ambassador to England destroyed any possibility of a reconciliation with Worrall. The English directors of MVTCo faced an awkward
choice: on the one hand, they could drop the founder of the
company, its managing director, and its chief protagonist or,
on the other hand, they could exclude the Grangers to whom
they were ideologically committed, and upon whom they felt
success depended. Director Neale explained the impasse as
frankly as possible to Worrall shortly before Wright arrived.
No one doubted that there were sound businessmen in the
American Cooperative Union, but "our hands are tied by our
own acts . . . you seem to imagine that we can undo what
has been done. . . ." The directors would negotiate with
Wright, and Worrall's organization would be approached only
if no understanding could be reached with the Granges. Re-
calling his trip to the United States, Neale offered little con-
solation to Worrall: "looks to me as if the Grangers' leaders
were anxious for a union with us."[34]

Recognizing the danger of Wright's mission to his scheme,
Worrall began a vicious propaganda campaign to undermine

the Grangers and reestablish his prestige in England. He knew, however, that without the participation of the Grangers in MVTCo, his efforts would be futile; hence his strategy was to drive a wedge between Granger leadership and the rank-and-file. As Wright later described it, Worrall and his friends "left nothing undone which they hoped would prevent my success. . . ."[35]

The Grange Executives were demagogues, Worrall wrote to Neale. "The honest Grangers are disgusted and joining us. They have never been consulted by Jones & Co. about the [MVTCo] and now they rebel. Have faith in me. . . ."[36] The secretary of the American Cooperative Union defended Worrall as "wise and far-seeing" in a letter published in the *Agricultural Economist,* a widely read English publication. The failure of so many of the Granger business enterprises was evidence of the incompetence of the Grange leadership that was now trying to gain exclusive control over MVTCo.[37] The Louisville press also sided with Worrall. The *Jeffersonian Democrat* combined an attack on the Grange executives with a demand to end the "treachery, deceit, trickery of the Wall St. rings."[38]

Despite Worrall's efforts, Wright received a warm welcome from the British when he arrived in February 1876. After touring the country to investigate the operations of various cooperatives, Wright returned to Manchester and opened negotiations to prepare new articles of association for MVTCo. Wright carried with him the resolution of the National Grange favoring international cooperation, an endorsement from the founder of the Grange, O. H. Kelley, and instructions not to commit the Order to any definite line of policy. He was merely to negotiate the removal of all difficulties in the laws of the company.[39] Worthy Master Jones warned that, while the Grangers hoped for the success of the reorganized company, the executive committee would never accept Worrall.

Wright found the English directors somewhat reluctant to abandon Worrall. He explained, however, that the Grange was prepared to admit non-Grangers into MVTCo "provided that this admission can be reconciled with the maintenance of the Grange organization undisturbed."[40] Worrall's insinuations and appeals to the membership over the heads of the Grange leaders represented a serious challenge to the very existence of the Order, and his participation in the direct trade organization was considered intolerable.

The long and arduous negotiations with Neale and other members of MVTCo were described by Wright in a pamphlet distributed to the state Granges. The result of his mission was an official change in the articles of association of MVTCo that was accepted by the Glasgow Congress of the English Cooperative Societies. There were three major changes: the name became Anglo-American Cooperative Trading Co. Ltd.; stock in the company was to be sold to cooperative associations, not individuals; and the position of managing director was abolished. These changes resulted from the activities of Worrall and his friends in the American Cooperative Union.

Under Worrall's direction, MVTCo had confined most of its work to the South, but Wright argued that Granges on the Pacific coast, the Northwest, and even in Canada, as well as the South, were interested in direct trade with Europe. The name of the company, therefore, ought to suggest the geographic scope of its operations. By limiting stock ownership to associations, the Grangers intended to decentralize the American branch of the company and prevent the formation of organizations like the American Cooperative Union. Finally, to guard against the possibility that the non-Grange directors of the American branch of MVTCo would accept the changes, Wright insisted on a provision that excluded Managing Director Worrall from the new company.[41]

Upon his return to the United States, Wright submitted copies of the articles of association of the new Anglo-American Company to the National Grange Executive Committee for approval. The "cherished scheme of international cooperation," he felt, was on the verge of being realized. The success of the Wright negotiations convinced Worthy Master Jones that "the time has arrived [to] take some definite action" and on 14 July 1876, he prepared a circular letter outlining a system of district agencies across the country to effect direct trade through the Patrons of Husbandry.[42]

Worrall's Louisville group remained undeterred by the new developments abroad. The *Cooperative Journal of Progress* began publication on 1 June 1876 as the official organ of the American Cooperative Union. It gave considerable space to the deepening of the mouth of the Mississippi through the Eads jetties: "This is a matter in which we naturally take a deep interest, and we hope before long to have our cooperation ships plying regularly between New Orleans and Liverpool. . . ."[43] At the MVTCo Executive Committee meeting on 15 June 1876, Worrall reported on his visit to Danville, Virginia, to organize a branch of the company. General Beauregard, a MVTCo vice-president, proposed to devote himself to the organization of a New Orleans branch.[44]

In a long report to the stockholders by the executive committee, the changes proposed by the Grangers in the articles of association were rejected. "The introduction of an Anglo-American Company is not friendly, but hostile to the original design and purpose for which the Mississippi Valley Trading Company was organized—the establishment of new connections with the vast population of the Mississippi Valley which has been deprived of its legitimate portion in commerce. The commercial facilities of the East need no improvement, and international cooperation does not require two companies. . . ."[45] The report defended Worrall and dismissed the Grangers as a small minority of the people of the Mississippi Valley who were eager for direct trade with England. These bold gestures failed to convince the English cooperative groups to conduct trade separately with themselves and the Grangers. The official organ of the American Cooperative Union ceased publication in August 1876, and there is no record of further correspondence between Worrall and the English directors after July 1876.

The Collapse of Direct Trade

The Grange press gave close attention to the organization of MVTCo, the struggle between Worrall and the Grange Executive Committee, Wright's mission to Europe, and the proposed Anglo-American Company.[46] By the opening of the Tenth Session of the National Grange in November 1876, the sentiment for action had reached a climax. Worthy Master Jones devoted most of his keynote address to the necessity of international cooperation and to the organization of the Anglo-American Company. Wright spoke at length on his mission and the anxiety of the English cooperators for speedy and decisive action. The issue was then referred to the Committee on Cooperation for a final report.[47]

Perhaps no document reveals the central elements of the Grange outlook better than the report on international cooperation prepared by T. R. Allen of Missouri, Joseph H. Osborn of Wisconsin, E. R. Shankland of Iowa, and two other Grangers. The Anglo-American Company rested on "certain facts which need but to be stated to all thinking farmers throughout our land to have their full assent." First, a large part of the surplus wheat, corn, cotton, wool, and other products had to be shipped to European consumers, chiefly in England. Second, numerous merchants and transportation agencies were amassing tremendous wealth in the transfer of these products from the producer to the consumer. "See how it is turned for them into huge store-houses, palatial homes, and luxurious living, while the farmer who receives these gifts from Mother Earth, as the reward of his labor . . . receives for his share a sum which rarely exceeds . . . his yearly expenses."

Under the plan of international cooperation, however, the profits of the intermediaries would be distributed more equitably between the American farmer and the European consumer. The heavy sampling, the too frequent handling, the incorrect weighing, and the exorbitant charges for warehouses, wharf storage, and freight might all be avoided if an effective system of direct trade was organized. "Think of the trade that may, with small and cautious beginnings ultimately flow in the interests of millions of farmers of our Western Continent to the ports of England through the Mississippi and its tributaries, through the Great Lakes and the St. Lawrence, from our seaports of the Atlantic, the Gulf, and the Pacific." Not all Granger business would be conducted through these channels, but there would be enough to offer a valuable corrective for the excessive marketing and transportation charges.[48]

Several Grangers did not support the Anglo-American Company. Brothers Lang, Hemingway, and Moore protested the entire action of the National Grange. "[It] is a scheme of business entirely unsuited to the wants and conditions of American farmers . . . it is the better policy for our farmers to buy and sell as near home as practicable."[49] But a motion to postpone action on resolutions favoring the general plan of the company lost twenty-three to sixteen, and international cooperation appeared close to realization.[50]

At the opening of the new year (1877), Neale sent congratulations to the Grange executives for promoting the "great cause of international cooperation."[51] Six months later his optimism had vanished. "[W]hatever enthusiasm there was for the enterprise originally has very much died down and we have now the disadvantage of being in a period of general dullness and commercial depression which weighs on the enterprise of everyone."[52] He warned Wright not to be surprised to learn that a meeting of stockholders in August would vote against the Anglo-American Company. When the Leeds Society, which held 2,000 of the 4,200 subscribed shares, withdrew from the company because of heavy losses in a fraudulent coal mining investment, the executives of the company refused to continue the enterprise.[53] The liquidator of the Anglo-American Trading Co. Ltd.[54] was appointed on 24 January 1878.

Worthy Master Jones reported a gratifying interest by Grangers in the Anglo-American Company; however, pledged subscriptions to the stock in the new company were meager.[55] Although the immediate cause of the collapse was British troubles, the decline in numbers and prestige of the Patrons of Husbandry by 1877 would have made it difficult, if not impossible, to continue the project even with the English. Too many Granger cooperatives had succumbed to financial mismanagement and embarrassment, and farmers were not interested in such a high-risk venture as the Anglo-American Company.[56]

Direct trade with Europe via New Orleans was no more successful in the 1870s than it had been before the Civil War. Much to the dismay of western and southern farmers, exports to European markets flowed along well-worn routes to the Atlantic seaboard, while agriculture remained ever more depressed. "Five-sixths of the exports are products of American farms," Brother W. W. Lang of the Texas Grange explained to President Rutherford B. Hayes in 1878. "By our industry, economy, and persevering will, we have changed the balance of trade from against us to near three hundred million of dollars in our favor. . . . Notwithstanding, Mr. President, our farmers are growing poorer and poorer."[57] Lang favored two proposals by which the government could provide relief to the farmers. These proposals, which were adopted by the National Grange, indicate that farmers had given up the illusion that direct trade with Europe was the answer for commercial prosperity and independence: "the national government should deepen and improve the channels of the Gulf ports, and establish a more perfect system of postal and reciprocal treaties of commerce with the Republic of Mexico, and the Central and South American States."[58]

This resolution was also the first sign of shift among all classes in the South and West toward the idea of developing new markets abroad. The opening of trade with Latin America and the Orient would outflank eastern commercial interests and enhance the wealth of the interior. The improvement of the Gulf and Pacific coast ports, as well as the national regulation of the railroads, were considered key elements to the success of this strategy. On the whole, however, transportation issues were obscured as the depression grew more severe and competitive railroad rates declined. The attention of agrarians focused on the currency and tariff issues and their impact on agricultural exports.

NOTES

1. Mississippi Valley Trading Company, Ltd. Papers, Library of the Cooperative Union, Manchester, England, Charlotte J. Erikson, ed. (microfilm in Minnesota State Historical Society). From introduction by Charlotte J. Erikson. (Hereafter cited as MVTCo MSS.) See also Philip Backstrom, "Edward Vansittart Neale and the Mississippi Valley Trading Company" (MSS, 1967). Professor Backstrom has kindly permitted me the use of his manuscript which is part of his projected biography of Neale.

2. Clifton K. Yearly, Jr., "Britons in American Labor: A History of the Influence of the United Kingdom Immigrants on American Labor, 1820–1914," Johns Hopkins University Studies, Series 75, no. 1 (Baltimore: Johns Hopkins University Press 1957), 247–76. This is the only published study available of the Mississippi Valley Trading Company and is based solely on the John Samuel Papers.

3. Erikson, Introduction, MVTCo MSS.

4. Beatrice Potter Webb, *The Cooperative Movement in Great Britain* (London: George Allen & Unwin Ltd., 1930), p. 46.

5. Erikson, Introduction, MVTCo MSS.

6. Louisville *Courier-Journal*, 6 October 1875. From speech by Worrall before the Louisville Board of Trade.

7. Manchester *Examiner*, n.d. (Reprint, Worrall's speech.) MVTCo MSS.

8. *Direct Trade Union*, circular by A. H. Colquitt to Patrons of Husbandry of Cotton States, 1874. Buck, *Granger Movement*, p. 264.

9. Branch Family Papers, no. 2718, Southern Historical Collection, University of North Carolina Library, Chapel Hill, North Carolina. I thank Denis Nordin for this and other documents related to MVTCo in the South.

10. Mississippi Valley Society, Prospectus, McCormick Collection, Wisconsin State Historical Society. All citations for the Mississippi Valley Society are from the McCormick Collection. Also see William T. Hutchinson, *Cyrus Hall McCormick* (New York: D. Appleton-Century, 1935), II, 595–600.

11. Broadside of *Southern Agriculturist of Louisville*, April 1876, MVTCo MSS. Jefferson Davis, president of the Mississippi Valley Society in 1876, spoke in Louisville for the MVTCo on Direct Trade. "Mr. Davis is in friendly cooperation with Dr. Worrall upon this subject, but there is no official connection between the Mississippi Valley Society and the Mississippi Valley Trading Company." Thomas D. Worrall to T. Wright, 24 October 1874, McCormick Collection. Wright was the secretary of the Chicago branch of the Mississippi Valley Society. "Direct Trade Between Great Britain and the Mississippi Valley," address by Dr. Thomas D. Worrall before the Mississippi Valley Society of London, 14 September 1874 (pamphlet, 1875).

12. Sees folders on St. Louis, Chicago, and New Orleans branches of Mississippi Valley Society, McCormick Collection.

13. C. R. Griffing, address before New Orleans Chamber of Commerce, 2 March 1874, McCormick Collection.

14. Chicago *Times*, 15 October 1874, clipping, Chicago branch folder, McCormick Collection.

15. Louisville *Courier-Journal*, 29 May 1874, clipping, in McCormick Collection. For a full discussion of the role of Davis in the Mississippi Valley Society see Hudson Strode, *Jefferson Davis: Tragic Hero* (New York: Harcourt, Brace & World, Inc., 1964), II, 404, 407, 415–419.

16. New Orleans *Price-Current*, 1 April 1874; New Orleans *Times*, 18 June 1874; Galveston *Daily Mercury*, 5 June 1874; Kansas City *Journal of Commerce*, July 1874: clippings, MVTCo MSS.

17. Gen. P. G. T. Beauregard to Worrall, 18 August 1874, MVTCo MSS.

18. A. P. Perkins to Worrall, 1 August 1874, MVTCo MSS.

19. Edward Vansittart Neale to officers and members of the National, State, and Local Granges of the Order of Patrons of Husbandry in the Mississippi Valley, April 1875, circular letter, Osborn MSS.

20. Worrall to John Neall, 27 April 1875, Worrall to H. R. Bailey, 29 April 1875: MVTCo MSS.

21. E. V. Neale to Order of Patrons of Husbandry, April 1875, Osborn MSS.

22. Dr. John Hunter Rutherford to the Cooperative Societies of the United Kingdom, circular letter, 10 July 1875, MVTCo MSS.

23. Dr. Thomas D. Worrall to John Cochrane, 21 July 1875, Osborn MSS.

24. Ibid. Cochrane scribbled his comment on the margin of Worrall's letter.

25. J. W. A. Wright, "Cooperation; Europe and the Grange," 1876 (pamphlet). Also found in National Grange, *Proceedings* (1876), 48–67. Neale was surprised to learn that three-fourths of the cotton for England was already exported direct from New Orleans. He later blamed Worrall for misleading him on this point. See *Cooperative* News, 20 November 1875. See also E. V. Neale to J. R. Buchanan, 3 July 1876, MVTCo MSS.

26. Thomas D. Worrall, *Manual of Practical Cooperation* (Louisville: American Cooperative Union, 3 November 1875).

27. National Grange, *Proceedings* (1876), 56–59.

28. National Grange, *Proceedings* (November 1875), 91–92.

29. Report of the Executive Committee, Changes in the Articles of Association of the Mississippi Valley Trading Co. Ltd., Manchester (Eng.), May 1876, MVTCo MSS.

30. Joseph Smith to Worrall, 28 October 1875, Letterbook, MVTCo MSS.

31. E. V. Neale to Worrall, 25 January 1876, Letterbook, MVTCo MSS.

32. National Grange, *Proceedings* (November 1875), 91–92.

33. National Grange, *Proceedings* (1876), 11–15.

34. E. V. Neale to Worrall, 25 January 1876, Letterbook, MVTCo MSS.

35. National Grange *Proceedings* (1876), 49.

36. Worrall to E. V. Neale, 21 January 1876, MVTCo MSS.

37. *Agricultural Economist*, 1 February 1876, MVTCo MSS.

38. Louisville *Jeffersonian Democrat*, 5 February 1876, MVTCo MSS.

39. National Grange, *Proceedings* (1876), 49.

40. Ibid., 59.

41. Report of the Executive Committee, Changes in the Articles of Association of the Mississippi Valley Trading Co. Ltd., Manchester (Eng.), May 1876, MVTCo MSS.

42. J. W. A. Wright to ?, 27 May 1876, MVTCo MSS; National Grange, *Proceedings* (1876), 8–10.

43. *Cooperative Journal of Progress*, 1 June 1876, MVTCo MSS.

44. American Section of the Mississippi Valley Trading Company, Minutes of the Executive Committee Meeting, 15 June 1876, MVTCo MSS.

45. American Section of the Mississippi Valley Trading Company, Minutes of Stockholders Meeting, Louisville, 17 June 1876.

46. *Rural Carolinian*, September 1876, pp. 410–411; *Cooperative News*, 29 July 1876, in John Samuel MSS; Wisconsin State Grange *Bulletin*, July

1876, January–February 1876, November 1876; London (Ont.) *The Granger*, February 1876: MVTCo MSS.
47. National Grange, *Proceedings* (1876), 48–67, 124–130.
48. Ibid., 144–152.
49. Ibid., 88.
50. Ibid., 168–169.
51. E. V. Neale to National Grange Executive, 3 January 1877, MVTCo MSS.
52. E. V. Neale to J. W. A. Wright, 10 July 1877, MVTCo MSS.
53. Ibid., 26 September 1877, MVTCo MSS.
54. Letterbook, 24 January 1878, MVTCo MSS.
55. National Grange, *Proceedings* (1877), 12.
56. Buck, *Granger Movement*, 260.
57. National Grange, *Proceedings* (1878), 122.
58. Ibid., 133.

4

The South and
Internal Improvements

THE CONFEDERATE soldiers returning from the war encountered widespread desolation. Fences were down, weeds had overrun the fields, and windows were broken. During the decade from 1860 to 1870, the value of southern farms decreased by $772 million, or 41 percent; the value of farm machinery and equipment by 37 percent; the number of hogs by 38 percent; and the number of beef cattle by 15 percent. And not until 1879 did the cotton crop exceed the one of 1860.[1]

Commerce also suffered from the ravages of the war. In 1865, one visitor to Charleston described it as a "city of ruins, of desolation, of rotten wharves, of deserted warehouses . . . and voiceful barrenness." In Mobile business was stagnant. Chattanooga and Nashville were ruined, and Atlanta's industrial sections were in ashes.[2] One of the greatest barriers to the revival of commerce was the havoc wrought to the transportation system and to public works. The war had destroyed or crippled well over half of the South's railroads. Track was torn up, freight cars burned, engines in disrepair; passenger and freight rates were high while service was slow and irregular.

Rehabilitation of the old rail lines did proceed steadily after the war. With the aid of federal credits and northern bondholders, the physical restoration of the South's railroads was practically complete by 1870.[3] Construction of new mileage in the South, however, was extremely slow by comparison to the boom in other sections of the country. Illinois alone built as much in the decade after the war as did the entire South, and by 1875 had mileage totaling over half that of the South. As before the war, heavy reliance was placed upon programs of state railroad aid to widen the transportation net.[4] The usual method was for the states to issue state bonds to the railroad in exchange for bonds of the company. Though sound in theory, the state aid programs were subject to graft and corruption, and large state debts were accumulated. The Conservatives, calling themselves variously the Democratic party, Conservative Union party, or the Democratic and Conservative party, attacked the state aid program of the Radical Reconstruction governments, and, once in power, succeeded in turning over the South's railroads to private interests, with which they were largely identified.[5] To the historian of southern railroads, the carpetbaggers "left behind a heritage of poorly constructed, financially weak railroads which were not prepared for the financial problems of the future."[6]

Neither the Reconstruction nor the Redeemer governments in the South provided significant aid for the waterways, harbors, or levee systems. For that matter, the legislature of Virginia, in 1871 and 1872, directed the board of public works to sell the state's interest in various internal improvement companies. There was some action in other states. West Virginia authorized certain counties to subscribe stock in the Little Kanahwa Company to improve navigation of the Little Kanahwa River. Kentucky made appropriations for improving the Kentucky River, but the state works on the Green and Barren rivers were ceded to a private company. Florida conferred the right-of-way through swamp lands upon certain canal companies. In other southern states, however, little was done to improve waterways.[7]

In addition to overseeing the construction of critical railroad mileage, the economic and political leaders of the South evolved a new strategy for obtaining other necessary internal improvements. After observing the agitation in the West for cheap transportation and the logrolling tactics of Congressman Philetus Sawyer in securing liberal federal grants for pet projects, the southerners abandoned their antebellum scruples against federal aid. "I belonged to that old school of democrats who were taught to go against all appropriations for internal improvements by the general government," Sen. Joseph E. Brown of Georgia told his northern colleagues. "You went 'for the old flag and an appropriation' before the war; we went for the old flag and the honors, and when the test came we found the appropriations a great deal heavier than the honors. I have concluded now to abandon that policy, to learn a lesson from you, and while you have taken your part of the appropriations we ask you to give us ours."[8] Brown and other leaders were aware that the great need of the South was for capital for internal improvements, and they correctly observed that the Federal Treasury was an important source of northern capital.

In the South, as elsewhere in the country, merchants supplied the driving force in the fight to secure internal improvement appropriations for cheap transportation. After 1868, conventions organized almost every year to petition or memorialize the Congress for cheap transportation. At the meeting of the National Board of Trade in Norfolk, Virginia, in 1869, the advantages of a canal connecting the James and Kanawha rivers were fully aired and the merits of an improved harbor at Norfolk discussed.[9] The Southern Commercial Convention, held the next year in Cincinnati, made direct trade between southern ports and Europe the first order of business. Congressman George Pendleton told the delegates that they should no

longer "submit to isolation." Instead, they should demand
the government provide free and easy access to the markets of
the world by the improvement of waterways.[10] Atlanta merchants were active from 1871 in pushing for the Atlantic and
Great Western Canal to link the Tennessee and Ocmulga
rivers. Using the financial scheme of the transcontinental railroads as a model, they proposed that the government grant a
million acres of land and promise to guarantee the interest on
the canal company's bonds.[11]

Of all the internal improvement projects advanced in the
South, none had more widespread support than the one for
the Mississippi River. For one thing, the value of the river
had been seriously diminished by the war. Snags had not been
cleared, banks had caved in, the levee system had been destroyed, and, most critically, the mouth of the Mississippi was
filling with mud, preventing the passage of ocean vessels to
dock at New Orleans. Because it was the most important river
serving the South, and because its improvement was deemed
necessary to the return of prosperity, the agitation about the
Mississippi came to symbolize the general struggle of the South
to win a larger share of federal appropriations.

Burwell and the Mississippi River

Not surprisingly, the New Orleans Chamber of Commerce
played the most active role in demanding the improvement
of the Mississippi River. The unofficial organ of the chamber
of commerce after the war was *DeBow's Review*. William M.
Burwell, who became its editor after the death of James De-
Bow in 1868, was also president of the New Orleans Chamber
of Commerce. He was a forceful speaker, a polished writer,
and generally considered one of the most thorough statisticians
in the South.[12] As the editor of one of the most widely read
periodicals in the South, Burwell formulated the ideology and

developed the practical strategy for government improvement of the Mississippi.

Burwell began with the assumption that the West and South occupied a single physiographic region. The integration of those regions depended upon the utmost development of the river systems, especially the Mississippi, which would draw the produce of every part of the valley to New Orleans. Burwell warned of the almost total domination of western trade by the northern water system and trunk-line railroads, and urged the development of competing trade routes, including the building of railroads, into the upper Mississippi Valley.[13]

The handling of the export grain trade of the West was the chief commercial prize that New Orleans wanted. Several preliminary steps were required to control that trade. First, Burwell asked members of the New Orleans Chamber of Commerce to reduce commission, drayage, storage, insurance, and other charges in order to become competitive with the Atlantic ports.[14] Second, grain elevators were needed. Grain was received and shipped in sacks and barrels, which necessitated extra work and expense, and could not be handled in bulk. The chamber of commerce, called upon Lewis J. Higby, who had accumulated a fortune in the elevator business in Milwaukee during the war, to solve that problem. He moved to New Orleans in 1868 and organized a stock company to build the first large elevator at a cost of over $200,000. By the end of the next year, Higby had sold his interests in Milwaukee (and part ownership in a flour mill at St. Louis) and transferred all his activities to New Orleans. He believed that New Orleans would "ultimately become the entrepôt for the foreign grain trade of the Mississippi Valley and the Northwest."[15]

As Burwell explained it, the New Orleans merchants "next found [they] needed the cooperation of the Western railroads running North and South."[16] There was little difficulty with the Illinois Central Railroad. The directors of that road hoped to induce businessmen to begin shipping grain to New Orleans by taking cargo in the name of the railroad. They also offered competitive through rates from Iowa and Illinois stations to New Orleans.[17]

None of those measures, however, would be sufficient unless the mouth and channel of the Mississippi River were deepened. New Orleans was reached after navigating ninety-eight miles of tortuous channel, and the huge sandbar at the entrance to the river discouraged the best and largest steamers from calling at the port. That problem worsened each passing year, as the size of ocean steamers continually increased with the fuller development of steam power and improvements in ship construction. Ships had to be 1,000 tons or less to reach New Orleans in 1868, and they made it only with difficulty and delay. Often, a part of the cargo had to be unloaded outside the bar, and outward-bound shipments were subject to spoilage or damage until high water was available. Such delays and losses made insurance premiums and freight rates higher than at other ports and hindered the development of New Orleans as an alternative route for the export of western foodstuffs. Only large appropriations from the national treasury could solve the problem.[18]

Still another related problem caused Burwell and his allies grave concern. Regardless of the port facilities for handling the northwestern trade, New Orleans was poorly located with relation to the principal trade routes to Europe. Even if both private capital for additional port facilities and government capital for the improvement of the river were to transform New Orleans into a first class port, the fear remained that Atlantic coast rivals would retain an overwhelming advantage in their proximity to the markets of Europe.[19] But if new markets in Latin America were found and opened for the trade of the West, then the Gulf ports would enjoy the proximity to those markets that the Atlantic ports enjoyed in relation to Europe.

Such reasoning had been heard in the South before the Civil War. The real difficulty lay in persuading western farmers, merchants, and politicians to join the South in a campaign to pressure the government to open the Latin American markets. In 1870, observing that European nations were already contemplating retaliatory duties upon American foodstuffs, Burwell admitted that the West was justified in embarking upon a program of industrialization to create greater economic independence. But surplus agricultural products would still remain. The continued immigration and the opening of new lands to settlement would actually increase the surplus and the West would therefore "require a market abroad." Somewhat overstating the case, Burwell went on to argue that the foreign market for this surplus could "alone be sought . . . south of the United States. For the railroad development of Russia and other nations of the north of Europe will so far increase the capacity of those nations to export that the European market will be filled with their products." The West had two choices: "First, to condense their provision products into manufactures [e.g., flour, beef, lard]. Second, to export their provisions to the continent of America."[20]

But the South American markets were largely blocked by tariff walls. Burwell persistently advocated, therefore, the negotiation of reciprocal trade treaties to open those markets. In his view, the improvement of the Mississippi River had to be accompanied by reciprocity treaties with Latin America. Before the Windom Committee in New Orleans during the fall of 1873, Burwell explicitly linked internal improvements to overseas economic expansion:

> I would say that in the estimation of many in this city, merchants and others, the *most important* object in improving the Mississippi River will be to establish a direct line of communication between the immense productive interior of the West and the consuming markets of and beyond the tropics. There is a physical

impediment in the way which we ask Congress to remove [the bar at the mouth of the Mississippi]; but there are diplomatic impediments also, which are even greater, as far as that line of trade is concerned, than the physical impediments. . . . The diplomatic impediments consist of the want of reciprocal trade treaties between the United States and the South American States that are adjacent to or lie South of us. [With reciprocity there would be] a draught of trade from the great interior West into the markets of gold and silver, of sugar and coffee, and . . . there would be a great gain to the people of the West in sending their trade in this direction, instead of being compelled to market it in Europe, and to import commodities received in exchange across the Atlantic ocean.[21]

Many groups and individuals, mostly from the South, joined Burwell in shaping their arguments for the improvement of the Mississippi around the trade possibilities in Latin America. The 1869 Mississippi River Improvement Convention in Keokuk, Iowa, called upon river and port cities in the valley to counteract the rivalry of cross routes by supporting subsidies to the steamers touching New Orleans, by demanding the appointment of diplomats and consuls from the Mississippi Valley states, and by insisting that Congressmen "examine the treaty relations between the United States and foreign powers with a view to obtaining such modifications or amendments thereof as will remove all obstacles to a free or reciprocal trade between the Mississippi River and such foreign powers."[22]

The Commerce Committee of the Mississippi Valley Commercial Convention of 1869, composed of delegates from Louisiana, Missouri, Illinois, Iowa, and Tennessee, resolved in favor of all governmental aid necessary for the removal of obstructions on the Mississippi River, "free and reciprocal trade with Cuba," and mail subsidies to steamships from New Orleans to South American ports.[23] Similar proposals were offered during the Southern Commercial Convention in 1870.

Gov. Thomas C. Fletcher of Missouri spoke of the "duty of the Government of the United States to encourage our commerce with . . . the Island of Cuba. [Cuba] has levied such amounts of duties on importations from this country as to amount to actual prohibition. . . ."[24] St. Louis merchants were enthusiastic advocates of increased trade with Latin America along an improved river route. One delegate to the 1867 River Improvement Convention in St. Louis suggested that direct trade with the West Indies and Latin America would place a large portion of the trade of the entire Northwest in the hands of St. Louis merchants.[25]

Perhaps the greatest tribute to the forcefulness of the arguments made by Burwell and others linking internal improvements with overseas economic expansion was paid by President Grant, in his first annual message to Congress in December 1869. A former resident of St. Louis, Grant manifested a clear interest and concern for cheap transportation. "The extension of railroads in Europe and the East [India] is bringing into competition with our agricultural products like products of other countries." Grant warned, therefore, that self-interest and self-preservation dictated the "necessity of looking to other markets for the sale of our surplus. Our neighbors south of us, and China and Japan, should receive our special attention."[26]

An Internal Improvements Coalition

In their bid for wider political support for internal improvement measures, southerners played on the animosity of westerners towards the eastern cities as much as on market expansion abroad. Improved waterways in the South would provide cheaper transportation for the West and loosen the grip of

eastern merchants, bankers, and railroad men. Such arguments
abounded in every discussion of the improvement of the Mississippi River. *DeBow's Review* reported that at an 1869 commercial convention in New Orleans, there was a "very unanimous hostility to the monopolies of Eastern capital and
transportation. . . . The West obviously regards the Mississippi
outlet as a means of escaping these exactions and will unite
on all governmental aid necessary for removing all obstructions."[27] Lewis Higby, an advocate of direct trade with Europe
as well as chairman of the Committee on Obstructions of the
New Orleans Chamber of Commerce, expressed a similar view
to Captain Howell of the Army Corps of Engineers. "The
West must and will be heard," exclaimed Higby after the failure of months of dredging at the mouth of the Mississippi,
"and a few resolute men can stir the People to demand it.
. . ."[28] Joseph H. Oglesby, president of the New Orleans
Chamber of Commerce, testified before the Windom Committee that to send western grain via New Orleans to Liverpool—
assuming a twenty-five-foot channel at the mouth of the Mississippi—would be fifteen cents a bushel cheaper by way of
New York. That saving would give the "farmer of the West
that which he has never received, namely, an adequate return
for his labor."[29]

The advocates of southern internal improvements, many
with less obvious practicality than the opening of the mouth
of the Mississippi, made a similar appeal to the West. Atlanta
merchants held a commercial convention in May 1873 and
memorialized the Congress on the need for cheap transportation and stressed the Atlantic and Great Western Canal. "To
the West and South," the memorial read, "this question [of
cheap transportation] is of peculiar importance. Their interests are in great measure identical, being the two great producing sections." High freight rates prevented the export of grain
from the West, though the surplus was sufficient to feed the
world. Moreover, expensive transportation compelled the South

to produce its own foodstuffs, and to that extent denied the western farmers a market. Given cheap transportation, not only would western and southern producers benefit, but, the memorial concluded, "our manufactories would increase, our exports would be doubled, our shipping interest revived, and the balance of trade would be largely in our favor."[30]

The unity of interest between the South and West on the question of internal improvements for cheap transportation to the seaboard was clearly evident in the hearings and report of the Windom Committee. One of the main arguments stressed by southern witnesses, and incorporated into the final report, was that high freight costs from the West to the South "compelled the planter to devote his cotton-lands to the production of wheat and corn, for which they are by nature unsuited, thereby reducing the product of cotton and diminishing the market for grain. . . ." Moreover, cotton exports were still far off the level of 1860, while other countries had greatly increased their exports. These disturbing statistics were "attributable to a large extent . . . to the system of internal improvements inaugurated in India by Great Britain, for the express purpose of rendering herself independent of us for the supply of cotton." Thus, the Windom Report concluded, joining South and West in a common cause, "every cent unnecessarily added to the cost of transportation is to that extent protection to the cotton-planter of India and the food-producers of Russia, against the farmers of the West and the cotton-planters of the South."[31]

Though appropriations were recommended and in June 1874 Congress made funds available for surveys on three east-west water routes, the most important practical result of the Windom Committee was the public attention it focused on the mud blockade at the mouth of the Mississippi and the need to unite South and West in securing its removal.[32] On the last day of the committee's hearings, Capt. James B. Eads, a brilliant engineer who had achieved an international reputa-

tion for the design and construction of the first bridge across
the Mississippi at St. Louis, presented his proposal for con-
structing jetties at the mouth of the river. Instead of a large
and expensive ship-canal skirting the river delta, as the Army
Corps of Engineers favored, Eads suggested the construction of
parallel walls across the sand bar in the Southwest Pass, in
order to prevent the river from spreading out as it entered the
Gulf. The river would then keep its velocity and power, removing the sand bar through the scouring action.[33] Senator
Windom was profoundly impressed with Eads's testimony, and
the Committee endorsed his proposal.[34]

But Eads had still to convince the House Committee on
Railroads and Canals. The ship-canal project had the backing
of the powerful Army Corps of Engineers. The Army thought
the Eads idea was preposterous. The canal was also supported
by the New Orleans Chamber of Commerce and most of the
valley press. With the help of the St. Louis Merchant's Exchange, the St. Louis Chamber of Commerce, and several
prominent engineers, however, Eads mounted a strong propaganda campaign against the ship-canal.[35] At the opening of
the Forty-third Congress, Eads appeared before the Railroads
and Canals Committee and presented his plan. To his great
disappointment and despair, the House committee voted
unanimously against his report.

But Eads did capture the imagination of one member of
the committee, George Frisbee Hoar of Massachusetts. Hoar
understood the reluctance of the Congress, during a period
of severe economic crisis and declining government receipts,
to appropriate $8 million merely to start the ship-canal proj-
ect when perhaps $7 million would be needed for its comple-
tion. He also understood the skepticism towards the jetty
system. "Captain Eads," Hoar inquired on the very day that
the jetty plan had been rejected, "can you not frame a bill
which will provide that you shall not have any money from
the treasury for your work until you have accomplished some-

thing. If you deepen the channel of the river a foot that will have done good. Suppose that you provide that when you have deepened the river a certain number of feet you shall have so much of your pay. . . ."[36] Eads eagerly acted on Hoar's suggestion. He publicly presented a plan, in January 1874, whereby the government would contract Eads to deepen the mouth of the Mississippi to twenty-eight feet, payments totaling $7 million to be made according to a schedule as the river deepened after eighteen feet. Not only did the Eads plan mean less government expense than the ship-canal, but Eads took all the financial loss if the plan failed.[37]

In June 1874, the House moved to reconsider its decision in favor of the ship-canal, and the Eads bill was offered as a substitute. The congressional debate over the Eads jetty bill revealed the unity of the Mississippi Valley for the removal of the sand bar and a profound resentment towards the East. Speaking in favor of the ship-canal, Rep. Erastus Wells of Louisiana concluded that relief from the economic depression in the Mississippi Valley depended upon the clearing of the mouth of the river to allow ocean steamers access to New Orleans.[38] In pleading for the jetty plan, Rep. John B. Clark of Missouri summed up a popular feeling in the South and West for cheap transportation. "Let me intreat you," he told his colleagues, "to do a tardy act of justice to the suffering South and West; we now come before you asking that we be paid back for all those years of toil."[39] Rep. Alvah Crocker of Massachusetts took offense at the course of the debate. The next day he reminded the House that the National Board of Trade, of which he was a member, had passed a resolution in favor of the opening of the Mississippi. "Sir, I yesterday heard of a South, sometimes coupled with a West, as if there were no East or North. Has the compass lost its attraction to the north pole?"[40]

A deadlock in the House and Senate over the different engineering proposals resulted in a compromise bill which established a seven-man commission of military and civil engineers to study the delta problem and recommend a solution. After six months of exhaustive investigations in the United States and Europe, the commission recommended the jetty system to Congress. Supporters of the ship-canal plan acquiesced in the commission's decision, and on 18 February 1875 the Eads Jetty Bill was approved by the Senate. Two months later work on the jetties began, and by 1876 Eads had succeeded in reaching a twenty-foot depth. By the end of 1878 a thirty-foot channel was available, and the government made full payment to Eads and his fellow stockholders.[41] As the president of the Illinois Central Railroad asserted, the Eads jetties marked the beginning of a new era in the commercial history of New Orleans, as important as the introduction of steam boats on the Mississippi River.[42]

The Eads Jetty Bill of 1875 also foreshadowed a new period of increased aid for internal improvements in the South. Always before, the Northwest had monopolized the river and harbor bill. For example, the 1870 bill had appropriated $2 million for the Northwest and only $460,000 for the South. Wisconsin and Michigan alone received more in the bill of 1872 than did the entire South.[43] But as more and more Republican governments in the South were redeemed, and Democratic party Representatives and Senators were elected to Congress, the South's share of the total allotment increased. The South had received 15 percent of the total in 1872; by 1875 the proportion had jumped to 24 percent.[44]

The river and harbor bill of 1875 was the last one constructed by Wisconsin Congressman Philetus Sawyer. The Democrats gained control of the House of Representatives in 1876 and took charge of the Committee on Commerce. Of a total appropriation of $5 million, $1.046 million, or 21 percent, went to the South. President Grant signed the bill, but aroused the Democrats when he sent a message to the House advising it that he objected to the many purely "local and private" matters in it.[45] One southerner surmised that Grant really objected "because a few dollars have been given to the downtrodden South."[46]

The importance of internal improvements to the South was dramatically illustrated in the aftermath of the disputed Hayes-Tilden election of 1876. As C. Vann Woodward has authoritatively shown, the Hayes Republicans sought the cooperation of the southern Democrats in the House in order to complete the official count of the electoral vote for Hayes. Among the most important promises given by Hayes was one that said his administration would look with favor on increased internal improvement appropriations for the South. Southern Congressmen had recently discovered a difference with their Democratic colleagues in the North who had shown a reluctance to vote for the Texas and Pacific Railroad subsidy, aid to clear the mouth of the Mississippi, grants for reconstruction of levees along the Mississippi, and other internal improvement measures.[47]

The alliance of southern Democrats and northern Republicans succeeded in placing Hayes in the White House. Shortly after the inauguration, he told the press he favored a "system of internal improvements calculated to benefit and develop the South." The Hayes Republicans even hoped, by promises of internal improvement appropriations, to gain enough southern votes in the House to elect James A. Garfield speaker and to organize the House.[48] The ex-Confederates, however, remained true to the Democratic party and voted to elect Samuel J. Randall of Pennsylvania speaker. For their faithfulness, the southerners exacted a reward from Randall in the form of the appointment of John H. Reagan of Texas as chairman of the Committee on Commerce. Reagan took charge of the river and harbor bill in the pattern established by Sawyer, and proceeded to cooperate with the Republicans of the Northwest to organize a two-thirds majority that could pass a large annual bill. A practical and durable internal improvements coalition between southern Democrats (of both the Whiggish and Jacksonian type) and the Republicans of the Northwest was effected by 1878, and it endured despite shifting alliances on other issues.[49]

One gauge of the strength of the new coalition was the attack from eastern Republicans. They began to assail internal improvement appropriations as treasury raids, and in their public statements dropped the Hayes policy of conciliation with the South. Headlines in the New York *Tribune* in 1878 denounced the "Hungry South" and the "Southern Maw." The *Tribune* raised again the old cry of "Rebel Claims," warning that if the South won its demands for improvements, and if the Democrats gained control of the Senate in addition to the House, uncounted millions of other southern demands would appear. "The country will not be able to pay the sums demanded by the South without dishonor and bankruptcy, ruin to its credit and prostration to its industry."[50] The eastern Republicans also accused the northern Democrats of aiding the South in a great treasury raid that would bankrupt the Republic.

In fact, however, northern Democrats joined the eastern Republicans in opposing the river and harbor bill of 1878. In the House, for example, Democrat Samuel S. Cox of New York claimed that many southern demands were for small, local projects like creeks and ponds. Cox reminded the southerners of the "old days of strict construction of the Constitution," and asked: "Gentlemen of the South, have those days gone to the rear and abysm forever?"[51] In the Senate, eastern Republican leaders James G. Blaine of Maine, Roscoe Conklin of New York, and Henry L. Dawes of Massachusetts led a similar attack on the bill. Blaine acknowledged that this was the first river and harbor bill he had ever voted against.[52]

Sen. Robert E. Withers of Virginia gave the southern reply. He remarked that it came with poor grace for northern Senators to arraign the southern Democrats for supporting an internal improvement bill when the northerners had for years received aid for "every inlet, creek, harbor, and everything else" in their states. And as for the Democratic party's old doctrines of strict construction of the Constitution, that had only meant advantages in wealth and power to the North, and comparative poverty and weakness in the South. "So far as I and my own section are concerned," Withers gave notice, "we mean to secure the development of our country by means of the same agencies and the same means, and I for one have no constitutional scruples upon the subject."[53]

Sen. William Windom of Minnesota spoke for other northwestern Republicans in defending the South. In one of the important speeches of his long career, Windom carefully analyzed the appropriations, and observed that most of the items were connected with either the Mississippi River or the northern water route. The Mississippi route to the seaboard had been revolutionized by the work of Eads, and would provide the people of the Mississippi Valley "a new and direct pathway to the markets of the world." It would transform the upper Mississippi and Missouri valleys into the battleground of commerce between the southward and eastward movements of trade. On the side of the southward movement, Windom listed the trade interests and enterprise of St. Louis, the north-south railroads, cheap transportation on the river, and the capital and enterprise of New Orleans. The eastward or northern route for the trade of the West had at its command the enterprise of Chicago, the trunk-line railroads, the northern water line (including the St. Lawrence River), and the capital and commercial strength of New York City. Windom did not exaggerate the disadvantages of the southern route, but he prophetically noted that, as the center of the grain crop moved west of the Mississippi River, farmers would refuse to bear a high burden of railroad transportation to the Atlantic coast. Instead, they would have grain transshipped to barges or steamer for New Orleans or use north-south railroads to the

Gulf ports. Windom concluded his speech with further demands for the improvement of the Mississippi.[54]

The Senate and House vote on the 1878 River and Harbor Bill showed that the South favored such appropriations overwhelmingly. Republicans from Michigan, Ohio, Indiana, Illinois, Iowa, Wisconsin, and Minnesota also voted for the bill.[54] Together, the two groups succeeded in passing a final appropriation of $8.3 million, of which the South received $2.8 million, or almost one-third.[55]

The Mississippi River
Commission

The congressional internal improvements coalition of southern Democrats and western Republicans was further strengthened by the evident success of the Eads jetties at the mouth of the Mississippi. Demands logically arose for the improvement of the whole length of the river, especially from St. Louis to New Orleans. Sen. Thomas N. Cockrell of Missouri had tried to persuade Congress to include authorization for a Mississippi River Commission in the 1878 River and Harbor Bill. The commission, five engineers appointed by the President, would survey the entire length of the river and make plans for a general system of permanent improvements. Cockrell explained that no general survey or plan for the Mississippi had ever been made and that no economical or judicious appropriation could be made until a general system was adopted. He predicted that a careful system of improvements could secure from ten to fifteen feet of water from St. Louis to the mouth of the river. Cockrell, however, had not organized enough support for his proposal, even in the South, and the commission was not approved.[56]

By 1879, the demands for the river commission had greatly swelled. Low water on the Mississippi halted navigation of grain barges from St. Louis; also, an epidemic of yellow fever at New Orleans in the fall of 1878 detained steamships in port days, weeks, and in some cases over a month. The cargoes which they finally obtained were at very low rates. One New Orleans shipper recalled that the steamship owners concluded that New Orleans was not such a bonanza as they had anticipated. "They went to the opposite extreme, and made up their minds that it was a delusion and a snare, and a place to be avoided by all steamers, unless provided with iron-clad charters, guaranteeing high rates of freight . . . (and) heavy payments in case of detention in loading. . . ."[57]

The low water on the Mississippi, and the yellow fever epidemic, also undermined the efforts of merchants in St. Louis and New Orleans to increase trade with Latin America. Capt. A. Browder, a barge owner on the St. Louis–to–New Orleans run, explained to Senator Cockrell his concern for improvement of the Mississippi. He was going to South America to develop direct trade in flour, pork, beef, and other products. Nearly all the goods sold in South America, Browder wrote, were produced in the Mississippi Valley, and yet they had to "pay tribute to the East in the shape of transportation commissions, etc."[58] The New Orleans Chamber of Commerce evidenced a similar concern for attracting western trade in their memorial to Congress for a steamship subsidy for a line from New Orleans to Rio de Janeiro. "Such portion of Western trade as may find a market in South America would be greatly relieved . . . [of the] expense of transportation across the country . . . if allowed to pursue a direct course between the producer and the consumer by way of the port of New Orleans."[59] The success of the new trade was obviously conditional upon cheap rail and water transportation to New Orleans.

Taking heed of these new pressures for the improvement of the Mississippi, Senator Cockrell was much more thorough in 1879 in his preliminary work to insure the passage of the Mississippi River Commission bill. He had a Senate Select Committee on the Mississippi River created, and in the House a new Mississippi River Improvement Committee was organized. The two congressional committees reported out a Mississippi River Commission bill that was similar to Cockrell's proposal of 1878.[60] In the House, Randall Lee Gibson of Louisiana summarized why the South would vote for the commission. The federal government had with "unstinted liberality" improved ocean front harbors, lakes, and upland rivers, he said, but had done almost nothing in comparison for the lower Mississippi. He outlined the navigation hazards which obstructed commerce on the river and made a strong plea for a systematic plan to prevent floods, to remove obstructions, and to provide deep water at all seasons of the year in order to unleash "the mighty commerce that carries the productions of the teeming millions who inhabit the great valley to the markets of the world. . . ."[61] Majorities in both parties heeded Gibson's plea and overwhelmingly approved the commission. Working under the direction of the Secretary of War, the Mississippi River Commission had, by 1881, completed enough surveys and plans to begin its system of improvements. But money was needed.

The Mississippi River Improvement Convention, the largest ever held, was organized late in October 1881 in St. Louis to insure that appropriations would be voted. Though the arguments at the convention were similar to those made in previous years, there was a new sense of importance generated by the tremendous export boom that had begun in 1878. From 1879 to 1881, the foreign market absorbed over 30 percent of the wheat crop, a higher proportion than for any three-year span between 1860 and 1914.[62] The magnitude of the American surpluses abroad convinced convention delegates, as well as many others, that the United States was a world power, and that a key element in that power was the existence of cheap transportation from the interior to the seaboard.[63]

The question of cheap transportation on the Mississippi had been made a national issue, explained the official call, by the "rapid growth and settlement of the Mississippi Valley, and with it the development and enlargement of the export trade —a trade made up in largely controlling proportions of its products. . . ."[64] Because the Mississippi Valley contributed so much toward the national revenue through its exports, it was entitled to obtain money for the improvement of a national river. Speaker after speaker demanded the improvement of the Mississippi. A delegate from Kentucky thought that as long as the Mississippi Valley remained the food supplier of the world, it would "continue to command the power to influence, and become the great seat of the empire of this region of the world." The chairman of the executive committee of the St. Louis Merchant's Exchange argued that the surpluses of the Mississippi Valley had turned the balance of trade in favor of the United States. Moreover, its products would soon "enable us to control the financial destiny of the world. . . ." Gov. John Gear of Iowa thought that the Eads jetties had already proven how much cheaper river transportation was than the all-rail route to the East for export shipments, and wondered what additional great savings would be made if the river were improved according to a comprehensive plan.[65]

The political strategy to be followed in Congress was outlined by former Rep. Edwin O. Stanard of Missouri. Stanard told the delegates of the importance of securing the votes of Wisconsin and Michigan Representatives (who were more interested in the lake route to the seaboard), as was done during the debate over the Eads Jetty Bill. No votes could be expected from the East in 1882, said Stanard, but if "adequate appropriations are secured for the improvement of the Mississippi and its great tributaries . . . we have got to have the votes of the Western members in Congress. . . ."[66]

The cogency of the strategy outlined by Stanard was revealed clearly in the allotments and votes of the 1882 river and harbor bill. Northern and southern Mississippi Valley Congressmen succeeded in passing a $5.468 million appropriation for the Mississippi River Commission, over $4 million of which was for improvements on the river south of the Ohio. In the House, the South, plus seven states in the Northwest, provided 90 of the 120 votes needed to suspend the rules and pass the bill; in the Senate, the same sections provided 25 of the 38 votes cast for the bill. The massive Mississippi River appropriations pushed the total bill for 1882 to $18 million, more than twice as large an amount as had ever been passed before. The South obtained 50 percent of the total appropriation.[67]

Though President Arthur had recommended, in a special message to the Congress, appropriations for the Mississippi River Commission, he nevertheless vetoed the river and harbor bill on 1 August 1882, on the grounds that it was designed to benefit particular localities instead of the general welfare.[68] Rep. George F. Hoar of Massachusetts recalled in his memoirs the strong sentiment throughout the Northeast in favor of the President's action, and the political danger of a vote to override the veto. As a matter of principle, Hoar voted against the President, but a storm of indignation greeted him on his return to Massachusetts. Only a strong speech on the importance of internal improvements to Massachusetts, and the fact that he was not standing for reelection, saved his political career.[69]

Hoar was an exceptional eastern Congressman, for it was the same coalition of southern Democrats and northwestern Republicans forged in 1878 that quickly overrode the presidential veto. In the crucial Senate vote, the southerners and Republicans of the upper valley states provided twenty-eight of the necessary forty-one votes.[70] The editor of the New York *Tribune* grumbled that it was "the worst River and Harbor bill that was ever invented." *Harper's Weekly* and the *Nation* were also critical.[71] In the Mississippi Valley, and especially in the South, the reaction was quite different. The New Orleans

Times-Democrat editorialized that the government had finally recognized "the duty that now devolves upon the entire river so that the people of the Northwest as well as those of the South may share the advantages of deep water to the sea."[72]

The Internal Improvements
Issue Fades

In the years after 1882, the South continued to receive from 35 to 50 percent of the river and harbor appropriations, and the Mississippi River Commission obtained $2 million to $4 million annually. Nevertheless, competition of the railroads, and the failure of various plans to make significant improvements in the navigation of internal waterways, caused the river boats to lose the cotton and grains business. They turned to the dirtier chores of carrying coal, ore, and petroleum. Defeated by trunk lines, the water freight on the lower Mississippi and its tributaries rose only slightly from 1880 to 1889. It then fell precipitously during the next decade. Traffic on the rivers in Virginia, the Carolinas, and Georgia dropped even more drastically.[73]

The importance of improvements on the Mississippi in order to secure cheaper transportation continued to be argued in the 1880s, but the stress was more on water routes as a regulator of rail rates. Increasingly, moreover, the lower river interests eyed large appropriations for the building of levees to protect and reclaim the lowlands. The Northwest grew somewhat envious of the lavish expenditures in the South for what appeared to be the protection of private property. As a result, in 1885 a split in the internal improvement coalition defeated the bill and no appropriations were made.[74] Large appropriations were resumed again the next year, but 1885 was a turning point, and the tariff and the money questions dominated the last two decades of the century.

If the internal river system was a victim of the rapid railroad building in the South during the 1880s, southern seaports (and especially the Gulf ports) were its beneficiaries. Exports from the southern states increased 95.5 percent in volume between 1880 and 1901, while exports from the rest of the country grew only 64.9 percent. Of the larger ports of the South, only Charleston and Norfolk suffered any appreciable decline. The greater gain was made by the Gulf ports. They increased the value of their exports 142.7 percent from 1880 to 1900. In the two decades after 1892, export values from the Gulf ports nearly quadrupled. New Orleans was second to New York and, for a time, Galveston was a close third in the value of exports.[75]

Much of the explanation for this enormous increase in exports from the southern ports involved the growth of trade in raw cotton and manufactured cotton, lumber, tobacco, oil, coal, pig iron, and other products of the South. But what heartened the leaders of the South was the diversion of western products from the Atlantic ports along the railroads that ran southward over the quickest and shortest route to the seaboard. By 1901, to take just one example, the southern ports shipped ten times the flour it had in 1880, and their share of this traffic had mounted from one-tenth to over one-third of the total.[76] The railroads played a key part in organizing the drive to improve the Gulf harbors and in reviving the antebellum idea of redirecting the course of western exports southward and on to new markets in Latin America and the Orient.[77]

NOTES

1.   Paul W. Gates, *Agriculture and the Civil War*, p. 373.
2.   William B. Hesseltine, *A History of the South* (New York: Prentice-Hall, 1936), p. 574.

3. John F. Stover, *The Railroads of the South 1865-1900* (Chapel Hill: University of North Carolina Press, 1955), pp. 39–58.

4. Ibid., p. 59.

5. John H. Franklin, *Reconstruction After the Civil War* (Chicago: University of Chicago Press, 1961), p. 143. For a discussion of the Conservatives' business interests, see C. Vann Woodward, *Origins of the New South, 1877–1913* (Baton Rouge: Louisiana State University Press, 1951), pp. 1–22.

6. Stover, *The Railroads of the South*, p. 98. For a different view, see Maury Klein, "The Strategy of Southern Railroads," *American Historical Review*, LXXIII (April 1968).

7. H. C. McCarty, "Federal and State Aid to Internal Improvements in the South," *The South in the Building of the Nation* (Richmond: Southern Historical Publication Society, 1909), VI, 333–339.

8. *Congressional Record*, 46th Cong., 2d sess., 1880, pp. 4015–4016.

9. *DeBow's Review*, Series 2, VIII, March 1870.

10. Baltimore *Gazette*, 7 October 1870.

11. *Windom Committee Report*, II, pp. 715–716.

12. *DeBow's Review*, Series 2, VIII, April–May 1870.

13. Henry Nash Smith, *Virgin Land*, pp. 169–170. *DeBow's Review*, Series 2, III, January 1867; Series 2, VI, June 1869.

14. *DeBow's Review*, Series 2, V, October 1868.

15. Field notes, Lewis J. Higby MSS, Wisconsin State Historical Society, Madison, Wisconsin.

16. *DeBow's Review*, Series 2, V, October 1868.

17. John Douglas to William Osborn, 9 November 1868, in Thomas Cochran, *Railroad Leaders, 1845–1890* (Cambridge: Harvard University Press, 1953), p. 316.

18. Wyatt W. Belcher, *The Economic Rivalry Between St. Louis and Chicago 1850–1880* (New York: Columbia University Press, 1947), p. 104.

19. *DeBow's Review*, Series 2, V, October 1868.

20. Ibid.

21. *Windom Committee Report*, II, 853–855.

22. New Orleans, Keokuk, and Louisville Conventions, Reports and Resolutions, *Cheap Transportation a Public Necessity* (Dubuque: Dubuque *Daily Herald*, 1869).

23. *DeBow's Review*, Series 2, VII, August 1869.

24. Cincinnati *Commercial*, 8 October 1870.

25. *Proceedings of the Mississippi River Improvement Convention*, St. Louis, 12 and 13 February 1867 (St. Louis: 1867).

26. James D. Richardson, ed., *Messages and Papers of the Presidents 1789–1897*, VII, 37.

27. *DeBow's Review*, Series 2, VII, July 1869.

28. Walter M. Lowrey, "The Engineers and the Mississippi," *Louisiana History*, V (Summer 1964), 244.

29. *Windom Committee Report*, II, 893–895.

30. U.S., Congress, House, Miscellaneous Documents, *Memorial of Commercial Convention, Atlanta, 20 May 1873*, 43d Cong., 1st sess., no. 106.

31. *Windom Committee Report*, I, 251–252.

32. Windom emphasized this in presenting the committee report to Congress. See also *Harper's Weekly*, 7 February 1891, "Mr. Windom's committee did some of the most important work ever accomplished in Congress. One of the results of its labors was the adoption of the jetty system. . . ."

33. *Windom Committee Report*, II, 963–970.

34. *Congressional Record*, 45th Cong., 2d sess., 1878, pp. 4538–4539. Windom later became a supporter of Eads's scheme for a ship-railway across the isthmus, and a business partner as well.

35. Florence Dorsey, *Road to the Sea: The Story of James B. Eads and the Mississippi River* (New York: Rinehart, 1947), pp. 166–180.

36. George F. Hoar, *Autobiography of Seventy Years* (New York: Charles Scribner's Sons, 1903), II, 270–272.

37. Dorsey, *Road to the Sea*, p. 178.

38. *Congressional Record*, 43d Cong., 1st sess., 1874, p. 4526.

39. Ibid., p. 4529.

40. Ibid., p. 4618.

41. Lowrey, "The Engineers and the Mississippi," p. 253.

42. New Orleans *Times-Picayune*, 15 January 1896.

43. For a full discussion of the congressional politics of internal improvements from 1867 to 1874 see Richard N. Current, *Pine Logs and Politics*, pp. 44–102.

44. Carl V. Harris, "The 'Confederate Brigadiers,' Congressmen of the New South" (Master's thesis, University of Wisconsin, 1965), pp. 113–114. The following section draws heavily from this excellent thesis and from several discussions with Harris. Harris computed the South's proportion of the total bill by adding up individual items from the United States Statutes at Large and dividing by the total appropriation. Percentages are approximate.

45. Richardson, *Messages and Addresses of the Presidents*, VII, 377.

46. Atlanta *Constitution*, 12 August 1876. Quoted in Harris, "The Confederate Brigadiers,' " p. 114.

47. Woodward, *Origins of the New South*, pp. 23–50.

48. Ibid., pp. 45–46.

49. C. Vann Woodward, *Reunion and Reaction: The Compromise of 1877 and the End of Reconstruction* (Garden City: Doubleday, 1956), pp. 251–252. Harris, "The 'Confederate Brigadiers,' " p. 115. Ben H. Proctor, *Not Without Honor: The Life of John H. Reagan* (Austin: University of Texas Press, 1962), pp. 203–260.

50. Woodward, *Reunion and Reaction*, p. 261. Harris, "The 'Confederate Brigadiers,' " pp. 115–116.

51. *Congressional Record*, 45th Cong., 2d sess., 1878, pp. 2740–2742.

52. Ibid., pp. 4642–4643.

53. Ibid.

54. Ibid., pp. 4358–4367, 4643.

55. Harris, "The 'Confederate Brigadiers,' " p. 120.

56. Ibid., pp. 123–129.

57. *Proceedings of the Mississippi River Improvement Convention,* held in St. Louis, October 26–29, 1881. This is from a letter of Forstall, Ross & Clayton to George L. Wright. For resolutions of the convention, see *Appleton's Annual Cyclopedia 1881,* pp. 609–610.

58. Capt. A. Browder to Sen. F. M. Cockrell, 26 November 1877, State Department Miscellaneous Letters, National Archives, Washington, D. C. This letter was forwarded by Cockrell to Secretary of State Evarts in order to obtain letters of introduction to consuls for Browder's trip to South America.

59. Memorial of Chamber of Commerce of New Orleans to Congress and the President, 19 December 1877, State Department Miscellaneous Letters, National Archives, Washington, D. C.

60. Harris, "The 'Confederate Brigadiers,' " pp. 123–124.

61. *Congressional Record,* 45th Cong., 3d sess., 1879, pp. 258–264.

62. Morton Rothstein, "America in the International Rivalry for the British Wheat Market, 1860–1914," *Mississippi Valley Historical Review,* XLVII (December 1960), 403.

63. *Proceedings of the Mississippi River Improvement Convention,* held in St. Louis, October 26–29, 1881. An editorial in the *Nautical Gazette,* reprinted in the official report of the convention proceedings, drew the connection between improved transportation and world power very explicitly. It asserted that, since the West had become the granary of the world, it must join the South in a drive to open up markets in Central America, "almost wholly monopolized by the English and Germans. . . . The men of the West must learn that England is her bitterest foe . . . that she has been working for years to get the whip hand of Americans." For other expressions of the link between the export boom, cheap transportation, and world power, see Lee Benson, "The Historical Background of Turner's Frontier Essay," *Agricultural History,* XXV (April 1951), 61–64.

64. Ibid.

65. Ibid.

66. Ibid.

67. Harris, "The 'Confederate Brigadiers,' " p. 125.

68. Edward L. Pross, "A History of Rivers and Harbors Appropriations Bills 1866–1930," 103. Pross argues that Arthur's veto marks a turning point in the reform of this legislation away from logrolling.

69. Hoar, *Autobiography of Seventy Years,* II, 112–119.

70. Harris, "The 'Confederate Brigadiers,' " p. 125.

71. Quoted in Pross, "A History of Rivers and Harbors Appropriations Bills," p. 104.

72. Quoted in *Grand Banquet to Captain Jas. B. Eads by Representatives of the Mercantile and Commercial Interests of New Orleans* (W. B. Stansburg Printer: 1882).

73. U.S., Bureau of the Census, *Report on Transportation Business in the United States at the Eleventh Census: 1890* (Washington: GPO, 1894), p. 449. For 1880, freight tons moved on lower Mississippi was 3,576,972; for 1889, the figure was 6,401,204. U.S., Department of Commerce and Labor, *Report of the Commissioners of Corporations on Transportation by Water in the United States* (Washington: GPO, 1909), Part I, 49–58. Tonnage dropped from 6,401,203 in 1889 to 2,546,187 in 1906.

74. *Bradstreet's,* 12 September 1885. This provides an excellent example of the regional conflicts over internal improvements.

75. Woodward, *The Origins of the New South,* pp. 125–126.

76. Ibid., p. 126.

77. See Chapter 7 for the role of the Illinois Central in this movement.

PART TWO

Railroad Regulation
and Economic Nationalism

5

International Aspects
of the Interstate
Commerce Act

THE DEBATE over cheap transportation to the seaboard did not
end in the 1880s, but became submerged in the stream of agitation over national regulation of the railroads. The anarchi-
cal expansion of the railroad network after 1879 generated demands from farmers, merchants, and railroad men for law and
order. The question was not whether but what kind of legislation would be enacted. Charles E. Perkins, president of the
Chicago, Burlington & Quincy (CB&Q) and a laissez-faire diehard, contended as early as 1878 that the "public will regulate
us to some extent—and we must make up our minds to it.
. . ."[1] Shippers and carriers clearly had different objectives in
seeking national regulation of the railroads. But there was one
common concern, which has been largely ignored in accounts
of the regulation struggle—that no law impair the economic
strength of the United States in its struggle for world power.

John H. Reagan, chairman of the House Committee on
Commerce, took up the cause of federal control of interstate
commerce in 1878 against a background of growing hostility

to railroad discrimination and arrogance. Reagan's bill called for an end to rebates and drawbacks, the prohibition of pools, the publication of freight rates and classifications, the elimination of higher charges for a short haul than a long haul, and an end to discrimination between shippers. The origins and motives of Reagan's action are still debated.[2] But the opposition strategy of appealing to economic nationalism was foreshadowed in the congressional debate on the Reagan bill in 1879.

Rep. Abraham S. Hewitt of New York spoke for the trunkline railroads. He advanced the concept developed by Charles Francis Adams, Jr., Albert Fink, and George R. Blanchard of a national railroad *commission* to strengthen the pooling machinery of the industry. The Reagan bill did not take that approach. Moreover, Hewitt argued, the long- and short-haul section was unfair to the West. The railroads should not be strictly regulated, as proposed by Reagan's bill, for it was often necessary "to put down rates to keep the foreign market." Cheap through rates would be destroyed by the Reagan bill. "The only thing that enables our grain to be sold in European markets in competition with rival nations," Hewitt exaggerated, "is that steamships are promptly loaded with full cargoes." A commission of competent experts would be "interested in developing this great foreign trade which at length is pulling us out of the quagmire into which we have been plunged. . . ." Hewitt consistently adhered to this position over the next several years both in and out of Congress.[3]

Rep. Clarkson S. Potter, also of New York, rose to point out that the long- and short-haul clause of the Reagan bill allowed the railroads to raise, not lower, the through rates. It therefore might discriminate against the West and destroy the booming export trade. "Look at our great foreign trade! How do we keep it up? How comes it that our vast surplus of grain is shipped abroad except that these crops are moved from where they are raised to the seaboard mainly without profit?" The Reagan bill, Clarkson concluded, would raise through rates and "thus destroy this the only prosperous branch of foreign trade we have left."[4]

Reagan did not answer such critics of his bill. Instead, he called for a vote. The bill passed the House, but the Senate declined to act upon it. As in 1878, the Reagan bill was pigeonholed in the committee on commerce. Only a more aroused public would be able to overcome congressional lethargy. The exposure of transportation abuses by New York State's Hepburn Committee during 1879 provided the needed spark for the advocates of federal regulation.

The committee itself arose from the protests of New York farmers and merchants against railroad disregard for the interests of the state. Excessively high costs of transportation, place discrimination, and railroad arrogance and corruption were the principal complaints advanced during the eight-month investigation. So startling and well documented were the charges that even William H. Vanderbilt of the New York Central and Hugh Jewitt of the Erie conceded that some type of federal regulation might be necessary.[5]

Before the investigations of the Hepburn Committee, agitation in the West for railroad regulation had been concentrated at the state level. "It is useless to go to Congress now with the subject. Congress cannot be approached upon any matter suddenly . . . ," argued Milton George, editor of the *Western Rural,* as late as 1 March 1879.[6] But as the revelations of the Hepburn Committee appeared in the columns of the *Western Rural,* and the flood of grain traffic resumed late in 1879, western farmers swung their full support behind the Reagan bill. The resumption of a large export trade in agricultural commodities dramatized the whole question of regulation for the West. "The rare opportunity of supplying the foreign demand for the products of our farms at *reasonable* prices must be in great measure lost," concluded George, "unless the intervention of Congress . . . can be secured as early as possible."[7] George had joined the argument of the railroad opponents of the Reagan bill. To him, regulation did not mean higher through rates and a consequent decrease in export shipments of farm surpluses. On the contrary, regulation would lower the general level of railroad rates and thereby allow farmers to profit from a growing export trade.

The campaign for federal regulation continued to gain momentum in 1880 as the railroads, pressed by large movements of crops, raised their rates. Average through rail rates on a bushel of grain from Chicago to New York increased from 17.56 cents in 1878 to 19.90 cents in 1880, a high for the decade.[8] From all over the nation, but especially from the Ohio and upper Mississippi Valleys, petitions and memorials swamped Congressmen. "While general prosperity pervades the land," read one typical petition from a local Grange in 1880, "agriculture, the corner-stone of our national progress, is depressed. The surplus from our farms is wrenched from us to enrich these giant monopolies. A buoyant market instantly enhances the freight rates of transportation, robbing the producer of well earned profits. . . ."[9] Westerners received support from New York merchants, who in 1881 organized the National Antimonopoly League to secure state regulation and the passage of the Reagan bill.[10]

The leaders of the railroad industry, especially the trunk-line presidents, took alarm at the new agitation and again attempted to head off the Reagan bill. First, they hoped to divide the railroad reformers with a bill of their own. Impressed by the testimony of Charles Francis Adams, Jr., and Albert Fink, the House Committee on Commerce, late in 1879, voted not to report out the Reagan bill. It endorsed the Henderson bill, designed by Adams and William W. Rich of Massachusetts. The Henderson bill provided for a relatively powerless National Board of Railroad Commissioners, recognized the existence of pools, rebates, and drawbacks, and was in every way antithetical to the Reagan bill. The spectacle of railroads pressing for a national commission caused Reagan and other supporters of regulation to shy away from this proposal, even though many conceded it was necessary. Such division over the best means of regulation, as the proponents of the Henderson bill predicted, had the effect of temporarily dissipating the whole regulation movement.[11]

At the same time that trunk-line officials pressed for a national commission, they again employed the technique of appealing to nationalistic sentiments to block the Reagan bill. The central figure in the second strategy was Edward A. Atkinson, a well-known political economist of the Adam Smith school and a vigorous opponent of railroad regulation. Atkinson believed in the adequacy of competition as a means of securing the proper conduct of business.[12] His first formulation of these ideas appeared in March 1880 in a lengthy pamphlet entitled "The Railroads of the United States, a Potent Factor in the Politics of that Country and Great Britain."

Atkinson attacked the critics of the so-called railroad monopoly. First, railroad rates had dropped precipitously since the Civil War. Second, the competition between products in the markets of the world, not the competition of railroads, set the limits on the cost of transportation. The railroad development of the Northwest, Atkinson observed, had transformed the agriculture of the eastern states. For a time the farmers of the East attempted to compete with those of the West, but the increase in transportation facilities soon placed them far behind in the race. They had to cease cultivating grain and turn to raising fruits, vegetables, poultry, and dairy products for local markets.

That process was causing a similar revolution in Great Britain. The tremendous flow of western grain and meat from the United States rendered the existing system of renting and working land in Great Britain unprofitable. Through rates of forty-five to sixty cents a bushel of wheat from Dakota territory stations to Liverpool on the Northern Pacific, for example, undermined the basis of power of the British land-holding aristocracy. The American farmer realized a large profit from those exports, which would cause a still greater increase in production. "Such being the condition," concluded Atkinson, "it seems very certain that we shall continue to supply Great Britain and Western Europe with our increasing quantities of bread and meat."[13]

The next year, as the tide of agitation for federal regulation swelled, Atkinson was invited by Joseph H. Reall, editor of the *Journal of the American Agricultural Association,* to revise his earlier piece in order to emphasize the dangers of government regulation more clearly. Atkinson obliged with his famous "Railroads and the Farmers." "The question of State interference with railroads is likely to come up in a serious way," Atkinson wrote to Reall, accepting the request to denounce the Reagan bill, "and I rather think the article will be a strong card on the railroad side of the question."[14]

Atkinson's argument proceeded from the assumption of a harmony of interest between the railroads and the farmers. After adducing charts and statistics which showed that the drop in railroad rates since 1865 was accompanied by increased agricultural production, Atkinson asserted that legislation—all legislation—damaged the underlying, fruitful harmony. Railroad men and farmers had a common interest in solving the most important problem of the future—the distribution, not the production, of the abundance of goods. He referred to his earlier article on the international implications of this problem and concluded that this "country never needed the world for a market so much as it does now."[15]

Leaders of the railroad industry were pleased with Atkinson's effort, and seem to have acted upon editor Reall's hope that if a copy of "Railroads and Farmers" were in the hands of every farmer "it would do them more good than a copy of the revised or any other edition of the New Testament."[16] Albert Fink, on behalf of the trunk lines, John Murray Forbes and Charles Perkins of the Chicago, Burlington & Quincy, and Collis P. Huntington of the Southern Pacific, joined forces to see that the article had wide circulation. Funds were provided to send copies of the article to 2,000 newspapers, and in all 32,000 copies of it were paid for by various railroad presidents.[17]

The leading advocate of federal regulation among the farmers of the West, Milton George of the *Western Rural,* viciously attacked the *Journal of the American Agricultural Association* as a "brazen attempt to make a monopoly apologist of a professed farmer's paper." The *Journal,* in his view, had insulted every farmer in the country by supporting railroad extortion. Reporting on a speech given by editor Reall, the *Western Rural* sarcastically commented on his statement that railroads and farmers were closer in interest than two peas in a pod. "Even this mild attempt to create competition might prevent Reall from getting the railroads to circulate the next issue of his farmer paper."[18] Thus, while rejecting the appeal of the railroads for a free hand, western farmers did recognize, as one Grange petition in 1880 phrased it, "the close interdependence" of agriculture and transportation which had helped to transform the United States into the "granary of the world."[19] It was the abuses of the railroad system, not the system itself, that the farmers hoped to eliminate through federal regulation.

Although no longer chairman of the House Commerce Committee, Reagan used the hearings of 1882 as a platform to push his own bill against a confusing array of other federal regulatory measures. The principal argument of the railroad witnesses at the hearings was that regulation would interfere with the export grain trade, the very key to the revival of prosperity in the nation. Chauncey M. Depew, president of the New York Central, set the pattern for other railroad executives in emphasizing the tie between the continuation of exports of American agricultural goods, the prosperity of the nation, and the freedom of the railroads to make rates so as to enable the American producer to compete in the markets of the world.

It was not the railroad monopolists, Depew explained, but the wheat grown on the steppes of Russia that controlled the rates on the New York Central from Chicago to New York. He recalled the tremendous export boom of 1880 that "had driven English farmers to despair . . . had discouraged development in Russia, and . . . had brought to a standstill the productions of Germany and of France. The results of that have been incalculable upon our prosperity. . . ." The export boom had turned the tide of debt between the United States and Great Britain, enabled the government to resume specie payments, set factories to work, encouraged railroad building, and given labor employment. But such conditions had begun to change in 1881 with short crops at home and large crops abroad. Clearly attempting to divert attention from the railroads, Depew charged that middlemen and speculators in the grain business bought up the short supply in order to raise prices, with the result that the export trade had not "received such a blow for a quarter of a century." British capital started to flow into Russian and Indian railroads, Egypt's production was stimulated, and finally, Depew lamented, "Europe became independent of us."[20]

Wayne MacVeigh of the Pennsylvania Railroad and George B. Blanchard of the Erie made similar remarks about such so-called natural causes that determined rates: they referred to water competition, value of domestic products, and foreign needs, markets and rivalries. Blanchard quoted Henry Varnum Poor, spokesman of the railroad industry, who in his 1881 "Manual of Railroads" had written that the railroads of the country "have been the instruments, of all others in placing it in its present position before the world, by enabling the wheat grower in distant Dakota to compete successfully with the wheat grower of Western Europe in his accustomed markets." Blanchard agreed with Poor's conclusion that all legislative endeavors to fix or regulate values would only hurt the country.[21]

But it was Albert Fink, nationally recognized authority on railroad affairs, who caused Reagan the most embarrassment. Like his predecessors, Fink emphasized the impact of domestic regulation on the foreign trade of the country. Fink pointed out to Reagan that, in order "to encourage industry and commerce, and enable the people of America to enter into competition in foreign markets," railroad companies offered special export rates, rates that were often less than the cost of transportation. Fink inquired if the Reagan bill would stop such a practice. Reagan acknowledged that was a correct interpretation of the bill. "Wherein does the injustice consist if railroad companies carry export freight to New York at less than domestic consumption?" Fink asked rhetorically. "Is it the duty of Congress," Fink sarcastically concluded, "to protect foreign nations against American competition by the passage of such bills as the 'Reagan bill?'"[22]

Many other criticisms were made by railroad opponents of Reagan bill. The antipooling clause, it was asserted, would only add to the competitive problems of the industry. The rule about posting rates and schedules would create undue railway expense and hardship. And the high penalties for violation were deemed unreasonable. One objection to the bill that was later stressed more strongly deserves special attention. The railroad presidents again appealed to nationalistic sentiment and testified that the strict regulation of the industry under the Reagan bill would encourage and promote the growth of Canadian lines to the detriment of United States lines.

Chauncey Depew played to the latent anglophobia of the American public, warning Congress to remember that British corporations were seeking to control American products for the benefit of British capital and the development of British territory. The Reagan bill would "take the American railway system by the throat, tie its hands behind it, and put it in the lap of the Canadian system." George Blanchard raised the specter of a completed Canadian Pacific Railway that would parallel the Northern Pacific and its trunk lines, and successfully divert traffic from the United States from ocean to ocean. The president of a railroad in Michigan submitted that the "majority of all interstate transportation to the Atlantic ports will by this bill be brought into the unjust, unwise, and suicidal competition with these Canadian lines."[23]

Biding his time for rebuttal, Reagan finally rose to defend his measure. Conceding that some of the bill might need amending, Reagan defended its theory and purposes. The resolutions of state legislatures, boards of trade, chambers of commerce, the state Granges in favor of his bill indicated that it was designed for the protection of the people against railway managers and corporations who did "things which all men know to be wrong."

Reagan concentrated his counterattack at the weakest point of the testimony of the railroad men. The greatest criticism hurled at the bill, he maintained in a purposeful distortion, concerned the fear of competition from Canadian roads. "Such fears . . . ought to excite our sympathy—the fears I mean, not the facts." Reagan correctly identified the Canadian Southern, one of the competitors ostensibly feared by the experts, as in fact part of the New York Central system. William H. Vanderbilt was the president and Cornelius Vanderbilt served as vice-president and treasurer. "And yet we are left to understand from the speeches of Messrs. Fink, Blanchard, De-Pew, and the balance," Reagan pounded home his point, "that these Vanderbilts are dreadfully afraid of the competition of these Canadian roads if the Reagan Bill shall become a law."[24] Depew's denial that the Canadian Southern was part of the New York Central system only served to put the railroad case in its worst possible light, and appeared to be proof of railroad arrogance and deceit. Reagan's counterattack on that point was effective, and it was not until Senator Cullom took a more active role in the regulation fight that the Canadian question once again assumed any importance.

The Transportation Versus Currency Debate

The tremendous export boom, from 1878 to 1881, had clearly helped such railroad stalwarts as Atkinson, Depew, Fink, and Blanchard in their opposition to the Reagan bill. They argued that cheap, competitive, and, most importantly, unregulated rates were in great part responsible for that boom. But farmers and merchants, especially in the West, complained that their share of the new prosperity was inadequate; they vigorously defended the Reagan bill. With the collapse of the export boom and the onslaught of another business depression (1883 to 1885), tension between the metropolis and the interior increased, and the push for federal regulation renewed. Moreover, debate on transportation, and a host of other issues, raged within the framework of the international competition of American agricultural exports in foreign markets.

The British minister to the United States, Sir Lionel Sackville-West, analyzed in 1885 the source of the economic problem. American prosperity depended "upon a profitable market for its surplus agricultural produce and, when, as at present this market is wanting, the Western farmer must necessarily forego his present social status." The competition of India and Russia in the British market, the minister pointed out, no longer guaranteed that poor harvests in Europe would increase American exports. He predicted, therefore, that the new foreign competition would produce a conflict "between the Western and Eastern States, which latter, under a restrictive tariff, have amassed wealth at the expense of the former by enhancing the cost of material life."[25]

Most Americans agreed that one of the crucial factors in the more severe competition of India and Russia in international markets was the increase in railroad and canal construction that facilitated large exports from those countries. Widely circulated and reprinted consular reports from Europe, Russia, and India in the 1880s often referred to these developments. The implications drawn from these reports provided an important focus in the campaign for railroad regulation and cheap transportation to the seaboard.

In 1883, Consul General H. Mattson, for example, reported from Calcutta alarming statistics on the increase of Indian wheat exports since 1879. In that year, only 2 million bushels were exported from India, but 37 million bushels were exported in 1882. By American standards, transportation and handling facilities were still very poor. But Britain was encouraging the development of wheat resources in India by building canals and better railroads to the seaboard, and in every other way giving aid, in the hope that India would ultimately become the grain supplier of the island. In order to maintain the American advantage in the British wheat market, Mattson insisted it was "absolutely necessary that America should keep pace with India in the efforts to reduce and maintain rates at the lowest possible minimum."[27]

Consul Albert D. Shaw of Manchester, England, was even more alarmed by railway and export developments in India at the end of 1884. He predicted that if the great increase in Indian wheat and cotton continued, those raw materials would find a market in the seaboard towns of the United States within a few years. Citing statistics on railway mileage and wheat acreage in India, Shaw did not even think it possible for the United States to compete by cheaper transport rates. "As the outlook now appears," he wrote, "the American markets and those of the South American states must soon mainly provide consumers for our American wheat."[28]

Many of the consuls in Europe reported that the railroads were either owned or controlled by the governments. One purpose of this arrangement was to encourage key industries and the development to exports. Consul Dunham J. Crain of Milan, for example, was greatly impressed with the administration of the railroads in Italy, and suggested that rate wars in the United States were injurious to the country and ought to be stopped by the government: "Reasonable and equitable rates, admitting of a steady and uninterrupted movement of our great staples to the ports, are essential to the sustenance of our commercial marine and the security of our markets in Europe." Stating the international importance of an improved internal transportation system, Crain concluded that economy of carriage must begin at the point of production and continue to the place of final destination. "The zone of consumption of American products is enlarged or diminished by the action of our railway companies. Ships are but a link in the chain. There must be coordinate railway and ship supervision."[29]

The large increases of raw material exports from other sources of supply, especially India, and of railroad regulation in Europe, heightened demands for river and harbor improvements in the West and South in the mid-1880s. For example, large conventions were held in 1885 in New Orleans, Kansas City, and St. Paul in the interest of cheap transportation in the Mississippi and Missouri valleys. The remarks of Iowa Congressman Jerry H. Murphy at the Northwestern Waterways Convention in St. Paul were typical. The urgent demands of farmers in Illinois and Iowa for waterways improvements resulted "because cheap transportation is indispensable to foreign markets for their surplus grain." If such improvements were not made, Murphy warned that "our producing rivals, Russia, Australia, and India will supply the Liverpool market instead of the United States of America. For if that market takes its supply from these nations, our surplus will be a burden: and believe me this is no dream of fancy."[30]

Aroused by the rapid fall in commodity prices, westerners argued that the competition of other nations in foreign markets also dramatized the urgency of national railroad regulation. Speaking on behalf of the growing National Farmers' Alliance movement, the *Western Rural* warned in 1884 that the "greed of railroad management will yet operate to shut our wheat out of the foreign market." Lower freights would not necessarily enable the United States to gain European markets, but the existing high rates made it impossible to hold the markets already gained. "It is a point that brings this question of railroad extortion more closely home to us than almost anything that has been presented," concluded the editors.[31] A year later, the *Western Rural* argued that the solution to the problem of increased competition from India was to be found in cheaper transportation and railroad regulation. "We are now forced to the conclusion that the alarming inroads made upon our former export demand for wheat is simply a question of internal transportation."[32]

Yet, even before the passage of the Interstate Commerce Act in 1887, that line of argument was used less in the pages of the *Western Rural*. Competitive anarchy within the railroad industry deepened, and through rates dropped precipitously. Noncompetitive local rates, however, remained relatively high. Thus, in considering the railroad problem, local—not through or export—rates were the greatest concern to the agrarians.[33] To be sure, increased railroad mileage, the Suez Canal, larger and faster steamships, and other world-wide transportation developments, especially in India, required improved through transportation if the new competition in the British commodity markets was to be met. But in a break with merchant and manufacturing interests, after 1885 agrarian spokesmen in the South and West emphasized the role of a changed monetary policy in order to reverse the depression of prices and the decline of American exports.[34]

The argument that the silver question was of greater importance than transportation developments in the new competition hinged on a complex analysis of the international role of silver. When Congress demonitized silver in 1873, the price of silver relative to gold began to fall. Consequently, the amount of silver that English merchants could purchase with gold increased. The cheap silver could then be used to purchase a greater quantity of wheat and cotton from India and other silver-standard countries. The farmers' spokesman concluded that, in effect, the demonitization of silver offered a premium to the British import merchant to purchase Indian wheat and cotton. This encouraged production of these staples in India and depressed commodity prices in the United States.[35] Thus, the increased construction of Indian railroads, for example, was seen as partly a consequence of international monetary policy. Morton Frewen, an articulate advocate of the demonitization of silver, summed up the problem in *Bradstreet's* in 1886. Indian railroads, Frewen claimed, were "largely the result of the cheap rupee. If it pays to sell the wheat, the corn, the cotton, the hides of the Punjab in London, of course it will be profitable to connect the Punjab and the ocean by railroads."[36]

The Cleveland administration largely avoided these arguments about transportation and silver by downgrading the importance of foreign competition in the British market. Secretary of State Thomas Bayard, for example, said in 1886 that Indian production and competition "seems distant and little to be feared."[37] Democratic Rep. John Findlay contended the same year that the comparative merits of silver and gold as a standard of value had no relation to a British attempt to encourage trade with India and other colonies. Silver advocates, he charged, were just "pulling the British lion's tail to the point of mutilation."[38] But Edward Atkinson, a vigorous supporter of the Cleveland administration's monetary policies, was one figure who repeatedly attempted to meet the arguments of the farmers directly.[39]

Atkinson refocused attention on the transportation issue, which he had studied earlier in connection with railroad regulation. Atkinson thought it "utterly untenable to allege that the depreciation of the rupee, in the exchange between India and Great Britain [had] worked an equivalent bounty on Indian wheat." Such depreciation may have stimulated wheat exports from India for a short time, but by 1887 silver was only a "side issue." The decline in the price of foodstuffs was not attributable to silver, but primarily to the "vast changes, in fact the social revolution, brought about by the railroad and the steamship. . . ." The prominent position of the United States in the supply of Great Britain was explained by the reduction of railway charges, especially on the long haul, that accompanied the extension westward of the railway network.[40] The heading of a graph, prepared by Atkinson for a speech entitled "What is Bimetallism," adequately explains his theory: A statement "showing the effect of the reduction in the charge for moving provisions long distances at the lowest possible rates, in enabling farmers to sell grain and meat for export which could not otherwise have been sold at all, thereby bringing about the restoration of specie payments. The balance of exports over imports for ten years has consisted wholly of farm products."[41]

The battle of the standards in the 1880s thus had a subtle influence on the railroad debate. Western and southern agrarians, fretting over the decline in exports of staple commodities and increased foreign competition, protested the existing monetary system. Although conscious of the role the worldwide communications revolution played in stiffer competition from countries supplying raw materials, the agrarians nevertheless confined the discussion of railroad regulation to discrimination, fraud, political influence, and high local rates.

Those issues allowed opponents of any regulatory legislation (or supporters of a weak national commission) once again to play on the real fears of farmers and others of meeting foreign competitors in the markets of the world. Regulation, if not carefully devised, they warned, would raise the cost of transporting export commodities and give these competitors an irretrievable advantage. The testimony before the Cullom Committee in 1885, and the public and congressional debates over regulation prior to and shortly after the passage of the Interstate Commerce Act, clearly illustrate this strategy.

"The International Element in the Railroad Problem"

Heightened agitation for regulation, abetted by the continuing depression, was reflected in the passage of the Reagan bill in the House on 8 January 1885 by a vote of 161 to 75. It had little chance of winning Senate approval, however. Shelby M. Cullom, chairman of the Senate Commerce Committee, endorsed a commission bill more acceptable to railroad interests. After rejecting the long- and short-haul clause, the Senate voted on 4 February 1885 in favor of the Cullom regulation bill. The two houses of Congress were then deadlocked, for neither house would agree to adopt the other's bill.[42]

"Cullom, we know nothing about this question; we are groping in the dark," Iowa's William Boyd Allison told his friend from Illinois when the latter again proposed his interstate commerce bill in the opening days of the Forty-ninth Congress. Allison suggested that a select committee ought to investigate the problem and report its finding to the Senate.[43] The advice made sense to Cullom, and he succeeded in organizing a committee of five senators to conduct the investigation from May until November 1885. The Cullom Committee took testimony in Boston, New York, Philadelphia, Buffalo, Detroit, Chicago, St. Louis, Des Moines, Omaha, Minneapolis, Memphis, New Orleans, and Atlanta. Railroad leaders, merchants, manufacturers, farmers, and many others either appeared before the committee to give testimony or sent accounts of their views.

The Windom Report of 1874 had made much of high charges, claiming that the general rate level was extortionate. But most of the complaints of shippers before the Cullom Committee stressed wildly fluctuating rates, rebates to favored shippers, heavier charges for shorter than for longer hauls, and the granting of favorable rates to one area at the expense of another. Cullom himself believed, by the end of his investigation, that the key problem to be dealt with by legislation was "unjust discrimination" between persons and places.[44] But, as in the Windom Report, numerous witnesses expressed concern for the influence of regulation upon the foreign commerce of the nation, and Cullom and others were forced to deal with that issue.

Many of the railroad men who had vigorously opposed the Reagan bill testified in favor of Cullom's plan for a national commission of railroad experts. But they warned again of the danger of iron-clad rules in determining rates. George R. Blanchard took the familiar stand that rates were limited by competitive factors, including the "value of wheat at and for Odessa and India." Despite the lowering of commodity prices, the general level of rates was not too high. Given the rates from Odessa to Liverpool, the British expenditures on irrigation and railways in India, and the fact that England made constant efforts to lessen the imports of American wheat, Blanchard concluded "our railway companies are standing more than their due share of the country's competitive burden of putting our products into foreign competing markets."

Albert Fink, who Cullom consulted privately in preparing his bill, repeated his concern at the hearings for the continuation of export rates in order that American wheat be able to withstand the "competition with grain from East India and the Black Sea." Albert Hamilton, a railroad lawyer, made the same point at greater length. Suppose that both India and the United States have a large surplus of wheat in the same year, hypothesized Hamilton: Indian wheat could then be sold in England "at much below what our American farmer can sell his wheat for. Now, either the American farmer has got to keep his stock on hand and not sell at all, or else he has got to go over to England and compete. . . . If he sends that wheat to England to compete with the Indian wheat he must have a railroad rate low enough to get it there, if possible in fair competition with the Indian farmer."[45]

A few of the large shippers in the West who cautiously accepted regulation or opposed it altogether, also showed great concern over the impact of new rates on foreign trade and competition. Charles Ridgely, president of an Illinois iron company, though favoring the commission system, contended that farmers had no ground for complaint against the railroads. Pointing to the industrialization of Illinois, Ridgely suggested that the underlying basis for the development of the West "has altogether depended [on] the possibility of sending our surplus products to European markets—a question of long distance transportation of commerce, not only between states, but across the ocean and with foreign nations."[46] Charles Pillsbury, wealthy Minneapolis flour miller, had no criticism of railroad rates to the seaboard. The competition of Granger and trunk-line roads contributed to an extremely profitable export trade, and Pillsbury opposed federal legislation which might change that situation. He acknowledged the complaints of Minnesota farmers against rates from their homes to St. Paul or Duluth. But that was not his concern. "You might say that the foreign price makes the price of wheat," Pillsbury suggested, noting that millers felt the competition of Indian and Russian wheat "very largely." But he denied that a reduction of rail rates for getting the wheat to the mill would allow the millers to lower the price of flour. The benefit of reduced local freights accrued entirely to the farmers and did not enable the millers to better compete abroad.[47]

Spokesmen for the farmers unanimously favored a strong regulation measure. But they avoided linking the regulation of railroads to the condition of the foreign market. The exchange between Herman C. Wheeler, secretary of the Iowa State Agricultural Society, and Sen. Isham G. Harris revealed the typical agrarian concern for local rather than through or export rates. Although, when questioned, Wheeler did admit their interrelationship. Was not the price of grain in the Chicago market controlled by the markets further East? Senator Harris inquired.

> *Wheeler:*   By the Liverpool market.
> *Harris:*   If it be true that the price of grain in Liverpool controls the price of grain in Chicago, and that the Chicago price controls the price here [Des Moines], does not the cost of transportation from here to Liverpool affect the price of grain in the hands of the producer?
> *Wheeler:*   Yes sir.
> *Harris:*   Then on what you sell at Chicago, the price you get depends upon what that grain will bring in Liverpool.
> *Wheeler:*   Yes sir.
> *Harris:*   And it makes the producer in Iowa directly interested in the freight from the field to the consumer in Liverpool, does it not?
> *Wheeler:*   Yes sir, with exceptions of big home demand, no export, or if they are short in Europe, then Chicago controls the price.[48]

The Worthy Master of the Tennessee State Grange, W. H. Nelson, gave an exceptionally direct reply to the critics of railroad regulation who appeared so concerned over the export situation. Agriculture and transportation had become and would remain interdependent, and, Nelson observed, the conflict between them was "more apparent than real." Farmers were not unmindful of the rate reductions on railroads over the years. But this was necessary, in part because "freight in excess of local demand must reach the seaboard at prices which will meet the foreign demand or exportation will cease." In years of short crops at home and weak foreign demand, railroads shared with other interests the impact of the depression. The trouble with the railroads was that, with a return to abundant crops and advancing prices abroad, rates were raised to "all the traffic will bear, thus making all seasons alike unpropitious to the farmer." Through that action so directly affecting the farmer, the railroads depressed every other interest in the land including their own. But Nelson concluded "these attempts to 'kill the golden goose to get the golden egg' should not be tolerated much longer by the American goose."[49]

Railroad men again raised the specter of competition between the regulated American carriers and the unregulated Canadian roads before the Cullom Commission. Albert Fink testified that it was most doubtful whether any legislation could prevent the Canadian roads from competing unfairly. He especially feared the Grand Trunk, stating that no law could prevent its charging a lower rate from Chicago to Montreal. George R. Blanchard made roughly the same statement. He explained that if the American law could apply to the Grand Trunk only between Chicago and the Canadian border, it could carry through business for less than its competitors.[50] John P. Green of the Pennsylvania told Cullom that his bill ought to be amended to include the Canadian railroads. "I have just returned from the West and in discussing this matter with some of the prominent railroad people there, they point to that as the defect of the bill." Without such an amendment, "our American roads will simply be at the mercy of their Canadian rivals."[51] Speaking before the Senate in 1886, when the question was reopened, Cullom minimized the importance of competition from Canadian railroads.⁵² During the next two years, however, he became convinced on the point and led the attack against the Canadian roads.

Cullom delivered the report of his committee to the Senate in January 1886. It emphasized that no general question of "governmental policy occupies at this time so prominent a place in the thoughts of the people as that of controlling the steady growth and extending influence of corporate power and of regulating its relations to the public."⁵³ The general contention of the committee was that unjust discrimination was the major evil to be remedied, and the various sections of the proposed bill were designed primarily to deal with this problem. But a section, "Relations of Internal and External Commerce to Agriculture," was included in the Cullom Report. It suggests that the arguments of those opposed to the Cullom bill were of this nature and had to be countered.

The American performance had "reversed the dictum of Malthus," Cullom asserted, because its food supply had outrun population. The excess had to be exported to "countries less fortunate." Rather than export the raw materials, however, Cullom favored condensation in order to save on the cost of transportation and to keep the profits from processing. But as surplus lands were occupied and the limit on production attained, the need to export farm commodities would cease. That would happen in the near future, he maintained. Moreover, South America, Australia, and Africa had immense areas of rich land and could easily expand their production. Thus, Cullom concluded, while the nation would respond to any foreign demand that might arise, "the principal markets, both for bread and meat, must henceforth be sought at home."⁵⁴

The question of foreign trade and regulation was not so easily dismissed during the public and congressional debates over the compromise bill which came out of the House and Senate Conference Committee of 1886. Sen. John Sherman of

Ohio, a supporter of the final bill, struck a responsive chord: "Everywhere there is a fear that this bill, intended to relieve the people of the United States, may destroy our export trade. . . ."[55] His concern centered on section 4, the long- and short-haul clause, which said that a railroad could not charge more for intermediate or short hauls over a longer route in the same direction than the price of shipping goods over the entire route. Even with the qualification that the Interstate Commerce Commission (ICC), to be established by the law, would determine the extent to which the railroads could be relieved from the operation of the clause,[56] many Congressmen feared the impact of the bill on foreign trade.

After listening to the debate on section 4 of his bill, Senator Cullom summarized the nature of the controversy. "There is a public sentiment and a public belief . . . that by means of the difference between the long and the short haul in this country the short haul people are terribly swindled, and that this is worse than the advantages from the cheap long hauls."[57] Opponents of section 4 were, therefore, shippers who benefited from cheap through rates and railroad men who feared that local rates would be reduced under the operations of the clause.

First among the groups opposed to section 4 were seaboard merchants. The New York Chamber of Commerce declared that section 4 would raise through rates from the West to the same level as local rates, "thus obstructing and materially decreasing the moving and exportation of cotton, grain, petroleum and other products."[58] The Boston Chamber of Commerce took a similar stand. "The bitterest opponent of the bill here" reported one Boston correspondent, "were the large export dealers, and European steamship lines, who interpret the new law as a direct blow at the foreign trade of this port."[59] In a lengthy editorial on the long- and short-haul question, the *Commercial and Financial Chronicle* called it a "cruel device for disorganizing the trade of the Far West. . . .

A Liverpool market for grain and an Oregon, Colorado, Kansas, or New York farm with the grain upon it, are the factors, and the problem [is] to bring them together."[60] Only cheap through rates accomplished this objective. The *Statist*, a British commercial journal, agreed that under section 4, through rates would be materially increased and American farmers would not be able "to sell their wheat at present prices so as to compete in the European markets with Russian, Indian, and Australian growers. Either the exports of wheat will, therefore, fall off very materially, or the price obtained by the farmer will be much smaller than he gets at present."[61]

It was not the western farmers, but western merchants and manufacturers (except those of the Lake ports), who joined the seaboard merchants in protesting the long- and short-haul clause. The Peoria, Illinois, Board of Trade sent Congress a resolution that section 4 would "unsettle all business interest throughout the West. . . ." The Minneapolis Board of Trade favored railroad legislation, but argued that section 4 "would ruinously depreciate the value of every bushel of wheat and every pound of beef produced in Minnesota by compelling the railroads to adopt a freight tariff on through shipments eastward which, if not prohibitory, would leave to our farmers no reward for their labor and invested means."[62] One Kansas City merchant wrote Sen. Francis M. Cockrell of Missouri that section 4 would force farmers in the West to use their crops for fuel, as they would be unable to compete with the farmers of Indiana, Ohio, or Pennsylvania in the Atlantic seaboard markets.[63] The flour millers of Minneapolis were among the most adamant opponents of regulation. John Crosby, president of the Millers' National Association, said that enforcement of the Interstate Commerce Act "would be injurious to the agricultural and manufacturing interests of the Northwest."[64] Agricultural implement manufacturers in Ohio protested that section 4 would not affect their domestic sales but that "it would break up their [export] business."[65]

To their own peril, spokesmen for the farmers in the West ignored the warnings of the merchants and manufacturers. In their view, section 4 would result in short-haul rates being lowered relative to the *existing* through rates and thus tend to favor the small-town shipper and farmer as against the merchants in primary or secondary markets. Gov. Knute Nelson of Minnesota told his farmer constituents, soon after the Interstate Commerce Act passed Congress, that Minneapolis and St. Paul millers and merchants would no longer be able to "lord it over us." He predicted that section 4 would have a "centrifugal" force in building up local manufactures and thus he considered it "the central, pivotal and vital part of the interstate law. . . . Extricate that from the law and you have simply an expensive commission."[66] The *Farmers Review* held that, under the imbalance of local and through rates, the big cities had "grown too fast," and that with section 4 they would be able to "rest awhile."[67] Milton George, editor of the *Western Rural*, was bitterly disappointed by the railroad industry's interpretation of section 4 of the Interstate Act. As through rates were raised week after week, George charged the railroads with purposely attempting to make the law "so obnoxious and oppressive that its repeal will be called for."[68]

Senator George F. Hoar provided the most thorough critique of the Interstate Commerce Act in terms of its impact on American foreign trade. Ironically, as a Representative, Hoar had written the first Interstate Commerce Act and had consistently gone along with the West in its demands for internal improvements.[69] But section 4 of the bill, he feared, would do special damage not only to Boston interests but to the nation's foreign trade. The foreign trade of Boston, as Hoar explained numerous times, depended upon a 5 percent rebate from the railroads to Boston exporters and importers. This was done by agreement of the trunk-line railroads to prevent rate wars and to make Boston port competitive with

New York, Philadelphia, and Baltimore. Boston interests feared that section 4 would disallow this rebate and jeopardize foreign commerce at the port. Hoar liked most of the features of the final bill, but he warned that under section 4 the railroads would raise their rates.

These fears caused others to join the railroad Senators in opposition to the bill. Hoar recalled how he had often helped withstand the railroads' clamor against river and harbor improvements so that western farmers would be able to send their grain to Europe. The real competitors of the western farmers were the Ganges and Bosphorous, and the central problem of statesmanship was to maintain the American farmer "in comfort, in honor and in wealth by a business in which he is to underbid the naked Oriental . . . in which he is to underbid as producer the subject of the power which is to be his principal competitor." The British had poured millions into Indian railroad development, yet the United States still had the best and cheapest railroad system in the world. "The result has been a balance of trade continually in our favor for the past ten years." But the Interstate Commerce Act would strike at American exports and render a "fatal blow" to Massachusetts and Boston.[70]

Defenders of the bill tried unsuccessfully to reassure Hoar that his fears were unjustified. Sen. Warner Miller of New York, a member of the investigating committee, explained to Hoar that if it were not for cheap transportation, the farmers of the West would find themselves shut out of the markets of the world. If section 4 would, in truth, stop export shipments, then Miller said he would vote against the bill. "I believe the people of the East do not desire to have taken away from our people as a whole the power to export our surplus wheat and produce . . . [if] you stop the shipment of the surplus abroad you will break down the entire West."[71] Sen. John Sherman also felt that the general cast of the bill was correct as long as exceptions were provided. The "most imperative" exception,

Sherman argued, was on export traffic in the application of the long- and short-haul clause. It appears, he concluded, "there ought to be some general and broad provisions which will . . . favor . . . our export trade [and] provide for competition between our wheat and the wheat of Russia and India."[72]

Senator Cullom was slow to understand Hoar's demand that special Boston rates on foreign commerce be fixed in the law rather than delegated to the discretion of the commissioners or courts. "I have no disposition to interfere with the foreign commerce of the country," Cullom told Hoar. "I would very much prefer to see the foreign commerce increase." Any law that prevented the "cheapest transportation to the seaboard of products which go to the people on the other side of the water . . . is a short-sighted system."[73]

Western Congressmen unanimously came to the defense of the regulation bill. Sen. John Ingalls of Kansas noted a "suspicious unanimity of assault" on sections 4 and 5 of the bill which proceeded "from those who prefer to have no legislation at all. . . ."[74] James Wilson, Senator from Iowa, did not accept what appeared to be an assumption of the critics of the bill that, given the existing railroad situation, farmers in the West received adequate compensation for their labors. The law would not make the fields of Iowa farmers waste places, Wilson told his colleagues. "They are being pushed in that direction without this bill."[75]

The attorney for the Chicago, Burlington & Quincy, J. Sterling Morton, summarized the sense of futility among the large group of western railroad men (including Jay Gould, Leland Stanford, Charles Perkins, Samuel Sloan, and Grenville Dodge),[76] who lobbied against any federal regulation. One day before the close of debate on the bill, Morton took a survey of the Senators and suggested to Charles Perkins in Chicago that he acquiesce in the legislation and work to make it innocuous. The problem was that Senators who had argued against the bill would vote for it for fear of political repercussions. In Morton's view, the law was based upon "public clamor, loudmouthed ignorance, and socialistic prejudice against capital combined with an unquenchable appetite for votes—more votes—begotten of a taste of and for office."[77] True to Morton's predictions, the Senate passed the bill on 14 January 1887 by a vote of 37 to 12. One week later the House approved the measure, 219 to 41, and it was signed into law by President Cleveland on 7 February.[78]

The Interstate Commerce Act was extremely vague, and its effect would depend upon the decisions of the commission established by the law. Many complaints, grievances, and questions were carried to the new commission on a large variety of issues, but the key problem, as during the congressional debate, was the interpretation of section 4. On the very day the commission opened for business (5 April 1887), Leland Stanford, president of the Southern Pacific Railroad, petitioned Judge Cooley for the suspension of section 4. "If a strict interpretation of the law were applied," Stanford wrote, the Southern Pacific would be "unable to compete with the Chinese and Japanese trade with the Suez Canal. . . ." The real question before the commission was whether through rates to and from Atlantic ports via the Southern Pacific could be made low enough to compete with the Suez Canal, regardless of the local rates charged along the line.[79] The southern railways were especially anxious to obtain relief from section 4 on the grounds that coastal shipping rates required low long-haul rates, to which local rates could not be adjusted.[80]

To the disappointment of many shippers, the commission temporarily suspended section 4 and embarked on an investigation of the matter. The Louisville and Nashville decision of 15 June 1887 effectively guided ICC policy for the next five years on the subject. It allowed the railroads to suspend section 4 if they judged that circumstances warranted suspension. The extenuating circumstances cited by the commission included unregulated water competition, railroads competing with intrastate lines, railroads competing with foreign lines, and rare and peculiar cases.[81]

As Gabriel Kolko has shown, the railroad men regarded the decision as a magnificent triumph. The *Railroad Gazette* editorialized that the commission and court interpretation of the law indicated that "it will be one of the most successful pieces of legislation ever devised." Many merchant groups who had earlier expressed fears about section 4 also praised the ruling. The St. Paul *Pioneer Press,* speaking for the commercial interests of that city, reiterated its view that section 4 was either harmful if enforced or meaningless if, under the new interpretation, the railroads remained at liberty to do as they pleased.[83] The radical western farmers, however, regarded the decision as a complete capitulation by the commission to railroad interests. "We are forced to the conclusion," wrote Milton George in the *Western Rural,* "that the commission is either lacking in ability or honesty . . . the commission is not the commission that we need and cannot see to anything that the roads do not want it to see." The hopes that the Interstate Commerce Act would solve the question of the "transportation monopoly" were dashed, and farmers increasingly advocated national ownership of the entire railroad system.[84]

Perhaps the key notion in the thinking of the commission in the Louisville and Nashville decision had less to do with favoritism to railroads or merchants than those interests themselves thought. The highly respected business journal, *Bradstreet's,* praised Judge Cooley, the author of the decision, in the highest terms. He had assured the continued, uninterrupted flow of exports from the interior to the seaboard. The decision showed that "the commission is thoroughly alive to the international element in the railroad problem, and that, as far as it is concerned the law will be administered with constant reference to that factor." The editorial recalled that Judge Cooley had served on the advisory commission of 1882 in the investigation of railway rates to the seaboard, and in those proceedings "the international element in the railroad problem was carefully considered and its importance set forth."

Canadian Railroad Competition

The awareness of railroad men that the ICC would administer the law with constant reference to the "international element" emboldened some industry leaders to use the specter of Canadian Railroad competition to modify or even repeal the law. Gen. James H. Wilson, a former railroad president, a Canadian annexationist, and suspected of being in the pay of the New York trunk-line railroads, appeared before the ICC in February 1888 to complain against the action of the Canadian Pacific and the Grand Trunk railroads in carrying trade between points in the United States. Wilson first argued that, because the coastwise trade was closed to foreign vessels, the analogous land traffic ought to be closed to foreign railways. Second, Canada was growing in population and strength, and with the backing of the British was becoming an increasing menace to American peace and integrity. Both the Canadian Pacific and the Grand Trunk, Wilson claimed, were military roads subsidized with British funds.[86] The New York *Sun,* which Wilson used in his campaign in 1888 against the Canadian railroads, summed up his objections: Congress must either make the practice of Canadian roads carrying American trade illegal, or protect American railroads by repealing section 4 of the Interstate Commerce Act.[87]

A few days later Wilson intensified his campaign. He presented the House Commerce Committee with a bill designed to repeal the "transit clause" of the Treaty of Washington under which the United States and Canada exchanged the privilege of carrying goods in bond through the other's territory.[88] A flood of resolutions descended on the House Committee, almost unanimously opposed to Wilson's bill. The Minneapolis Chamber of Commerce claimed that the legislation had been introduced at the instigation of the trunk-line railroads who wanted to "force exorbitant rates between the West and the East. . . ." The Detroit Board of Trade and the Milwaukee Merchant's Association resolved that the Wilson proposal would inflict disaster upon the entire Northwest. Chicago, Duluth, and Portland, Maine, added their disapproval.[89] Despite those outcries, Wilson reappeared a few months later before the same committee defending his bill and attacking the Chicago Board of Trade. Its resolution, he asserted, had been prepared by an agent of the Grand Trunk.[90]

Wilson's efforts would probably have gone unnoticed except for a convergence of other circumstances. First, in May 1888, the Canadian Pacific gained a controlling interest in the Soo railroads which connected Minneapolis with Sault Ste. Marie, giving flour millers a route to Boston 500 miles shorter than via Chicago and New York.[91] That gave some credence to Wilson's allegations of Canadian malevolence. Second, Wilson gained support for his assault on the Canadian Pacific from the American transcontinental railroads, which unanimously opposed the Interstate Commerce Act and which suffered increasingly from the diversion of through traffic between Portland, San Francisco, and other ports in California and Oregon. Finally, the whole range of American and Canadian issues, from the fisheries to the tolls on the Welland Canal, were before Congress; the railroad question was easily introduced as a part of American foreign policy.[92]

Playing on the general feeling against Canada, Sen. Shelby Cullom introduced a resolution on 25 July 1888, requesting the ICC to inquire into the allegation that the Canadian Pacific, a foreign corporation operated in the interest of a foreign government, was ignoring and defeating the operations of the Interstate Commerce Act. So important did the matter appear to Cullom that he decided to lead an investigation by the

Interstate Commerce Committee of both water and rail transportation between the two countries.[93]

Shortly before the Cullom Committee hearings opened in May 1889, a three-way correspondence between Joseph Nimmo, Charles Perkins, and William Van Horne revealed the purposes and tactics of the railroad witnesses. Nimmo was the former chief of the Bureau of Internal Commerce, and was employed as a Washington agent for the transcontinental railroads. He wrote several articles for American newspapers in the spring of 1889 attacking the Canadian Pacific as the arm of the Canadian government that received British subsidies for a line of steamers between Vancouver and the Orient, diverting large amounts of "states to states" traffic from the American railroads.

William Van Horne, president of the Canadian Pacific, foresaw the attempt to prevent his road from competing for American trade, and answered Nimmo's charges point by point. He then accurately concluded that "what appeared in the American press about the Canadian Pacific Railway for a year or two back has resulted from its having been used as a bugbear by the American lines in opposing the Interstate Commerce Act and in seeking to evade its enforcement." Nimmo retaliated with a lengthy letter designed to increase Van Horne's apprehension. The letter was forwarded to Charles Perkins, president of the Chicago, Burlington & Quincy and leader of the transcontinental executives opposed to the Interstate Commerce Act. Perkins liked the letter but he suggested that Nimmo "bring out more strongly than you do the idea that nobody can blame or ever thought of casting blame on the Canadian Road for the policy it follows. But that in view of that policy you think our own government is making a very great mistake in tying the hands of our Pacific Roads for the benefit of the Canadian Pacific . . . take the occasion to rub it in that the policy of our government is permitting the Canadians to carry off the plunder."[94] As Van Horne had understood, Perkins and others hoped to use the Canadian issue as a means of further modifying or repealing the 1887 law.

The Cullom Committee took testimony in New York during 1889 on the effect of the Canadian roads on American lines. The members of the committee were uniformly hostile to the Canadian companies, asking repeatedly whether the foreign roads were not injurious to the United States, if they did not attempt to evade the interstate commerce law, and if Canada did not discriminate against United States vessels on the Welland Canal. None of the railroad executives proposed that the Canadian lines be shut out of the country. They wanted either the extension of the Interstate Commerce Act to cover the Canadian roads or relief from its provisions. George B. Roberts, Albert Fink, and other trunk-line officials charged that the Grand Trunk, not subject to section 4 of the act, cut its rates on business in the United States, recouped the losses in Canada, and thereby was enabled to offer inordinately low rates on exports. Nimmo submitted a statement reiterating his charges against Canadian Pacific aggression for the transcontinental railroads. When the committee visited Boston and Chicago during the summer, however, they discovered that the Canadian lines, especially the Grand Trunk, had many friends. The testimony was largely in their favor.[95] Given such conflicting interests, Cullom commented even before the investigation closed that no legislation was likely to be introduced.

Meanwhile, Sen. George F. Hoar was conducting his own investigation of American-Canadian commercial relations. This offered railroad men another opening to attack Canadian competition and the Interstate Commerce Act. The most embittered assaults on the Canadian government and the Canadian Pacific Railroad were made by representatives of the transcontinentals. The general manager of the Southern Pacific asserted that the Canadian Pacific and its steamships were examples of England's "movements for the maintenance of commercial supremacy, the invasion of American commerce, and the absorption of the benefits of American prosperity. . . ." The vice-president of the Northern Pacific stated that the subsidized steamships of the Canadian Pacific diverted foreign trade "naturally tributary to the transportation lines of the United States. . . ." As for domestic business, he insisted that if the Interstate Commerce Act was not modified to eliminate section 4, then the Canadian Pacific would have the American transcontinentals at their mercy. Joseph Nimmo also appeared, again making his usual charges against the Canadian Pacific.[96]

Testimony by shippers in the Northwest and in New England again clearly indicated a united stand against interference in the use of the Canadian Pacific. And not even all shippers on the Pacific coast were opposed to the Canadian Pacific. Before the opening of the Canadian Pacific's Soo railroads, as *Bradstreet's* explained, a shoe manufacturer in Haverhill, Massachusetts, had to pay a high local freight to Boston and the Boston rate to the West. Under the new conditions, the arbitrary local rate was wholly absorbed. The same lower rates prevailed on shipments of flour and other products from Minneapolis and Dakota points to the seaboard.[97]

Despite such opposition, the transcontinentals persisted in their fight. "Nimmo is out again in full war paint" warned William Raymond, the Canadian Pacific agent in Washington, in writing Van Horne in 1890. He suggested that the Canadian government revise its tolls on the Welland Canal to prevent the discrimination against American vessels. Such action, he felt, would disarm the American railroad opposition to the Canadian Pacific.[98] Nimmo, however, continued his efforts to "secure adequate protection against Canadian Pacific competition," as well as the repeal of sections 4 and 5 of the Interstate Commerce Act, and subsidies for steamships from Pacific coast ports to the Orient.[99]

Except for a brief period in 1892, Nimmo received little encouragement from Washington officials. "In my opinion Mr.

Blaine has been the chief obstacle to a just consideration of Canadian Pacific aggressions," he explained to Perkins, "not perhaps from a spirit of opposition, but for the reason that he has given his whole attention to South America." John W. Foster, who succeeded Blaine in June 1892, was more receptive to Nimmo's protestations. He was important in moving Secretary of the Treasury William Windom, and even President Harrison, to transform the fight into a live issue during the closing months of the Republican administration. Though Nimmo hoped that Cleveland might show some sign that he was "not a patron of British interests . . . by a policy of defense against British and Canadian outrage and aggression," the opposition of New England and northwestern shippers who enjoyed the benefits of Canadian competition dissipated his plans. Moreover, Cleveland chose Venezuela rather than Canada as the place to prove his Americanism.[100]

The use by railroad men of economic nationalism as a weapon to modify or oppose federal regulation began with the Reagan bill in 1879 and continued well after Nimmo's futile efforts in the formative years of the Interstate Commerce Commission. The first major congressional amendment to the Interstate Commerce Act, the Elkins Bill of 1903, for example, created a major stir over the impact that the filing of export and import rates would have on the nation's foreign trade.[101] Similar questions were raised by representatives of railroads, foreign trade associations, and shippers from all sections of the country regarding provisions of the Hepburn Bill in 1905.[102] The utility of the foreign trade and foreign policy arguments was that it enabled railroad men to acclaim publicly their support for the principle of regulation, while acting to modify it in their own interests.

At the same time, the effectiveness of the strategy spoke to the widespread economic nationalism in the United States. Farmers, especially, realized the importance of the railroads in the commercial strength of the nation. But that group manifested economic nationalism more directly in the debates on the silver, tariff, subtreasury, and alien land questions. In the general push for enlarged overseas markets, however, the farmers had the support of the railroads and the Interstate Commerce Commission.

NOTES

1. Gabriel Kolko, *Railroads and Regulation 1877–1916* (Princeton: Princeton University Press, 1965), pp. 37–38.

2. Ben H. Procter, *Not Without Honor: The Life of John H. Reagan* (Austin: University of Texas Press, 1962), pp. 229–234. For a contrary view of the origins of Reagan's bill, see Gerald Nash, "Origins of the Interstate Commerce Act of 1887," *Pennsylvania History*, XXIV (July 1957), 181–190.

3. *Congressional Record*, 45th Cong., 3d sess., 1879, p. 101. For further evidence on Hewitt, see Allan Nevins, *Abram S. Hewitt: With Some Account of Peter Cooper* (New York: Harper & Brothers, 1935), pp. 401–409. *Banker's Magazine*, June 1882, XXXVI, 935.

4. *Congressional Record*, 45th Cong., 3d sess., 1879, p. 99.

5. Lee Benson, *Merchants, Farmers, & Railroads*, pp. 115–132.

6. *Western Rural*, 1 March 1879.

7. Ibid., 25 October 1879.

8. *Yearbook of the United States Department of Agriculture, 1899* (Washington: GPO, 1900), p. 847.

9. HR 46A-H 6.6, National Archives, Washington, D.C. See also Indiana State Grange, *Journal of Proceedings* (1880). Indiana Grangers wanted "measures that will give to the farmer the benefit of a rise in European markets" by the regulation of railroads.

10. Lee Benson, *Merchants, Farmers, & Railroads*, pp. 150–173.

11. Ibid., p. 219.

12. Harold Francis Williamson, *Edward Atkinson: The Biography of an American Liberal 1827–1905* (Cambridge: Riverside Press, 1934), p. 137.

13. Edward Atkinson, *The Railroads of the United States: A Potent Factor in the Politics of that Country and Great Britain* (Boston: March 1880).

14. Edward Atkinson to J. H. Reall, 7 March 1881, Edward A. Atkinson MSS, Massachusetts Historical Society, Boston, Massachusetts. (Hereafter cited as Atkinson MSS)

15. Edward Atkinson, "The Railroad and the Farmer," *Journal of the American Agricultural Association*, 1881, I, 178–179. The article was extensively used by railroad men at the 1882 hearings.

16. J. H. Reall to Atkinson, 11 June 1881, Atkinson MSS.

17. Atkinson to Albert Fink, 21 March 1881; Fink to Atkinson, 25 March 1881; Atkinson to J. M. Forbes, 4 April 1881; C. P. Huntington to Atkinson, 13 June 1881; Charles E. Perkins to Atkinson, 15 June 1881: Atkinson MSS.

18. *Western Rural,* 2 December 1882, 23 December 1882.

19. HR 46A-H 6.6, National Archives, Washington, D. C.

20. U.S., Congress, House, Miscellaneous Documents, "Arguments and Statements before the Committee on Commerce in Relation to Certain Bills Referred to that Committee Proposing Congressional Regulation of Interstate Commerce (1882)," 47th Cong., 1st sess., no. 55, 204–206.

21. Ibid., pp. 6–8, 96, 103–105, 154. See also Henry V. Poor, *Manual of the Railroads of the United States . . . for 1881* (New York, 1882). See volumes for 1885 and 1889, as well.

22. Ibid., pp. 171–172.

23. Ibid., pp. 52, 103, 207.

24. Ibid., pp. 257, 258.

25. Quoted in Edward Crapol, "'America for Americans': Economic Nationalism and Anglophobia, 1876–1896" (Ph.D. dissertation, University of Wisconsin, 1968), p. 230.

26. *Western Rural,* 14 July 1883.

27. United States Consular Reports, 1883, X, 19–24.

28. Ibid., 1885, XV, 308.

29. Ibid., 1883, IX, 66.

30. Northwestern Waterways Convention, *Proceedings* (St. Paul: 3 September 1885). See also remarks of Mark H. Dunnell before Committee on Rivers and Harbors, HR 49 A-F34.1, National Archives; and U.S., Congress, Senate, Reports, 49th Cong., 1st sess., no. 46, Part I, Appendix 110–125, 168, 170. (Hereafter cited as *Cullom Report.*)

31. *Western Rural,* 19 April 1884.

32. Ibid., 31 October 1885.

33. Kolko, *Railroads and Regulation,* pp. 30–31. Benson, *Merchants, Farmers, & Railroads,* pp. 239–240.

34. See, for example, W. Scott Morgan, *History of the Wheel and Alliance, and the Impending Revolution* (Fort Scott, Kans.: J. H. Rice and Sons, 1889), p. 558.

35. Numerous examples of these arguments can be cited. Rep. Richard Bland, foremost proponent of the free coinage of silver, argued in Congress in 1886 as follows: "We find that European countries, by purchasing bullion silver and sending it to India, are stimulating the industries of India to such an extent that its wheat and cotton are coming into competition with ours. . . . [India's] wheat and cotton are driving our wheat and cotton out of European markets. Again silver, being worth more as money in India than as bullion in England, is imported into India for the purpose of employing laborers in building railways and in opening up wheat and corn fields, and in this way India . . . is

destined to drive us out of European markets. . . ." See also *Western Rural*, 24 October 1885, 21 November 1885, 9 January 1886.

36. *Bradstreet's*, 13 November 1886. See also *Congressional Record*, 49th Cong., 1st sess., 1886, pp. 3217–3225, 3274.

37. *Bradstreet's*, 10 April 1886. *Bradstreet's* found Bayard's analysis and arguments "not satisfactory." See also *Farmer's Review*, 7 April 1886.

38. *Congressional Record*, 49th Cong., 1st sess., 1886, p. 3294.

39. Atkinson to Hon. W. Hunter, Acting Secretary of State, 24 September 1883; Atkinson to Hon. John K. Kenox, 3 June 1884; T. H. Farrar to Atkinson, 6 September 1885; Atkinson to Chas. S. Fairchild, Secretary of Treasury, 20 July 1887; Edward Taussig to Atkinson, 24 February 1888: Atkinson MSS.

40. U.S., Congress, Senate, Executive Documents, "Report Made by Edward Atkinson, of Boston, Mass.; to the President of the United States upon . . . Bimetallism in Europe," 50th Cong., 1st sess., no. 34, 23–27. For an excellent review of Atkinson's role in Cleveland's monetary difficulties, see Jeanette P. Nichols, "Silver Diplomacy," *Political Science Quarterly*, XLVIII (1933), 573–577.

41. Ibid., p. 30.

42. James W. Neilson, *Shelby M. Cullom, Prairie State Republican* (Urbana: University of Illinois Press, 1962), pp. 91–92.

43. Shelby M. Cullom, *Fifty Years of Public Service* (Chicago: A. C. McClurg and Company, 1911), p. 314.

44. Neilson, *Shelby M. Cullom*, p. 108.

45. *Cullom Report*, Part II, 99–112, 144–146, 787–790.

46. Ibid., pp. 62–64.

47. Ibid., pp. 1242–1245.

48. Ibid., p. 1011.

49. Ibid., Part I, Appendix, 113.

50. Ibid., Part II, 112, 156, 160.

51. John P. Green to Shelby M. Cullom, 30 October 1886, Shelby M. Cullom MSS, Illinois State Historical Library, Springfield, Illinois.

52. Neilson, *Shelby Cullom*, p. 128.

53. *Cullom Report*, Part I, 2–3.

54. Ibid., pp. 25–28.

55. *Congressional Record*, 49th Cong., 2d sess., 1887, p. 641.

56. Kolko, *Railroads and Regulation*, pp. 49–50.

57. *Congressional Record*, 49th Cong., 1st sess., 1886, p. 3869.

58. St. Paul *Pioneer Press*, 8 June 1887.

59. *Northwestern Miller*, 28 January 1887.

60. *Commercial and Financial Chronicle*, 1 January 1887.

61. *Statist*, 22 January 1887, 26 March 1887.

62. *Congressional Record*, 49th Cong., 2d sess., 1887, p. 607.

63. Ibid., p. 635.

64. *Northwestern Miller*, 21 January 1887.

65. *Congressional Record*, 49th Cong., 2d sess., 1887, p. 643. Ohio farmers, on the other hand, favored section 4.

66. St. Paul *Pioneer Press,* 8 June 1887.

67. *Farmer's Review,* 1 June 1887.

68. *Western Rural,* 2 April 1887.

69. George F. Hoar, *Autobiography of Seventy Years,* I, 270–272; II, 112–119.

70. *Congressional Record,* 49th Cong., 2d sess., 1887, pp. 634–635.

71. *Congressional Record,* 49th Cong., 1st sess., 1886, p. 3876.

72. *Congressional Record,* 49th Cong., 2d sess., 1887, p. 641.

73. Ibid., p. 485. See also *Commercial and Financial Chronicle,* 15 January 1887, which belittles Cullom's defense.

74. Ibid., p. 652.

75. Ibid., p. 647.

76. Neilson, *Shelby Cullom,* p. 116.

77. J. Sterling Morton to Charles E. Perkins, 13 January 1887, Chicago, Burlington, & Quincy Railroad Archives, Newberry Library, Chicago, Illinois.

78. Procter, *Not Without Honor,* p. 260.

79. *Interstate Commerce Reports,* "Decisions and Proceedings of the Interstate Commerce Commission . . . May 1887 to June 1888," I, 16–17.

80. Kolko, *Railroads and Regulation,* p. 50.

81. *First Annual Report of the Interstate Commerce Commission,* 1 December 1887, pp. 64–85.

82. Kolko, *Railroads and Regulation,* p. 51.

83. St. Paul *Pioneer Press,* 18 June 1887.

84. *Western Rural,* 6 August 1887. See also *National Economist,* 30 March 1889, 22 March 1890.

85. *Bradstreet's,* 18 June 1887.

86. Chicago *Times,* 11 February 1888, clipping, James Harrison Wilson MSS, Library of Congress, Washington, D. C.

87. New York *Sun,* 8 February 1888.

88. Ibid.

89. HR 50A-H6.1, National Archives, Washington, D. C.

90. New York *Sun,* 17 March 1888.

91. *Railroad Gazette,* 14 September 1888.

92. *Congressional Record,* 50th Cong., 1st sess., 1888, p. 6769. *Bradstreet's,* 11 August 1888. Charles C. Tansill, *Canadian-American Relations, 1875–1911* (New Haven: Yale University Press, 1943), pp. 412–420.

93. Neilson, *Shelby Cullom,* p. 128.

94. William Van Horne to Joseph Nimmo, 27 March 1889; Joseph Nimmo to Charles Perkins, 3 April 1889; Joseph Nimmo to William Van Horne, ? April 1889; Charles Perkins to Joseph Nimmo, 9 April 1889: Chicago, Burlington & Quincy Archives.

95. U.S., Congress, Senate, Committee on Interstate Commerce, *Transportation Interests of the United States and Canada* (Washington: GPO, 1890), pp. 20–42, 55–70, 417–503.

96. U.S., Congress, Senate, Reports, *Relations with Canada,* 51st Cong., 1st sess., no. 1530, Part I.

97.   *Bradstreet's,* 11 August 1888, 8 June 1889.

98.   William C. Van Horne to Sir John Macdonald, 26 June 1889, John Macdonald MSS, National Archives of Canada, Ottawa, Canada.

99.   Joseph Nimmo to Charles Perkins, 23 August 1890, Chicago, Burlington & Quincy Archives.

100.   Ibid., 23 April 1892, Chicago, Burlington & Quincy Archives.

101.   *Eighteenth Annual Report of the Interstate Commerce Commission* (Washington: GPO, 1904), p. 49.

102.   U.S., Congress, Senate, Documents, 59th Cong., 1st sess., no. 243, *Hearings on Regulation of Railway Rates,* 1905–1906, II, 1473–1590.

PART THREE

*Trunk-line Railroad
Executives in Quest of
World Markets*

6

John W. Garrett,
the Baltimore & Ohio,
and European Trade

PRIOR TO 1865, export products of the western states reached the Atlantic seaboard chiefly by the Lakes, the Erie Canal, and the Hudson River; New York enjoyed almost a monopoly of that commerce. Railroads were not organized to compete with the waterways for the bulk commodities trade of the West. The trunk-line railroads, for example, had track gauges of different widths so that each road could serve its own terminal city exclusively. Railroad cars from the West had to be ferried across rivers or have their wheels realigned to a different gauge. Timetables were not standardized. But after the Civil War the trunk-line roads were welded into a national system. They increasingly diverted grain traffic destined for European markets from the canal route, and heightened the rivalry between port cities.[1]

The career of John W. Garrett, president of the Baltimore & Ohio Railroad from 1858 to 1884, illustrates how, by the 1870s, at least one trunk-line railroad came to predicate its own prosperity on a prosperous agriculture at home, including a large export demand. Of equal significance, perhaps, was that the extensive involvement of the B&O in the export trade did not lead President Garrett to publicly advocate national policies that would sustain or increase foreign trade. His efforts remained almost exclusively at the entrepreneurial level of maximizing profits.

Garrett was a member of a prominent merchant family in Baltimore that had developed its interest in the western trade, and in railroading, in the 1830s.[2] Garrett left Baltimore to go West when he was seventeen, and later recalled that it was there he "learned the true foundations on which might be built the prosperity of Baltimore."[3] After several years of training, Garrett became president of the B&O in 1858. He held the position for twenty-six years; as president and owner of practically a controlling interest, he "was the virtual dictator of its policy."[4]

As the most southern of the four east-west trunk-lines, the B&O was gravely disrupted by the war. It was exposed along its entire flank to attack and destruction by both the Union and Confederate forces. The Washington, D. C., branch, which served as the feeder from the North to the Virginia military railroads, suffered least; but the main stem, from Baltimore to Wheeling, West Virginia, on the Ohio River, was a constant Confederate objective and suffered destructive raids throughout the war. Over 100 miles of lines were occupied by troops under Stonewall Jackson on 28 May 1861, an operation that cut east-west communication. Locomotives and rolling stock were stolen, bridges blown, machine shops and engine houses damaged, and telegraph lines torn down. When the tide of battle surged in the opposite direction in 1863, the destruction of track, bridges, rolling stock and other property continued. Union troops, for example, burned the trestle work at Harper's Ferry and over the Chesapeake and Ohio Canal. All told, the railroad was in the possession of the federal government for about eight months of 1862 and six months of 1863.[5]

Despite the severe dislocations of the war, the company prospered, with a highwater mark of $10 million in earnings for the fiscal year of 1865. The war was a business stimulant, and the growth of Washington, D. C., along with the constant movement of Union troops, quickly increased passenger and freight traffic. During the war, track was relaid and equipment restored to operating condition.[6] Although a short recession followed the close of hostilities, Garrett prepared for the anticipated expansion of traffic from the Middle West. The main stem was double-tracked, and plans were made to push the road beyond the Ohio River at Wheeling and Parkersburg. The company purchased a substantial interest in the Central Ohio and the Marietta & Cincinnati railroads. Bridges across the Ohio River at Wheeling and Parkersburg were completed in 1870, and by 1873 connections had been made into Pittsburgh, Cincinnati, and St. Louis.[7]

The chief objective of B&O officials during the first decade after the Civil War was to acquire through connection to Chicago. Only then would the road be able to compete with the other trunk lines in the growing export trade (especially in grain) of the West. The first step on the way to Chicago was to gain access to Lake Erie at Sandusky, Ohio, in 1869.[8] As one New York observer remarked that year, the destiny of the B&O could not "be fulfilled, except by taking to [Baltimore] a large share of the trade of the West."[9]

Encouraged by the response of the Chicago Chamber of Commerce, President Garrett told the Board of Directors of the B&O in June 1870 that "the whole commercial, agricultural and manufacturing interests of the West" would have the advantage of "the shortest and cheapest outlet to the ocean" when the B&O reached Chicago.[10] The B&O pounded its way into Chicago in August 1874, undaunted by the scarcity of capital that followed the financial panic of 1873.

Garrett's strategy was double-pronged. Not only did he move to complete a through line to the West, but he acted to acquire port facilities and steamship connections to European and South American markets.[11] Immediately upon the close of the war, the board of directors decided to inaugurate a line of steamships from Baltimore to Liverpool. By establishing its own line, the company hoped to demonstrate to European steamship interests that a large and permanent business existed at Baltimore. The B&O purchased three propeller steamers which had been in the coastwise trade. The first boat sailed on 30 September 1865.

President Garrett reported to board members upon his reelection in December 1865 that their anticipations were being realized. An increase in the trade of Baltimore was observable from the "pressure of exports brought to our mart for England and the continent." The new steamers were needed not to create business, but rather to handle the existing large flow of passenger and freight traffic.[12] Monthly cross-Atlantic trips were made by the wooden vessels, but they soon proved unsuited for the trade. They had very limited carrying capacity either for cargo or passengers, were slow, and consumed large amounts of coal.[13]

The Baltimore city council and mayor were critical of the B&O for using its connections through Philadelphia and New York.[14] Merchants in central and southern Ohio also complained. Although Baltimore was the best market for cattle, tobacco, and produce generally, they told Garrett, the greater facilities for export at New York and Philadelphia prevented them from using the B&O to Baltimore. One Cincinnati meat packer, for example, expressed great "anxiety to have the cattle business transferred" to Baltimore.[15]

By 1868 the situation had become critical because the wooden vessels could not compete with the foreign lines. They were withdrawn in the fall of that year. The B&O contracted with the North German Lloyd Line for two first class steamers to run from Baltimore to Bremen via Southampton. Garrett thought the expenditure of $750,000 for the steamships fully justified "in view of the increase and impetus that would result to the commerce and growth of the port of Baltimore, and the consequent reactive effects upon the business of the road."[16] Then, in the spring of 1869, two more new steamers were added to provide semimonthly runs.

A change in the customs regulations in July 1870 gave an important assist to the traffic of the B&O and the other trunk lines. The new law permitted the importation of goods without valuation at the port of landing. Chicago, St. Louis, Louisville, Cincinnati and other interior markets had been clamoring for the change, which would better equip them to compete with seaboard rivals. Moreover, direct exportation was stimulated as business houses in the interior made commercial arrangements with merchants abroad.[17]

President Garrett was enthusiastic about the new law. Speaking to the Southern Commercial Convention in Cincinnati in October 1870, Garrett argued that direct trade with Europe would abolish the charges of middlemen and stimulate trade in the South and other sections of the country. It would also secure for each section "the shortest and most economical route to the ocean" and the development of home industries.[18] To the president of the Ohio & Mississippi Railroad, Garrett suggested that representatives from their companies be established in France, Switzerland, and Germany to increase "our homeward and outward business." The new law, Garrett's colleague replied, would allow these agents to take goods at a fixed rate of freight from the manufacturing centers of the interior, all expenses included. "Such an agency in Havre would, by giving information in time develop the exports from the country through which our roads pass: shipments of grain, pork, etc. to France from Baltimore are rare to what they should be."[19] By the end of the year, the general freight agent for the B&O had completed arrangements with the Allan Steamship Company for a schedule of through rates between western cities and Liverpool.[20] Having achieved gauge uniformity, completed bridges, fast freight tracks, and other improvements, direct trade was the accepted procedure for the export business of the trunk-line roads of the outports after 1870.[21]

Though most of the increase in the export trade of the B&O after the war came in Europe, the company did not neglect other markets. Before the Civil War the trans-Atlantic trade had been small compared with Latin American trade. In the year 1860, approximately 84,000 tons cleared Baltimore for Latin America, while clearances for Europe were only 59,000 tons. But trade with Brazil was seriously hampered by the war. Coffee imports dropped by almost two-thirds in 1862, when Baltimore was cut off from its principal markets in the West.[22] In cooperation with Baltimore merchants, after the war the B&O struggled to regain its old markets in Latin America, especially in Brazil.[23] George R. Blanchard testified before the Hepburn Committee that, as an operator for the B&O, in 1870 he "offered all sorts of inducements to bring to Baltimore . . . flour for Brazil, and to get the coffee coming back."[24] An officer of the United States Brazil Steamship Company enlisted Garrett's help in 1871 to obtain a subsidy from Congress to increase its service to Brazil. "With a trade on a proper footing," the steamship representative suggested, "there must be a much larger interchange of our products for those of Brazil and the freights over the [B&O] Road will of course be greatly benefitted."[25]

The public notice given the B&O steamship ventures, and their success, caused other steamship companies to begin operations in Baltimore. One Rotterdam firm offered to establish a direct line of steamers to Baltimore if the B&O would subscribe at least half the capital stock of the line. "We think it is really absurd," wrote the steamship representative to Garrett, "that two places of the importance of Baltimore and Rotterdam should remain without direct steamer communication but as long as you are the principal proprietor of the German line and having at the same time in your hand the regulation of freight to the interior, nobody will start a line to Baltimore without your assistance."[26] Baltimore was soon linked not only with Rotterdam, but also with Antwerp, Havre (and with Liverpool when the Allan Line began making regular stops on its east-west passages after 1871). The rising stream of immigrants from Germany, and the flow of trade from Baltimore, prompted Garrett to order two additional steamers from the North German Lloyd Line as well, thus giving twice weekly departures between Baltimore and Bremen in each direction.[27] Garrett complained to his German contact at the beginning of 1873 that "six times the capacity of the steamers could be readily filled by business pressing from Western cities."[28]

To accommodate the steamship traffic at Baltimore, Garrett launched a program for the development of the B&O terminal at Locust Point in 1872. Of first importance was the improvement of the channel and harbor of Baltimore to a minimum depth of twenty-four feet at low water. In his campaign to obtain a congressional appropriation for the improvements, Garrett had the help of the city of Baltimore, western merchants, and noncompeting railroad interests. One shipper of Salem, Ohio, thought that the improvements would enable the West to escape the "blackmailing in New York," and Baltimore would become one of the main foreign trade centers in the country.[29] Jay Cooke of the Northern Pacific Railroad promised to use his considerable influence in Congress to get the appropriation. Cooke wanted to run a line of Lake steamers from the Northern Pacific terminal at Duluth to the B&O terminal at Sandusky (and thence ship to Baltimore) in order to provide an alternative route to the trunk-line roads of New York City.[30] "I have always considered Baltimore as a natural outlet of the vast northwestern trade," Cooke wrote Garrett, "now being rapidly developed by the Northern Pacific Railroad."[31]

An appropriation of $400,000 for the dredging of Baltimore harbor was obtained before the close of the Forty-second Congress, and the Army Corps of Engineers reported to Garrett in June 1873 that the desired depth had been obtained.[32] Meanwhile, the B&O had been busy constructing huge wharves (on which freight trains could roll up to the side of the ships), great coal bins, warehouses, and, most importantly, two storage structures with a combined capacity of 2 million bushels of grain. When finally completed in 1873, these structures contained 331 storage bins, 21 receiving elevators, and 11 shipping elevators, providing Baltimore with the finest grain-handling facilities in the country.[33]

The Trunk-line Scramble
for Export Trade

By the early 1870s, railroad improvements and lower rates placed the trunk-line railroads in effective competition with the Lakes in transporting to the seaboard all the agricultural products of the West. Flour had been the first commodity of comparatively low value which the railroads carried in competition with the water lines, and by 1869 the diversion of the bulk grain trade of the Lakes to the railroads also began. But high rates and heavy traffic taxed the capacity of all carriers to the seaboard and delayed a full battle for the export grain trade (the key eastbound traffic for which rival cities and roads fought) until the Panic of 1873.[34]

Confronted by hard times after 1873, the trunk lines (and the cities identified with them) pushed hard to enlarge or protect their share of the export grain traffic. The diversion of agricultural commodities from water to rail impressed the railroad industry with a full realization of their dependency upon a prosperous agriculture. To a very great extent, argued the editors of the *Railroad Gazette* in November 1873, "the prosperity of this country is dependent upon the quantity and price of its crops. For, with the exception of petroleum these are the only things of which we produce a surplus. . . . When the farmers are prosperous, when they have large amounts of cotton, grain, and cattle to sell, and the foreign demand is sufficient to make the prices high, then usually other business is prosperous. . . . Now the railroads, while they share more or less the general prosperity or adversity, are especially affected by the condition of agriculture, for the products of the soil form the largest part of their traffic, these products being for the most part enormous in bulk, and going great distances to reach the consumer."[35] The editors of the *Gazette* concluded that, despite the general depression in the country and the decline in the prices of railroad securities, the outlook for traffic in 1874 was good. The crops were expected to be large and export demand would hold up prices.

Certainly that was Garrett's belief—and hope. The collapse of the stock market in August 1873 caught Garrett in Europe. He urged his general manager, John King, to reduce company purchases to a minimum and to maintain revenues by handling cash freight where possible and giving paper "whenever advantageously large crops must [be] moved [to] Europe."[36] But such devices were only stop-gap measures. Passenger business nearly halted, and in 1873 freight to Baltimore dropped precipitously.

As had occurred so many times in the past, the paucity of traffic initiated a series of severe rate wars among the trunk-line railroads, and rates dropped to as low as ten cents a hundred-weight from Chicago to New York.[37] According to Garrett, the New York Central and the Erie were responsible for the drastic rate cutting because of their unwillingness to yield trade to ports nearer points of production. The only way to restore the prosperity of the B&O, Garrett decided, lay in the increase of exports of agricultural goods,[38] and all means would be employed to that end.

The policy was strikingly successful for almost a year. The value of foreign merchandise exported from Baltimore in 1874 doubled over the previous year.[39] Additional ships for the Bremen-Baltimore run were arranged, and a weekly communication with Southampton was obtained on the promise of "liberal facilities" from the B&O.[40] Even the company's new banker in London, J. S. Morgan, seemed assured by the burst of activity. Garrett suggested to Morgan that a new line of steamers be arranged for a connection between Baltimore and Marseilles. "In view of your connection with our financial history," Garrett wrote, "I shall feel it a duty to continue to pay attention to the development of the B&O RRd."[41] Garrett also established credit and foreign exchange houses in Bremen and Paris to handle the increased trade. "At the present moment" wrote *Scribner's Magazine* in 1874, "it may fairly be said that Baltimore is the fashion. . . . Baltimore may with reason be called the 'Liverpool of America.' "[42]

But even before the close of the year, the optimism faded. Sharp skirmishes between the trunk lines in 1874 had further lowered rates, and Garrett's refusal to participate in a trunk-line railroad conference in Saratoga Springs, New York, meant a continuation of the struggle.[43] Prospects for increased export trade to balance rate losses were not good, either. The general freight agent for the B&O informed Garrett early in September 1874 that half the business from Cincinnati had been lost in less than a month. "I can see nothing on which to base a good business for September" he concluded. "The prospect for a good foreign demand is hardly to be hoped, and nothing else will help us."[44]

Rate levels on the trunk-line roads, however, did not go out of control until early in 1875. The contest was at first limited to the B&O and the Pennsylvania, but by March 1875 the New York roads, fearing that lower rates to Philadelphia and Baltimore were diverting traffic from New York, broke the Saratoga compact and brought the rate structure of the trunk-line roads to near anarchy. Alarmed by the decreasing revenues, the bankruptcy of the Erie, and the inability of the trunk lines to settle their affairs, the British banking firm, A. J. Drexel's, intervened to make a temporary truce.[45] Garrett sought to assure the Drexel people that with the rate agreements all would soon be well. "The increased demand for our cereals, arising from the reported condition and prospects of crops in Europe," he argued in July 1875, "will aid our railway interests, and I hope create a material improvement in business during the approaching autumn and winter."[46]

To the satisfaction of Garrett and Baltimore merchants, the substantial improvements and extensions of the B&O and its excellent terminal facilities were reflected in the growing percentage of export to Europe from Baltimore in 1875.[47] The railroad wars indicated that lower rates might be offset, at least temporarily, by gains in shipments that had been handled by lake and canal carriers. One of the B&O vice-presidents complained in June 1876 that Philadelphia and the Pennsylvania Railroad were getting more of the traffic than they would if the B&O had more grain cars. Garrett replied later in the year, inquiring whether "the advance in the prices of grain caused by the latest European intelligence [will] keep up our business in corn without reduction in rates."[48]

By the end of 1876, Commodore Vanderbilt of the New York Central decided upon an aggressive campaign against the rate differential system that tended to push traffic to Philadelphia and Baltimore. The rapid innovations in transportation now meant that the advantage of one or two cents a hundred on grain changed the course of trade from New York to Baltimore, and Vanderbilt hoped to bring his competitors to terms by an all-out rate war. Rates of eight and ten cents a hundred for grain from Chicago to New York give some indication of the severity of the new fight. The situation became so critical that even the maverick of the industry, President Garrett, organized the famous trunk-line pool of 1877, which established the enforcement machinery for an agreed-upon schedule of port differentials.[49]

Despite fears by English investors of continued rate wars, Garrett made preparations in 1877 to float a B&O bond issue through the House of Morgan. Vanderbilt and other trunk-line presidents, he told Morgan, would agree on new differentials and freight classification that would restore rates to levels near those of 1873 and thereby increase revenues.[50] Moreover, prospects for a large increase in export demand would greatly relieve the situation. The war which threatened between Russia and Turkey would "prove beneficial here," he wrote. "We have vast crops of corn and provisions and the advances in price which have already taken place, will create much wealth and increased business in our agricultural sections. The railway companies are already experiencing very favorable effects in increased traffic at advanced rates. Should the war involve other European Powers, the demand upon this country for great varieties of supplies cannot fail to restore activity and profits in many classes of business."[51]

Regardless of the assurances to Morgan, the B&O was in a severe financial crisis, and Garrett had to apply for a large cash loan in May 1877. The Morgan firm thereupon investigated the company's records and was startled by what it found. "I am somewhat staggered by the amount of your floating debt," J. S. Morgan told Garrett, "I see enough ahead to show me that the position is a very grave one. [It] will require great care and be handled with great good judgment if we would bring the ship safely around upon its course again." Morgan warned Garrett that further difficulties would develop unless a conservative policy was adopted and the affairs of the road were set in order.[52]

Almost as if in defiance, the B&O became embroiled in a severe strike in less than two weeks. Responding to the pressures from abroad, the action of other railroads, and the deepening depression at home, Garrett called for a 10 percent across-the-board wage cut on 11 July 1877. He had assumed that his men lacked unity and were, thanks to the depression, amenable to company discipline. He was mistaken. The day the wage cut became effective, the firemen at Camden Junction deserted their trains and inaugurated a strike that spread to the whole line of the road.

President Garrett displayed hair-triggered readiness to call upon public authorities to break the strike. He cabled President Hayes that it was impossible to move freights, and, after noting the intimidation and attacks upon loyal employees, asked the President to take immediate action to prevent the "rapid increase" of the difficulties. By presidential proclamation, Federal troops were ordered to Martinsburg, West Virginia, on 18 July 1877 to counter the alleged insurrection. The troops opened the line of the road (after putting down several small riots sparked by their presence), and the strike gradually subsided. President Garrett stated that nearly all lines were in operation on 1 August 1877. The strikers had been beaten and no concessions were made to them.[53]

Under the strained circumstances of rate wars, unstable finances, and labor troubles, Garrett agreed to establish the Trunk-Line Pool of 1877, the first formal recognition of the international nature of the railroad problem. The self-defeating rate wars had proven the need for pools, and the railroad managers were in the mood to accept them. The object of the differentials and pool was to settle on rates, in the words of Albert Fink, arbitrator of the pool, "with a view of securing to each of the competing railroad companies a fair share of the traffic without at the same time unjustly discriminating between the commercial communities, each of which must have an equal chance, unrestricted by arbitrary charges, to compete with the other in the markets of the world."[54] Fink thus recognized, as did the railroad managers, that the trunk lines had become simply links in the through route between common points of competition in the United States and foreign countries. The portion of the through rate which they could charge was determined with regard to competition in the export trade.[55]

Yet the Trunk-Line Pool of 1877 failed to provide an immediate guarantee of peace and plenty for the B&O. Such agreements were hard to enforce in periods of slack, because each road was desperate to fill its empty cars at rates that would defray fixed costs, if not provide a profit. Thus, suspicion between the roads was rife. Meetings among the trunk-line officials went on regularly, and accusations of rate cutting were made openly.[56] When, at the end of 1877 William Vanderbilt made such a charge against the B&O, Garrett gave this (no doubt unsatisfactory) reply: the low through rates from Chicago to Liverpool via Baltimore arose, not from breaking the trunk-line agreement, but "from the very low ocean rates, caused by an almost total cessation of exports via our port." Even the low rates of the ocean steamers failed to attract traffic, he told Vanderbilt, and had resulted in vessels at foreign ports declining to take cargoes to Baltimore.[57] By 1877, the B&O was brought to the lowest financial ebb of its history.

Recovery and Collapse

The depression of the 1870s convinced many sectors of the business community that increased agricultural exports were the key to economic recovery. George M. Weston, an editorial writer for *Banker's Magazine,* suggested in 1877 that such exports at high prices would enable the United States to pay off its foreign debt. That, in turn, would open new markets to industry which "languishes because supply outruns existing markets."[58] The *Commercial and Financial Chronicle* noted in 1878 that for three consecutive years exports, mostly of agricultural products, had exceeded imports. Such a "remarkable" development in the balance of trade insured a return to at least the level of prosperity before 1873.[59] Observing the large exports of grains and provisions to England in 1878, the widely read *Rural New Yorker* predicted that "our capability of supplying them can continue. In this promised enlargement of our own best and convenient market lies the most hopeful prospect of our agriculture."[60]

Railroad executives, who generally held some type of over-investment theory to explain economic cycles, believed that expectations of heavy future traffic at high prices from the export of agricultural goods encouraged new investments, and thereby would help to end the depression of the 1870s.[61] The *Railroad Gazette* paid such close attention to fluctuations in the British grain market and its impact on the movement of grain to the seaboard that in 1876 the editors noted that "doubtless some readers are tired of it."[62] John W. Garrett, like other business and railroad leaders, counted heavily on an increased export trade to restore a measure of prosperity to his company.

"Our spring weather here is delightful," Garrett wrote in 1878 to John Walter, a member of Parliament, "and the crops of every description promise full yields. The good crops of the past year have produced improved results with our railways."[63] Garrett also went to Europe in the summer, and while there spoke to Walter about the desirability of corn meal as a substitute food for the masses. It was healthful and nutritious and could be furnished at half the price of wheat flour. "It appears to me," Garrett suggested, "that no greater boon could be conferred on the laboring classes of Great Britain than to explain its advantages, and induce its general use."[64] Garrett did not have to add that corn, not wheat, was the most important grain crop in the territory of the B&O.

Grain receipts at Baltimore during 1878 showed a remarkable upsurge to 40 million tons from only 28 million tons of the previous year. The rate differentials of 1877 had definitely established Baltimore as an outport for western grain.[65] The increased trade did not come soon enough, however, to save the company's interest in the North German Steamship Line. The manager for the B&O reported that, at the end of 1878, the steamship company was in debt almost 1 million marks. The decline in immigrant traffic from Germany after 1873, and the general reduction of rates and fares, made it doubtful whether even the existing ruinous prices could be sustained.[66] The B&O, like other railroads, dropped out of the intensely competitive and expensive steamship business.[67]

Bumper crops in the United States, disastrous harvests in all of Europe, and the refinement of the trunk-line differential system contributed to the rising prosperity of the B&O from 1878 until 1881. Wheat exports from Baltimore, which had been below $1,000 in 1867, had climbed to about $12 million in 1878—and they zoomed to $43.5 million by 1880. That was a record until World War I.[68] The annual report of September 1881 called attention to remarkable increases in tonnage of through traffic both eastbound and westbound. Gross earnings for the entire system were over $4.2 million over 1879. The B&O, indeed, had reached the peak of its prosperity.[69]

The flow of such heavy traffic again raised the old issues of freight capacity and adequate steamship connections. The master of transportation reported to Garrett in 1879 that a bottleneck had developed, and over 2,500 cars of grain were waiting on the main stem to unload. Any more grain traffic, he warned, would tie up all the other cars on the road, and it would be impossible for the company to handle local business or accommodate other rolling freight.[70] The same year, Garrett sent his son to London to establish the Barrow and Baltimore Line of steamships. "Under the new system of arbitration between the trunk lines," Garrett explained to a British investor, "we look for a steady and great improvement in our business, as the large differences in favor of Baltimore will be maintained with firmness and uniformity. Our prospects for great harvests in all regions through which our lines pass are excellent, and the time is so advanced as to be well assured." There was no more advantageous time, concluded Garrett, for the commencement of a new steamship line.[71]

Despite the revival of prosperity, a minor episode in 1879 underscored Garrett's view that only the continuation of large exports would enable the company to sustain its recovery. The move of the British government to control the flood of American agricultural imports threatened a growing trade of the B&O. Imports of American cattle and pork products were prohibited in 1878, on grounds that they were contaminated. Whether in fact the animals were particularly diseased was open to question, but the laws had the effect of cutting the influx of American food products to Europe. American farmers rushed to Washington for help.[72] One proposal, in 1879, called for a bill to provide for the inspection of stock cars and cattle intended for export before leaving for Europe. Garrett favored the bill for, as the general freight agent in Baltimore explained, it was "desirable in view of the efforts being made by foreign countries to prevent exportation of cattle from this country."[73]

Later in the year, when the British passed a law requiring that American cattle be slaughtered within ten days of arrival at a British port (on grounds that American cattle had pleuropneumonia), Garrett promptly responded. He was a free-trade Democrat, and he suggested in a conversation with Thomas Potter, an old friend and member of Parliament, that perhaps Great Britain was moving away from its vaunted policy of free trade. Potter assured Garrett otherwise. "I believe the matter rests with the United States government." Strict attention to the health of the cattle, both in transit and on the range, "would go far to satisfy the English law which any government is bound to carry out. I am confident that there is no intention on the part of the [government] to check the importation of American cattle on protectionist grounds."[74] Garrett was apparently not satisfied with the explanation, and a year later Potter sent him a letter from the chief of the British Veterinary Department explaining that the inspection system of the United States did not insure against the introduction of pleuropneumonia and that therefore the slaughter laws could not be modified.[75]

More serious for the B&O than discrimination against cattle exports was a gradual erosion of the Baltimore trade with Brazil. New York had acquired an increasingly large share of the business by 1879, because it offered a better market for mixed cargoes and it had regular steamship connections with Rio de Janeiro. Despite Baltimore's advantages of greater proximity to the West, cheaper handling expenses, and a head start in commercial contacts with Brazil, Baltimore could not compete with New York unless it made a faster change from sail to steam. A British steamship company, known as the King Line, was established in 1874 to make the triangular voyage between Brazil, Baltimore, and Liverpool. But after two years of operation the venture failed because of the depression and the difficulty of securing full cargoes on each leg of the journey.[76]

Baltimore merchants, who had assisted in the defeat of a steamship subsidy to a line which would run from New York and New Orleans to Brazil in 1878, were prepared the next year to obtain their own connection. The B&O used the full weight of its power to win the help. President Garrett candidly explained his concern to the House of Morgan. The importance of a line of steamers handling the triangular trade touching Baltimore could not be overestimated "inasmuch as Baltimore, in comparison with New York is rapidly losing ground as a port of entry for coffee and clearance port for flour and lard whereas up to within the past six months she almost equalled New York in her receipts of coffee and stood first as the export market for flour and lard to the Brazils. This decline is solely due to the fact that New York has regular lines of steamers to Brazil while Baltimore has none, and is therefore alone dependent upon the few sailing vessels yet remaining in the trade."[77] Garrett promised the merchants the full support of the B&O road in supplying traffic and distributing coffee for the steamers, and also provided them with a letter of introduction to the Morgan firm.[78]

Whether the merchants succeeded on this mission is uncertain; but the number of steamers (mostly foreign-owned) clearing Baltimore for Brazil increased from two vessels in 1875 to thirty-eight in 1885, and steamers entering Baltimore from Brazil increased from three vessels to twenty-two in the same years. The greater concentration of the Brazilian trade at New York continued, however, primarily because of Baltimore's lack of demand for mixed cargoes and less rapid employment of steamers.[79]

John W. Garrett had served almost a quarter century as president of the B&O by 1881, and the heavy responsibility had taken its toll. He showed an increasing preference for working at home, and his son, Robert, who was being groomed to take over as president, ran the day-to-day operations of the company.[80] In legend, at any rate, the older Garrett has been spared the burden of responsibility for the rapid eclipse of the B&O. At the time of his death in 1885, rate wars, parallel tracking, and heavy indebtedness in the railroad industry foreshadowed the fall of the B&O into government receivership during the next decade.

In perspective, the career of John W. Garrett—1865 to 1881 —illustrates several general considerations about the relationship between trunk-line railroads and the increasing commercial expansion of the United States. First of all, Garrett understood that the essence of the struggle to make Baltimore a seaport for the commerce of the B&O lay in the number and frequency of its steamship connections with foreign ports. He

made extraordinary efforts after 1865 to induce foreign carriers to put in at Baltimore. The channel and harbor were
deepened, terminal facilities improved, and an import traffic
developed in high-value commodities so as to balance ocean
freight costs in both directions. In order to provide additional
tonnage, to control the arrival and departure of vessels, and
to load and unload immediately, the B&O also entered the
steamship business between 1865 and 1868. It later contracted
with, and held stock in, the North German Steamship Company for regular service out of Baltimore.

Garrett realized that the local hinterland of the B&O did
not provide enough business for either the port of Baltimore
or the B&O. A policy of consolidation, uniformity, and expansion was thus inaugurated, and connections made to
Philadelphia and New York. The chief object was to win a
greater share of the export traffic in provisions, flour, and
wheat from the Middle West. The virtual monopoly once enjoyed by New York over the valuable export traffic of the
West was gradually and inevitably overthrown by the extensions of the B&O and other trunk lines of the outports. The
Trunk-Line Pool of 1877, to which Garrett adhered, was
merely an attempt to stabilize and systematize these new conditions wrought by the vigorous competition for the export
traffic of a common hinterland.

Throughout the depression of the 1870s, Garrett linked
the prosperity of the B&O to the increase it could gain in the
competitive export traffic from the West. Certainly his efforts seem less concerned with raising the total amount of the
foreign commerce of the country than in influencing the routes
of trade within those markets where the United States already
had a foothold. For example, Garrett did not question the
overall unfavorable balance of trade between the United
States and Brazil or the British domination of that trade.
Rather, he feared its shift away from Baltimore and the B&O
to New York and the other trunk-line roads.

Nevertheless, the stability of rates and the increase in the company's earnings depended, in Garrett's view, as much upon the European demand for American agricultural commodities as on any pooling agreement. Although his own ability to influence this demand was small, Garrett closely watched changes in European tariffs, European crop reports, and signs of war or peace. On one occasion he attempted to introduce corn meal as a substitute for wheat flour in European markets. And he actively, though privately, opposed the British restriction on American cattle imports.

Ironically, the tremendous boom in agricultural exports from 1878 to 1881, and the general prosperity it produced, only increased the difficulties of the trunk lines during the decade of the 1880s. This is clearly borne out by the experience of the B&O, which finally succumbed to receivership in 1896.[81] The new prosperity caused Garrett to favor the extension of old lines and to build a branch road parallel to the Pennsylvania Railroad from Baltimore to Philadelphia. Other ambitious managers extended their roads as well. New capital poured into such stock-jobbing enterprises as the West Shore and Nickel Plate. Those activities upset the existing traffic pattern of the trunk-line territory, and made it impossible to implement and enforce the Pooling Agreement of 1877. Rate wars resumed with even greater intensity after 1882. Trunk-line presidents placed little faith either in their own ability to regulate themselves or, as Garrett had so often done, in a resurgence of a large export demand. Increasingly, they looked to the national government to save them from their competitive destructiveness.[82]

NOTES

1. George R. Taylor and Irene D. Neu, *The American Railroad Network, 1861–1890* (Cambridge: Harvard University Press, 1956), pp. 1–7.

2. Baltimore *American*, 2 June 1881, John W. Garrett MSS, Library of Congress, Washington, D. C. (Hereafter cited as Garrett MSS.)

3. For sketch of Robert Garrett and family, see Clayton C. Hall, ed., *Baltimore, Its History and Its People* (New York: Lewis Historical Publishing Co., 1912), II, 455–461.

4. *Bradstreet's*, 10 September 1887.

5. Thomas Weber, *The Northern Railroads in the Civil War 1861–1865* (New York: King's Crown Press, 1952), pp. 75–82. Festus P. Summers, *The Baltimore and Ohio in the Civil War* (New York: G. P. Putnam's Sons, 1939), pp. 15–63.

6. Edward Hungerford, *The Story of the Baltimore and Ohio Railroad, 1827–1927* (New York: G. P. Putnam's Sons, 1928), II, 64–65.

7. Ibid., pp. 69–70.

8. Ibid., p. 69.

9. Quoted in Taylor and Neu, *The American Railroad Network*, pp. 29–30.

10. *Railroad Gazette*, 25 June 1870. See also T. M. Eddy to J. W. Garrett, 11 June 1870, Garrett MSS.

11. For the activities of the B&O in the South see John F. Stover, *The Railroads of the South 1865–1900*, pp. 65–67, 103–104.

12. Address of John Garrett to the Board of Directors of the Baltimore & Ohio Railroad upon his reelection as president (Baltimore: 1865), Baltimore & Ohio Railroad Archives, Maryland Historical Society, Baltimore, Maryland. (Hereafter cited as B&O Archives.)

13. Fred B. C. Bradlee, "Baltimore's Experiment in Trans-Atlantic Steam Navigation," *Maryland Historical Magazine*, XX (1925), 297.

14. John W. Garrett, speech before the Baltimore City Council, 1866, Garrett MSS.

15. B. F. Grove to John W. Garrett, 24 May 1866, B&O Archives.

16. Baltimore and Ohio Railroad, Annual Report, 30 September 1868.

17. Lee Benson, *Merchants, Farmers, & Railroads*, p. 33.

18. Baltimore *Gazette*, 7 October 1870, clipping in B&O Archives.

19. A. N. Chrystie to J. W. Garrett, 28 August 1871, B&O Archives.

20. John W. Garrett to Hugh Allan, 27 December 1870, B&O Archives.

21. Taylor and Neu, *The American Railroad Network*, pp. 5–7.

22. T. Courtenay J. Whedbee, *The Port of Baltimore in the Making 1828–1878* (Baltimore: Schneidereith & Sons, 1953), pp. 81–82.

23. Frank R. Rutter, *South American Trade of Baltimore*, Johns Hopkins University Studies in Historical and Political Science, Series 15, No. 9 (Baltimore: Johns Hopkins Press, 1897), 398.

24. Hepburn Committee, *Proceedings*, III, 2999.

25. D. B. Allen to J. W. Garrett, 6 November 1871, B&O Archives.

26. Plate Reuchlin & Co. to J. W. Garrett, 22 November 1872, B&O Archives.

27. Whedbee, *The Port of Baltimore in the Making*, p. 86.

28. John W. Garrett to G. A. Von Lingen, 2 January 1873, B&O Ar-

chives. See also John W. Garrett to H. H. Meier, 23 August 1873, Garrett MSS.

29. Ludsow Street to J. W. Garrett, 6 February 1872, B&O Archives.

30. Jay Cooke to H. E. Johnston, 17 October 1871, B&O Archives.

31. Jay Cooke to J. W. Garrett, 8 February 1872, B&O Archives.

32. William P. Craighill, United States Army Corps of Engineers, to John W. Garrett, 23 June 1873, Garrett MSS.

33. Hungerford, *The Story of the Baltimore and Ohio Railroad*, II, 73.

34. George G. Tunnell, "The Diversion of the Flour and Grain Traffic from the Great Lakes to Railroads," *Journal of Political Economy*, V (1897), 340.

35. *Railroad Gazette*, 3 November 1873. For a generalized statement of this thesis, see A. Piatt Andrew, "The Influence of the Crops upon Business in America," *Quarterly Journal of Economics*, XX (1906), 323–352.

36. J. W. Garrett to John King, telegram, 29 September 1873, Garrett MSS.

37. *Statistical Abstract of the United States for 1891* (Washington, D. C.: GPO, 1892), p. 65. Lee Benson, *Farmers, Merchants, & Railroads*, 38, Garrett MSS.

38. Garrett, toast notes, n.d. probably 1874, Garrett MSS. The notes read: "History to 1873—inadequate facilities up to that panic. . . . Basis reached for renewed prosperity—agriculture—200 millions excess of exports."

39. *Statistical Abstract of the United States for 1891*, p. 65.

40. J. R. Stebbing to J. W. Garrett, 2 May 1874; J. W. Garrett to J. R. Stebbing, 12 May 1874: Garrett MSS.

41. J. W. Garrett to J. S. Morgan, 28 January 1874, 31 July 1874, Garrett MSS.

42. Quoted in Whedbee, *The Port of Baltimore in the Making*, p. 89.

43. Benson, *Farmers, Merchants, & Railroads*, p. 39.

44. M. L. Doherty to W. Guilfand, 9 September 1874, B&O Archives. Copy of this letter was sent to Garrett.

45. Benson, *Farmers, Merchants, & Railroads*, p. 40.

46. J. W. Garrett to J. S. Morgan, 23 July 1875, Garrett MSS.

47. Rutter, *South American Trade of Baltimore*, p. 417. For example, in 1875, the proportion of flour exports from Baltimore destined to Great Britain was 9 percent; in 1884 it was 40 percent. This rapid increase occurred while the exports to Brazil remained stationary.

48. Vice-President to President 28 June 1876; J. W. Garrett to Vice-President, 5 October 1876, B&O Archives.

49. Benson, *Farmers, Merchants, & Railroads*, pp. 42–43.

50. Ibid., p. 50.

51. J. W. Garrett to J. S. Morgan, 2 May 1877, Garrett MSS.

52. Benson, *Farmers, Merchants, & Railroads*, p. 51.

53. Clifton K. Yearly, "Baltimore and Ohio Railroad Strike of 1877," *Maryland Historical Magazine*, LI (1966), 188–211.

54.   Albert Fink, "Report upon the Adjustment of Railroad Transportation Rates to the Seaboard, 1881," in John B. Daish, *The Atlantic Port Differentials . . . 1877–1917* (Washington: 1918), p. 11.

55.   R. W. Harbeson, "The North Atlantic Port Differentials," *Quarterly Journal of Economics*, XLVI (1932), 644–670.

56.   Benson, *Farmers, Merchants, & Railroads*, p. 235.

57.   J. W. Garrett to W. K. Vanderbilt, 1 December 1877, B&O Archives.

58.   *Banker's Magazine*, July 1877, p. 40.

59.   *Commercial and Financial Chronicle*, 31 August 1879.

60.   *Rural New Yorker*, 8 February 1879.

61.   Thomas Cochran, *Railroad Leaders, 1845–1890* (Cambridge: Harvard University Press, 1953), p. 103.

62.   *Railroad Gazette*, 3 November 1876. See also *Railroad Gazette*, 29 September 1876 and 27 October 1876.

63.   J. W. Garrett to Hon. John Walter, 7 May 1878, Garrett MSS.

64.   Ibid., 10 January 1879, Garrett MSS.

65.   Whedbee, *The Port of Baltimore in the Making*, p. 95.

66.   Y. Loffman, manager's report, 30 January 1879, B&O Archives.

67.   *Commercial and Financial Chronicle*, 16 March 1901, p. 507. This information is in an article entitled "Steamship Lines as Extensions of Railroad Systems."

68.   Whedbee, *The Port of Baltimore in the Making*, p. 90.

69.   Quoted in Hungerford, *The Story of the Baltimore and Ohio Railroad*, II, 131.

70.   John King, Jr., to J. W. Garrett, 27 October 1879, B&O Archives.

71.   J. W. Garrett to Richard Potter Esq., 24 June 1879, Garrett MSS.

72.   James L. Erlenborn, "American Meat and Livestock Industry and American Foreign Policy 1880–1896" (Master's thesis, University of Wisconsin, 1966), pp. 15–24.

73.   Milton H. Smith to J. W. Garrett, 27 May 1879, B&O Archives.

74.   Thomas B. Potter to J. W. Garrett, 11 December 1880, Garrett MSS.

75.   Ibid., 21 October 1882, Garrett MSS.

76.   Whedbee, *The Port of Baltimore in the Making*, p. 91. See also Rutter, *South American Trade of Baltimore*, p. 72.

77.   J. W. Garrett to Messrs. J. S. Morgan & Co., 9 May 1879, B&O Archives.

78.   J. W. Garrett to Messrs. Wolff & Seligsberg, 9 May 1879, B&O Archives.

79.   Rutter, *South American Trade of Baltimore*, pp. 426, 432, 449.

80.   Hungerford, *The Story of the Baltimore and Ohio Railroad*, II, 159. This is also reflected in the paucity of letters in the Garrett manuscripts after 1880. Company correspondence in the archives terminates at the same time.

81.   Ibid., p. 232.

82.   Gabriel Kolko, *Railroads and Regulation 1877–1916*, pp. 3–45.

7

Stuyvesant Fish,
the Illinois Central,
and Latin American Trade

SEATED AT his editorial desk in the offices of the Louisville *Courier-Journal,* Col. Henry Watterson surveyed the alternatives open to the New South as a result of the ignominious defeat of Spain in 1898. Watterson implored his readers to look to South America and the Orient, for there would be found power, glory, wealth, and renown for all Americans. The millions to be fed and clothed in those lands would provide markets for the industrial nations of the world—and in the great commercial battle among nations that would be the hallmark of the twentieth century, the United States had the greatest advantages. Chief among those was the control of the Nicaragua Canal. It tied the Orient and South America geographically and commercially to the United States—and especially to the South.[1]

To the newspaper readers of 1899, such pleas had become almost trite. The "great debate" between the Imperialists and the Anti-Imperialists had already produced a clear majority in favor of economic expansion abroad.[2] But Colonel Watterson's analysis of how many southerners came to accept that view was strikingly bold and perceptive. All efforts at direct communication between the South and Europe, he began, had been "embarrassed by the increased distance on the one hand and the dominancy of the great Northern cities on the other." To continue exclusive trade with Europe meant only "fiscal and geographic dependency" for the South. In a popular (and strongly geopolitical) idiom, Watterson summarized his argument: "As the map now is [the South] will always have to pay tribute to the ship owners and money changers of New York, and its collateral branches, Philadelphia and Boston. But taking the map of the whole continent of America, both North and South, and starting from any point upon the Gulf of Mexico, look South and West. . . ." There, in South America and the Orient, was the key to the prosperity of the South and its economic and political independence from the Northeast.

The president of the Illinois Central Railroad, Stuyvesant Fish, was very impressed by the extracts of Watterson's editorial that appeared in the New York *Herald.* "I can endorse most fully all that Col. Watterson says. I sincerely trust that the position now taken by the *Courier-Journal* will mark a new era, in which the South . . . will turn its attention to the development of its unbounded resources, very much on the lines suggested by Col. Watterson."[3] To Fish, the editorial was "a text from which many sermons could be preached," and he instructed the company's chief attorney to distribute a hundred copies along the line of the road.[4]

There is a touch of irony in the enthusiasm of a railroad president, whose home office was located in New York's financial district, for an editorial that attacked the "money changers" of that city. Yet, from his earliest years with the Illinois Central, Stuyvesant Fish identified his interests with the agrarian West and South which the railroad traversed. The rampant discontent of those sections in the 1880s and 1890s often found expression in attacks on the middlemen, money lords, and railroad magnates of the East, and any diversion of shipments or economic realignment that would loosen the grip of the metropolis was keenly desired.[5] That approach naturally suggested, to Watterson and others, the reestablishment of the antebellum alliance between the South and the West, and the idea was especially strong within the states along the main line of the Illinois Central Railroad. After 1890, the leadership of the Illinois Central hoped to make its outport at New Orleans the key point in an alternate route for the export of farm commodities. Unlike Garrett and the B&O, this effort led to direct involvement in the shaping of such national policies as tariff legislation, the Nicaragua Canal, and the Spanish-American War.

A New Highway to Latin America

Sen. Stephen A. Douglas had long dreamed of a Lakes-to-Gulf railroad that would serve to bind the South and West together. After years of effort, Douglas secured a 2.5-million-acre federal land grant (the first in the nation's history) in 1850 for the promotion of a line to run south from Chicago. As a result of the federal largesse, the Illinois Central (IC) came into being in 1851. To make good on its land holdings, and to lay the basis for future agricultural traffic, the IC initially functioned more as a land company promoting settlement than as a carrier.[6] Nevertheless, in a short time the road extended from Cairo, Illinois, at the meeting of the Ohio and Mississippi rivers, northward in the form of a Y, one terminal in the Northeast at Chicago, and the other in the Northwest at Dunleith. The IC had further extended into Iowa by the end of the Civil War, and was one of the most prosperous roads in the country. It hauled huge quantities of freight from the interior of Illinois into Chicago to be forwarded to eastern and foreign markets, and moved tons of supplies and thousands of soldiers for the government during the war.[7]

Ironically, the Illinois Central's early success almost caused its extinction. By the end of the 1870s, the IC main line was tapped by rival roads at no less than forty-nine different points. Competition from eastern trunk lines not only caused a decrease in the Lakes trade, but cut into the interior trade as well. The fierce intensity of this competition, coupled with the panic and economic depression of the 1870s put the company's future in jeopardy.[8]

The president of the road during the boom period, William H. Osborne, acted effectively to save it from certain bankruptcy. Cutting costs, he reasoned, was at best a stop-gap measure. The road could survive only by expanding trade to increase its earning power. Osborne's frontier for expansion seemed a desperate gamble. He pinned his hopes on a revival of the port of New Orleans by extending the Illinois Central south from Cairo, through the prostrated states of Kentucky, Tennessee, and Mississippi. As a first step, the Chicago, St. Louis, & New Orleans Railroad was acquired by the IC in 1877, providing the first and only through line from Chicago to New Orleans. Stimulated by the successful clearing of the mouth of the Mississippi, and the return of a modicum of prosperity in the South, the new acquisition proved a complete success. Within three years the value of traffic on the IC southern division increased six-fold.[9] Stuyvesant Fish, who was the son of Secretary of State Hamilton Fish and was appointed to the IC Board of Directors in the company's darkest hours, later recalled that the extension to New Orleans "proved to be the salvation of the property."[10]

The interest of the Illinois Central in developing the commerce of New Orleans in the 1880s grew rapidly from a somewhat passive appreciation of the work of commercial organizations in the Mississippi Valley to an all-out effort to make

New Orleans a seaport comparable to any on the Atlantic coast. The central figure in the change was Stuyvesant Fish, who assumed the presidency of the company in May 1887. At a banquet for the celebration of the Illinois Central's golden anniversary in 1901, railroad magnate Edward H. Harriman (a member of the board of directors of the IC) spoke of the very different leadership offered by Fish. "Its grandfathers," he claimed, "had become first conservative and then restrictive and apparently did not care to do anything more. But finally young men came in and things began to change."[11]

Fish ran the Illinois Central from his offices in New York, but he was acutely aware of the interdependence of a prosperous agriculture and successful railroad. After only six weeks in office, Fish requested his general manager to prepare and send him every four days a condensed report on the condition of crops and the prospects for business.[12] Fish also realized that agriculture along the road from New Orleans to Chicago would not be profitable unless the surplus productions were marketed in the cities or abroad. In the early years of the company's history, Chicago had served as the principal outlet for these surpluses. But the competition from the eastern trunk lines, which had initially prompted the IC to extend to New Orleans, also gave New Orleans an increasingly important role as the terminal for the road's through business. If the export trade was to grow, however, the development of a northbound business from New Orleans was necessary. The inadequate import trade of New Orleans meant returning empty freight cars, and Fish considered a change in that pattern to be essential to the successful operation of the company. The increase in the banana trade of Central America and the sisal trade of Yucatan, for example, were watched closely by company officers in the late 1880s.[13]

During his first two years as president of the IC, Fish found little to produce satisfaction. The expectations for the wheat, oats, flax, and corn crops of the western Iowa branch were not realized in 1888. The good prospects for corn in eastern Iowa and Illinois at remunerative rates were dimmed by the sudden reduction of rates from central Illinois to New York from twenty-five cents to twenty cents a bushel by the Pennsylvania Railroad. The other trunk lines also cut through rates to the seaboard, forcing the IC to set rates to Chicago which Fish claimed barely paid the cost of handling.[14] At the same time, the company had to increase its construction account and, as a result, a large floating debt was created. Many of the Granger roads were in similar competitive and financial difficulties, and in 1889 they sought help from J. P. Morgan to enforce some kind of controls on the industry. The IC, however, maintained an attitude of strict independence. Aside from the fear of harsh public criticism for such involvement, Fish predicted that the Morgan effort would collapse (which it did) and that the unique interstate character of the IC rendered cooperation less advantageous for it than for the other roads.[15]

Perhaps Fish also hoped that the IC could profit from a growing sentiment in the West and South to export its surpluses to Latin America via the Gulf ports. The steady decline in prices for the staple commodities of wheat, corn, and cotton in the South and West had provoked resentment against the level of railroad charges for hauling those items to the markets of the East. The farmers, who were organizing National Farmers' Alliance chapters, the Populist party, and other protest organizations, believed that the improvement of the Mississippi River to New Orleans, the completion of several deep water ports on the Gulf, and the use of north-south railroads, would enable them to secure a larger share of the quoted market price for their produce.[16] Such a strategy involved the opening of new markets in Latin America, and the government would be asked to assist. To be sure, the farmers did not spare the Illinois Central from its more general attack on the mendacity of railroads, but the lines of solidar-

ity between them were very strong. All agreed on the wisdom
of redirecting the export trade southward along the shorter
north-south axis.

The common interest of the farmers and the Illinois Central first appeared in their mutual support of the expansionist
foreign policy of Secretary of State James G. Blaine. The Harrison administration, which realized the political dangers of
the farmers' revolt in the West and South, sought to stifle it
by adopting the demands for enlarged markets.[17] From his acceptance of the office of Secretary of State to his resignation
in 1893, Blaine energetically pushed for closer commercial
ties, including improved transportation with Latin America
as a way of creating new markets for the surpluses of the West
and South. The first step in that direction was the calling of
Pan-American Conference of 1889–1890.[18]

News of the conference sparked Stuyvesant Fish's interest in
Latin American trade. To William E. Curtis, the most active
publicist of the conference and the first director of the Bureau of American Republics, Fish suggested that the Latin
American delegation visit New Orleans and the whole Mississippi Valley. Fish offered to put the facilities of the Illinois
Central at the disposal of the delegation.[19]

The Pan-American Conference failed to produce Blaine's
objective of a Customs' Union which, in his conception, would
have been controlled by the United States. It did, however,
create the public climate and pressure for the inclusion of
reciprocity provisions in the McKinley tariff, and Blaine took
the lead in that fight. The competition of Russia and India
in the British grain market was seriously hurting American
farmers, he argued. The only alternative was the development
of new markets to the south. In a public letter to Sen. William
Frye, Blaine complained that there was not a single section
or line in the McKinley tariff that would "open a market
for another bushel of wheat or another barrel of pork." Reciprocity was an opportunity "for a Republican Congress to

open the markets of forty million of people to the products of American farms." The activities of the Secretary of State were not immediately successful in moving the Ways and Means Committee of the House to action, but they did have a great effect upon the people of the Mississippi Valley.[20]

One western Congressman wrote that "Blaine's plan had run like a prairie fire all over my district." Iowa papers warned their representative on the Ways and Means Committee that, before he voted against reciprocity, he would be wise to "come home and see the folks. The mails are too slow and the telegraph wire is too small to convey to him a proper idea of Iowa sentiment on that question."[21] The southern press tended to favor reciprocity too, but it was suspicious of Blaine's political motives. The Fort Worth *Gazette*, for example, claimed that Democrats had been teaching the doctrine of wider markets in Latin America for years and suggested to Blaine that while he may have been converted, his party had not. "You [Blaine] have now an excellent field for evangelization among brethren. . . ."[22]

Since theirs was the principal trunk line of the Mississippi Valley, the leadership of Illinois Central recognized the value of reciprocity treaties with Latin American nations. When the reciprocity provisions were finally attached to the McKinley tariff at the last moment and the treaties concluded, President Fish commented that the only fault he found in the system was that "they do not go far enough."[23] Furthermore, in anticipation of the conclusion of the reciprocity treaties with Latin America, President Fish dispatched his industrial commissioner, George C. Power, and an assistant, Adolphe Schreiber, on a four-month commercial tour of the major South American ports in 1891. "The Illinois Central has sent commissioners to Cuba, Mexico, and Central and South America," Fish explained to the delegates of the first Western States Commercial Congress, "to inquire into and stimulate reciprocal trade by way of New Orleans, which was the original and is the natural outlet for the products of the Mississippi Valley."[24]

The two commercial ambassadors sent regular dispatches to Fish discussing their meetings with business and political leaders. The Central American trade, Fish learned, was "practically in the hands of Europe because of lower through rates to West Coast ports via Panama." When Power and Schreiber returned to the United States in May 1891, they wrote a report for Fish which was published by the Illinois Central for distribution along the line of the road and printed in part or in full in the local papers and commercial journals of the Mississippi Valley.[25] The Power-Schreiber Report can be read as the keynote address of the Illinois Central's thrust into world trade.

Its first proposition held that the American merchants and manufacturers had failed to compete successfully in Latin America despite the superiority and cheapness of their goods. Second, the advantages of proximity to the markets of Latin America by the conduct of trade through Gulf ports were lost through the monopoly of Atlantic coast ports on steamship connections to Latin America. The solution to these vexing problems was simple: form a trading company controlling its own line of steamers via New Orleans, thereby providing direct communication between the Mississippi Valley and Latin America. The report made a direct appeal to Chicago capitalists to invest in such a trading company, claiming that a line of steamers between New Orleans and Havana, Progresso, and Vera Cruz "run in connection with the Illinois Central would save between 600 to 800 miles in distance as compared with New York and both for exports and imports place Chicago at an advantage."[26]

The report also summarized the trade possibilities with individual countries. Of first importance was direct relations with Cuba, for 71 percent of Cuba's exports, mostly sugar, went to the United States, while only 23 percent of its imports were purchased from the United States. This discrepancy was attributable, the report argued, to the differential duties established and maintained in favor of Spanish producers. "Under this system it has been found possible to ship American flour to Barcelona and thence to Havana, where it was sold at a profit as Spanish flour. Should reciprocity do away with the system, there is little doubt that the bulk of Cuba's supply of flour would be taken from the United States."

Power and Schreiber reported that a large, profitable, and immediately available trade was possible with Mexico via New Orleans. The business of Central America was largely in the hands of merchants from Hamburg, Bremen, and Havre, and unless the policy of the Pacific Mail Steamship Company and the Panama Railroad changed, little could be expected. With a regular line of communication via Colon, trade with Ecuador and Peru would be stimulated. Although New York controlled the Colombian and Venezuelan export trade, steamship service from New Orleans would revolutionize that pattern. The Illinois Central, concluded the editors of the *Northwestern Miller* after a full-page review of the Power-Schreiber document, "does not seem to wait until it is pushed into carrying our exports out through the Gulf, but it is taking initial steps, in a thorough and businesslike way. . . ."[27]

The Power-Schreiber suggestion for a trading company to establish steamship connections out of New Orleans took on life in August 1891. In its corporate capacity the Illinois Central never participated in the steamship business despite considerable pressures to create such a subsidiary: as Fish explained in 1898, every attempt by railroad companies to run their own steamship lines had failed. But the IC did encourage other groups, both in the United States and abroad, to establish connections at New Orleans. The Pan-American Transportation Company was incorporated in August 1891 by a group of Chicago capitalists. Among the company's officers were James C. Clarke and Harold C. Ruttan, executive officers of the Illinois Central. "The general idea of the scheme," explained Dr. W. O. Kalp, treasurer, "is to establish steamship lines from our southern coast to all the South American ports . . . made possible by reciprocity."[28] The Chicago *Evening Post* reported that the company had been contemplated since the beginning of negotiation for reciprocity treaties with South America, and the success of the deep harbor conventions in securing a large appropriation from Congress for work at New Orleans and Galveston. The company would benefit the whole valley, while Chicago would practically monopolize the South American trade in flour and packing products.[29]

Toward the end of 1891, the Illinois Central received a flood of petitions from bank presidents, commercial exchanges, and grain merchants to erect elevator facilities in New Orleans for the handling of export grain. The flour millers of the Northwest were particularly active, and under the auspices of the Illinois Central visited Cuba.[30] The New Orleans *Times-Democrat* chided the merchants of that city for allowing the Illinois Central to take the lead in promoting trade with Latin America. President Fish had been the first to see the opportunities of increased trade, the article reported, and was disseminating information to merchants, manufacturers, and farmers of the area served by the IC.[31]

The vigorous promotion of Latin American trade by Fish involved him in 1892 in the politics of foreign affairs. Though Fish once described himself as a free-trade Republican, he abjured partisan politics as unnecessary and dangerous to the interests of the Illinois Central. Nevertheless, when the Bureau of American Republics, with commercial headquarters in Washington, came under fire from Democrats in the House and Senate, Fish was in the forefront of the counterattack. The Democrats called for the dismantling of the Bureau because the participating Latin American states were not contributing to the expenses of the operation.[32] William E. Curtis, executive director of the bureau, pointed to the war in Chile, the revolution in Brazil, and the financial collapse in Argentina as legitimate excuses for default on payments, and began to organize known friends to save the bureau.

Fish responded to Curtis's pleas with assurances that he would contact Senators Vest, Randall L. Gibson, and Representatives William C. Breckenridge, James B. McCreary, John F. Andrew, and George D. Wise—all on important Senate or House committees.[33] To Andrew of the House Foreign Relations Committee, Fish candidly explained his concern for the Bureau of American Republics. "The interest which we have in the matter is obvious, when you come to consider that the Illinois Central Railroad runs . . . the whole extent of the food producing country which must supply Central America and the West Coast of South America with breadstuffs, beef, and hog products for many years to come." Moreover, the company had invested considerable capital since 1875 in building a return trade in bananas from Honduras. Unless the United States government assisted private entrepreneurs in the development of Latin American trade, Fish predicted that trade would collapse. "With any assurance that our merchants will receive the same protection in Latin America which is given by Great Britain, Germany, and other European nations," Fish concluded, "we can command that trade for all time to come without peradventure."[34] To Representatives McCreary and Wise, Fish made a similar appeal and added that the Illinois Central or any other company could not afford to do the educational work necessary for an understanding of the advantages of increased trade with Latin America. The government was the only means.[35] Fish tried to emphasize the nonpartisan character of overseas market expansion to Democrats and friends of influential Democrats. Often he referred to so good a Democrat as Thomas Jefferson "who well knew that other commercial nations had grown rich by the trade with less civilized races living to the South."[36] To Fish's satisfaction, the Bureau of American Republics did survive the partisan onslaught of the Democrats.

The same year, Fish renewed his demand for the government completion of the Nicaragua Canal. His actions highlight the persistent, sustained, and energetic efforts of the Illinois Central to expand its foreign business. It seemed obvious to Fish that the development of the commerce of New Orleans depended in great measure upon some means of piercing the isthmus. "We have watched for years the fiasco at Panama and have also waited patiently for Captain Eads and his friends to build their Ship-Railway," Fish wrote to Sen. John T. Morgan, the leading advocate of the Nicaragua Canal project, "and have only reverted to the original American project of the Nicaragua Canal when all other means . . . seem to have failed." Fish thanked Morgan for his work in Congress, and added that the people in the whole Mississippi Valley were grateful as well.[37]

Fish himself invested $5,000 in the stock of the Nicaragua Canal Company. More importantly, he supported the publicity campaign of Capt. John F. Merry. According to the historian of the Illinois Central, Merry was "agricultural agent, industrial agent, immigration agent, and publicity representative rolled into one."[38] Merry's work for the Nicaragua Canal was unstinting. He joined the Nicaragua Canal Association and became its president in 1892. He wrote long articles for local newspapers on the importance of the canal to the Mississippi Valley. He corresponded with Senators on behalf of the canal. He provided President Fish with statistics and arguments to be used at a congressional hearing on the canal.[39] And he was also, no doubt, the principal author of *The Ten Best States of America*, a fifty-page publication of the Illinois Central prepared for distribution at the Chicago World's Fair. Though written in flowery language, it illustrates perhaps more clearly than any other document the economic and political rationale behind the Illinois Central's concern for the success of the Nicaragua Canal project.

The "ten best states of America" were quite naturally those in the railroad net of the Illinois Central, running from Wisconsin at the North to Louisiana at the South. With the completion of the Nicaragua Canal, the wheat from the north and cotton of the south would find 600 million additional consumers in Japan, China, and Australia. It would revolutionize the commerce of the world. New Orleans would be 11,000 miles nearer San Francisco and within 1,300 miles of the Pacific. Although England had more than twice the foreign commerce of the United States, it did not have the natural resources or great agricultural supply which, with the canal, would transfer commercial supremacy to the United States. While the importance of the canal to the whole nation was also mentioned, the pamphlet described the project as the "extension by water of the Great Highway [the Illinois Central] that spans a valley teeming with the material to freight ships that will pass between its banks for the continents beyond. . . . The levee wharves of New Orleans . . . will groan under the burden of products that seek the markets of the Eastern world through the Isthmus waterway. The floods of commerce from the Allegheny to the Rocky Mountains will pour down the Mississippi Valley through this passage to the East Indies, whose commerce has made the colossal fortunes of the world." In sum, the Nicaragua Canal would restore the commercial basis for the designation of the Mississippi Valley as a regional unit and in particular give to the Illinois Central Railroad the occupation of the "vantage ground of the world."[40]

By the end of 1892, discussion of the Nicaragua Canal and the distant China market gave way to more mundane matters concerning construction, purchases, repairs, and other preparations for World's Fair passengers to Chicago. But interest in the commercial development of New Orleans did not wane. "Can't you stir up the New Orleans papers," Fish inquired of the IC agent in New Orleans, "to an appreciation of their advantages under the incoming Democratic Administration to such an extent that they will insist on having a mail-route [i.e., steamships] from New Orleans and some of the Gulf ports?"[41] Fish had noticed an increase in grain receipts at New Orleans during 1892 sufficient to place New Orleans ahead of all other Atlantic ports except New York.[42] If the trend were to continue, steamship connections to Latin America would be indispensable.

The Crises of the 1890s

The downward course of the business cycle that began in May 1893 did not at first alarm the Illinois Central officials. The location of the IC lines provided it with a decided advantage over other railroads of the country. Its main tracks ran north and south and tapped the cotton, rice, and sugar regions of the South, and at the same time penetrated the great midwestern grain fields and the industrial sections around Chicago. Poor crops in one region or an industrial slump in another did not reduce the earnings of the system as much as otherwise would have been the case.[43] Nevertheless, as the depression deepened and financial panic struck Wall Street, a shrill note appeared in President Fish's correspondence.

Two important circumstances conditioned Fish's response to the economic crises of the 1890s. Though he presided over a western and southern railroad, his birth, education, and experience made Fish view the world as a banker. Second, the majority of the stocks and bonds of the Illinois Central were still held by English investors, to whom Fish was responsible.[44] He therefore vigorously opposed agrarian proposals for the remonitization of silver as the solution to the depression.

Fish pinned his hopes for relief, in the spring of 1893, on reports of a poor wheat crop in Great Britain, for that turn of events would stimulate exports from the United States and thereby stop the outflow of gold from the treasury. By the prompt movement of export freights to the seaboard, the railroads could help alleviate the problem. Fish suggested to his New Orleans agent that the company change its bills of lading to allow for through billing via New Orleans to Liverpool, not only from Memphis and Vicksburg and other large collecting points, but from any station at which there were cotton compresses. It was of the "utmost importance," he said, "that freights intended for export should be carried to the sea promptly and that railroad companies make good reports of net earnings."[45] Nevertheless, Fish believed that the ultimate solution to the nation's financial crisis remained in the hands of the politicians who would have to repeal the Silver Purchase Act of 1890, and pledge the national credit to a single gold standard.[46]

Although Fish had no great apprehensions for the Illinois Central's financial standing during the depression, he did fear the downturn in tonnage of the road. For that reason the Illinois Central sought to increase its traffic at New Orleans. In his report to the board of directors for 1894, Fish wrote with gratification that New Orleans receipts for that year had come near to equalling those of Chicago. "We cannot ignore New Orleans," Fish proclaimed. "It is almost as important a station to us . . . as is Chicago."[47]

The old questions of the tariff and the Nicaragua Canal were also reassessed in the light of the need for more traffic at New Orleans during the depression. The Wilson-Gorham tariff of 1894, Fish believed, had not gone far enough towards free trade. And, because the hope of the railroads lay in increased tonnage, "anything which in the slightest degree restricts the absolute freedom of trade, either foreign or domestic, tends to diminish the volume transported and to that extent injures carriers." The threat of a 20 percent duty on bananas, oranges, coconuts, and other fruits in the new tariff schedule greatly aroused Fish's ire.[48]

President Fish visited Secretary of State Roger Q. Gresham in November 1894 to discuss the building of the Nicaragua Canal. Gresham and Cleveland, he felt, were fully committed to the enterprise; but the change in Congress since the election would prevent them from taking any action. Fish also discussed the matter with Sen. Shelby Cullom of Illinois. Though his money interest in the project was very small, Fish explained, "as representing the principal line of railway serving the great central Valley, I have the matter very dearly at heart, and will gladly do anything in my power to foster it." Thereafter, Cullom drew upon the publicity resources of the Illinois Central for arguments, statistics, and pamphlets on the need for the Nicaragua Canal.[49]

Much to the satisfaction of the leaders of the Illinois Central, New Orleans commanded an ever larger share of the nation's export traffic after 1894. The increasing traffic of grain from Illinois and other northwestern states was especially noteworthy. From 1894 to 1898 wheat exports from New Orleans increased by 10 million bushels and flour exports trebled. In the decade after 1894 all Gulf ports together increased their proportion of wheat exports from 10 to 22 percent.[50]

The press of this new traffic, and the failure of repeated attempts by the IC to obtain the approval of the New Orleans City Council for the construction of wharves, tracks, and warehouses led to a showdown between Fish and the city in December 1895. Unless permission were granted for more facilities, Fish warned the mayor, the company would divert its traffic to Mobile. The published ultimatum argued that, of the six railroads serving New Orleans, the Illinois Central forwarded and received more tonnage than any other road and therefore had the greatest interest in the commercial de-

velopment of New Orleans. There were a great many export
and import articles that would naturally seek the port of
New Orleans, the report suggested, if facilities were on a
parity with other ports.[51]

The ultimatum had the desired result. On 14 January 1896,
the New Orleans city council granted the Illinois Central the
right to establish wharfage and trackage on their property
along the Mississippi River. The next day Stuyvesant Fish
was interviewed by the New Orleans *Times-Picayune*. The
council action, Fish said, "marked the beginning of a new
era in the commercial history of New Orleans . . . second
only to the introduction of steamboats on the Mississippi
River and the opening of its mouth by Eads jetties."[52]

No company played a more important role in ushering in
the new era for New Orleans than did the Illinois Central.
By January 1897 the Stuyvesant Docks (named in Fish's
honor) were completed. A million-bushel grain elevator and
a half mile of sheltered wharves lined the port. Within two
years, the number of foreign seaports brought into connection with New Orleans doubled.[53] In his usual careful man-
ner, President Fish began to collect data and read up on commercial matters. He wrote Merry for statistics on the value
of exports and imports for the United States, and the percentages of them that moved through each of the major ports.
Along with the statistics, Merry sent Fish a copy of Archibald
R. Colquhoun's "Key to the Pacific," which emphasized the
value of the Nicaragua Canal to New Orleans and the Mississippi Valley.[54] To Fish's satisfaction, the Chicago and New
York papers began to take alarm at the diversion of trade to
New Orleans. "I have been working for many years to build
up trade through New Orleans. . . . I see her future opening
brightly and very early," Fish commented in September 1896.[55]

But there were weaknesses in the situation. The phenome-
nal growth in the export trade of New Orleans had not been
accompanied by a similar growth in the import trade. The

result was that ships charged extra for the round trip, and empty cars had to be carried northbound on the Illinois Central. The IC took a full-page ad in the New Orleans *Times-Democrat* Import Trade edition of October 1896, and distributed the edition to its Latin American agencies. A company official was also directed to give all his time to increase the import business of New Orleans by seeking out merchants in the valley who might as easily buy through New Orleans as through New York. Nevertheless, as Fish told the New Orleans Chamber of Commerce, the Illinois Central and other railroads could do little to solve the import problem: "the merchants here and in the interior must now take up the laboring oar."[56]

President Fish was also alarmed by the presidential campaign of 1896. He viewed the issues of the election very much in terms of their impact on the Illinois Central's foreign business. Fish never had any doubt that McKinley would defeat Bryan and that the gold standard would be maintained. But he roundly condemned the agitation for free silver. That would mean the decline of dividends to the company's shareholders, and he preferred the Socialists to Bryan and "his crew of repudiators."[57] The grievances of the Populists were real enough but they did not lie with the so-called money power. Rather, the troubles arose from weak financial legislation by the Congress, and in particular, the National Bank Notes. The need was for "a wise system of banking that will give people a safe, sound, monetary system, elastic enough to prevent panic and to prevent the sacrifice of our great export-merchandise, cotton, grain, and provisions." With such a system, the United States would be in a "position to compete, on fair terms, with foreign nations" in the markets of the world.[58] Fish considered the revival of prosperity that began in 1897 to be the result of large crops and an increased export demand. "The excellent crops which now seem assured," he told the *Manufacturers' Record* in July 1897, "came at a most opportune time . . . giving the basis, just at the time it was most needed, for trade improvement, for good crops mean business for the mills, for the railroads, for every line of trade."[59] Fish accurately predicted that an increasing share of the grain trade would be exported via New Orleans because of its greater proximity to the constantly westward movement of the center of surplus grain production, the increased growth of cereal crops in the border states, and the cheaper land for elevators in New Orleans than on the Atlantic coast. By the end of the year, Fish was satisfied that the Illinois Central had successfully emerged from the depression.[60]

The optimism engendered by increased trade along the entire line of the Illinois Central was suddenly dimmed, however, by the talk and activity concerning United States intervention in Cuba early in 1898. At McKinley's behest, Congress passed a $50 million emergency military appropriation on 9 March. Stuyvesant Fish immediately telegraphed Under Secretary of the Navy Theodore Roosevelt for a meeting. Fish wanted to use his influence to have New Orleans made the supply depot for any war on the island. While in Washington, Fish also proposed to meet the two senators from Louisiana (and others) to secure—war or no war—a share of the $50 million for the merchants of the Mississippi Valley.[61]

As he wrote President McKinley, Fish thought that war with Spain was avoidable and that it would be a calamity for the United States to go to war. But, he added, peace must be maintained with honor. A trip through the South had convinced Fish that though that section was generally opposed to the McKinley administration, it would support any war effort. "The whole South stands behind you," Fish told the President after McKinley had refused to remove the United States consul-general of Cuba at the insistence of the Spanish government, "as it has never stood behind any of your predecessors, Republican or Democrat."[62]

Though Fish approved of each step taken by the administration toward Cuba, he failed to discern the drift toward war. In private correspondence he railed against interference in Cuba as senseless and profitless, and continued to believe to the very end that war was avoidable.[63] Nevertheless, Fish made every effort to promote the interests of the Illinois Central and New Orleans in the event of war. He outlined a plan for blockade designed to starve the Spanish in Havana and then arm and feed the insurgents from New Orleans. For Gen. Nelson Miles and other members of the War and Navy departments, Fish prepared a four-page memorandum indicating that the Spanish had rightly found that New Orleans was "the cheapest and best market for all supplies destined for Cuba." With the supplies available in the Mississippi Valley hinterland, the railroad and water transportation to New Orleans, the superb storage and elevator facilities, and the proximity of the port to Cuba, no other city on the Gulf or Atlantic could serve as well as New Orleans.[64] With the help of southern and western Congressmen, New Orleans was chosen as the army supply base over Mobile and Tampa during the Spanish-American War.

Even after the war began, Fish maintained that American action had been cowardly and unprovoked. The war would produce vast and unknown complications. A permanent navy, subsidies for steamships, and power in the Pacific were all elements which Fish somewhat regretfully described as the abandonment "of our traditional policy of isolation." Fish did not question that the United States had a legitimate grievance against Cuba for the interruption of trade. "My trouble arises," he explained to a New Orleans merchant, "from an absolute incapacity to see what we could do with Cuba at the end of the war, or with Spain either."[65]

Fish gradually came to accept the consequences of American imperialism, its opportunities as well as its complications. The action of the United States could not be defended on legal or moral grounds, but it was "part of the evolution of nations—the survival of the fittest—and is practically in line with the conduct which has always been pursued by the stronger to the weaker nation." Moreover, the Cubans would benefit from American rule. As Fish wrote to one minister shortly after the war, "unless Great Britain and the United States are to dominate future civilization, the rate of progress will be perceptibly slackened."[66]

In the flush of enthusiasm generated by the war, the Illinois central looked for a large increase in traffic with Cuba. The abrogation of the Spanish duties on imports from the United States opened up new possibilities for direct trade between the Mississippi Valley and Cuba via New Orleans. The trade from Chicago, Fish told the editor of the Chicago *Times-Herald,* had heretofore been eastward with Europe and thus was taxed by the merchants and bankers of the seaboard cities. The new trade to be developed with Latin America "can and should be made free to Chicago, St. Louis, Omaha, St. Paul and the northwest—which originate and should control it throughout from factory and field to ultimate consumer."[67]

The only line of steamers with regular service between New Orleans and Cuban ports, however, was controlled by the Southern Pacific Railroad. Many groups in the Mississippi Valley, especially the flour millers, found the service inadequate and urged the Illinois Central to provide its own steamships. The Mobile and Ohio Railroad had ordered four steamers to run from Mobile to Havana, they pointed out, and the Louisville and Nashville Railroad also had connections from its Pensacola terminal.[68] Fearing this competition from the other Gulf ports and railroads, Fish confided to his vice-president in February 1899 that he was increasingly inclined to organize a steamship company, but added that he had not been able to find anyone who understood the business.[69] Fish needed to learn, among other things, whether the expenditure for steamships was justified by trade prospects. Accordingly, he sent two company agents to Cuba. The reports were not very encouraging. Fish feared that the growth of the trade would be very slow, but in March 1899 he went to Cuba for a week to verify that estimate. He returned from Cuba with a sense of "utter disgust with the natives, who are past redemption." The wealth of Cuba had been overstated, the people lazy, and the prospects for trade too small for the company to invest in steamships.[70]

Although Fish did not find much value in American expansion into Cuba, he accepted expansion as a fact, and insisted on legislation that would allow the United States to seize the benefits of increased foreign trade. The amendment of banking laws, the establishment of a merchant marine, and the building of the Nicaragua Canal were among the measures he favored. Such legislation would allow the United States to "win and win speedily" the competition with Europe for the trade of the world.[71]

When Stuyvesant Fish retired as president of the Illinois Central in 1906, New Orleans had been restored almost to the position it had held before the Civil War as the entrepôt for all commerce of the Mississippi Valley. New Orleans was second only to New York in aggregate exports for 1905, and exceeded New York in the export of corn and wheat by more than 1 million bushels. As Fish recognized, the new importance of the Gulf route was largely a product of railroad development and railroad ingenuity. In 1900 he told Iowa Sen. William B. Allison, in appealing for support of increased appropriations for the improvement of the mouth of the Mississippi, an enlarged merchant marine, and the completion of an isthmian canal, that the South "is strongly, almost unanimously in favor of a Policy of Expansion. Nowhere have I heard such outspoken and all-embracing views expressed."[72]

Through the influence of the railroads, ocean transportation facilities were rapidly regained by the southern ports; they no longer had to depend upon mere tramp steamers, but had direct connections by the most modern vessels with all the countries of the world. The Atlantic ports and the railroads feeding those ports manifested the most alarm at the diversion of traffic southward. Rate wars between eastern and southern roads resulted, and various differentials respecting trade via the two groups of ports were agreed upon from time to time.[73] Nevertheless, in the fight between southern and eastern roads and ports, the post–Civil War pattern had largely been reversed. Ironically, the dream of reestablishing the antebellum alliance between South and West was realized only when sectionalism had been dissipated by the forces of industrialism and expansion. As with so many other Granger and Populist programs that were denounced as radicalism at the time, the economic alignment of South and West and the diversion of trade to the Gulf ports was an accepted fact only after the demise of these groups. The Illinois Central had played a major role in effecting the new alignment.

NOTES

1. New York *Herald,* 15 July 1899. Reprinted from Louisville *Courier-Journal* and found in Fish to James Fentress, 17 July 1899, Stuyvesant Fish Papers, Illinois Central Archives, Newberry Library, Chicago, Illinois. (Hereafter referred to as Fish MSS.)

2. William A. Williams, *Tragedy of American Diplomacy* (New York: Dell, 1961), pp. 37–39.

3. Fish to James Fentress, 17 July 1899, Fish MSS.

4. Fish to Bruce Haldeman, 17 July 1899, Fish MSS. Watterson's interest no doubt was the Louisville & Nashville whose president, Horatio V. Newcomb, strove for a Lakes-to-Gulf route to Latin American markets, diverting trade from New York. See George R. Woolfolk, *The Cotton Regency,* p. 152.

5. John D. Hicks, *The Populist Revolt* (Minneapolis: University of

Minnesota Press, 1931), pp. 74–75. C. Vann Woodward, *The Origins of the New South, 1877–1913*, pp. 182–198.

6.   Paul W. Gates, *The Illinois Central Railroad and its Colonization Work* (Cambridge: Harvard University Press, 1934), pp. 32–35.

7.   Carleton J. Corliss, *Main Line of Mid-America: The Story of the Illinois Central* (New York: Creative Age Press, 1950), pp. 196–207.

8.   John F. Stover, *The Railroads of the South, 1865–1900*, pp. 155–185.

9.   Board of Directors of Illinois Central Railroad to Shareholders, *Annual Report, 1877*, 1 February 1877, Chicago, Illinois.

10.   Quoted in Robert L. Brandfon, "Political Impact: A Case Study of a Railroad Monopoly in Mississippi," *The Railroad and the Space Program* (Cambridge: MIT Press, 1965), pp. 182–201.

11.   Corliss, *Main Line of Mid-America*, pp. 321–322.

12.   Fish to E. T. Jeffery, 26 July 1887, Fish MSS.

13.   Ibid., 2 December 1887, Fish MSS.

14.   Fish to Sidney Webster, 5 January 1889, Fish MSS.

15.   Fish to E. T. Jeffery, 22 January 1889, Fish MSS. See also Herbert L. Satterlee, *J. Pierpont Morgan* (New York: Macmillan, 1939), pp. 249–254.

16.   Hicks, *The Populist Revolt*, pp. 61–62. *National Economist*, 1 March 1890, commented that the effect of rate wars had been to raise rates at all noncompeting points and was therefore "simply a method of taking from the country and giving to the city." For the agitation for a deep-water harbor at Galveston see Grenville Dodge Papers, Iowa State Historical Society, and proceedings of the Trans-Mississippi Commercial congresses, 1891–1895.

17.   L. T. Michener to Halford, 8 November 1890, Benjamin Harrison MSS, CXIV, Nos. 25593–25594 (microfilm). Michener, who was Harrison's chief political advisor, wrote that the farmers demanded legislation for the improvement of the Mississippi River to compete with the railroads, or they would swing over to the Populists.

18.   Alice Tyler, *The Foreign Policy of James G. Blaine* (Minneapolis: University of Minnesota Press, 1927), pp. 165–190. Mary Abigail Dodge [Gail Hamilton], *Biography of James G. Blaine* (Norwich: Henry Bill Publishing Co., 1895), pp. 677–689.

19.   Fish to William E. Curtis, 14 January 1890, Fish MSS.

20.   Gail Hamilton, *James G. Blaine*, p. 687.

21.   Ibid., p. 688.

22.   Fort Worth *Gazette*, 7 August 1890. For a picture of editorial sentiment in the South and West, see scrapbooks entitled *Reciprocity* in the William E. Curtis Collection, Princeton University, Princeton, New Jersey.

23.   Fish to Wakeman, 6 February 1894, Fish to James Fentress, 26 March 1892, Fish MSS.

24.   Western States Commercial Congress, *Proceedings*, Kansas City, Missouri, 1891.

25.   For printed copy of report, see Fish In-Letters, LXXX, No. 3,

22 July 1891, Fish MSS. See also New Orleans *Times-Democrat,* 2 August 1891; New Orleans *Times-Picayune,* 2 August 1891; *Northwestern Miller,* 16 October 1891; Schreiber to Fish, 28 April 1891, **Fish In-Letters,** LXXVIII, No. 43, Fish MSS.

26. *Northwestern Miller,* 16 October, 1891.
27. Ibid.
28. Chicago *Evening Post,* 3 August 1891.
29. Ibid.
30. Chicago *Tribune,* 20 November 1891. New Orleans *Times-Democrat,* 14 February 1892.
31. Ibid.
32. *Congressional Record,* 53d Cong., 1st sess., 1892, p. 3672.
33. Fish to William E. Curtis, 28 March 1892, Fish MSS.
34. Fish to Hon. John F. Andrew, 29 March 1892, Fish MSS.
35. Fish to Representatives Wise, McCreary et al., 29 March 1892, Fish MSS.
36. Fish to C. P. Huntington, 30 March 1892, and Fish to A. C. Hultrian, 30 March 1892, Fish MSS.
37. Fish to John T. Morgan, 24 February 1893, Fish MSS.
38. Corliss, *Main Line of Mid-America,* pp. 299–300.
39. Chicago *Herald,* January 16, 1893. The editorial says that the new president "thoroughly understands the subject." Fish to J. F. Merry, 10 March 1894; J. F. Merry to Fish, 13 December 1894; Sen. J. P. Dolliver to J. F. Merry, 3 December 1892: Fish MSS.
40. *The Ten Best States of America for Agriculture, Horticulture, and General Industries Traversed by the Illinois Central Railroad* (Cedar Rapids: Republican Printing Company, 1893).
41. Fish to M. R. Spelman, 20 February 1893, Fish MSS.
42. Fish to E. L. Corthell, 4 December 1893, Fish MSS.
43. Edward G. Campbell, *The Reorganization of the American Railroad System, 1893–1900* (New York: Columbia University Press, 1938), pp. 276–277. See also Fish to Bossevein, 1 May 1895, Fish MSS.
44. Thomas Cochran, *Railroad Leaders, 1845–1890,* pp. 46–48.
45. Fish to J. C. Welling, 3 August 1893; Fish to S. R. Spelman, 3 August 1893, Fish MSS.
46. Fish to (?) Harris, 2 August 1893, Fish MSS.
47. Fish to Board of Directors, 4 October 1894, Fish MSS.
48. Fish to Wakeman, 6 February 1894; Fish to C. P. Huntington, 12 March 1894; Fish to W. B. Allison, 12 March 1894: Fish MSS.
49. Fish to Cullom, 13, 15, 17 December 1894, Fish MSS.
50. *Statistical Abstract of the United States, 1900* (Washington: GPO, 1901), pp. 280–281; United States Department of Agriculture, Bureau of Statistics, Bulletin 38 (Washington: GPO, 1906), Table 1, p. 5.
51. Fish to William Bossevein and other foreign stockholders, 16 January 1896, Fish MSS. Fish to mayor and board of aldermen of New Orleans, 19 December 1895. For the background of the dispute, see John

S. Kendall, *History of New Orleans* (Chicago: Lewis Publishing House, 1922), II, 509–514.

52. Fish interview with Francis Chisman of New Orleans *Times-Picayune*, 15 January 1896, Fish MSS.

53. Kendall, *History of New Orleans*, II, 604; Fish Memorandum, April 1899, Fish MSS.

54. Fish to J. F. Merry, 4 December 1895, 20 January 1896; Fish to Worthington C. Ford, 28 January 1896: Fish MSS.

55. Fish to Brown, 28 September 1896, Fish MSS.

56. Fish to Harahan, 18 November 1896, Fish MSS.

57. Fish to J. Fentress, 10 October 1896, Fish MSS.

58. Ibid., 26 November 1896; Fish to William Dodge, 24 March 1897; Fish to Fentress, 23 November 1896: Fish MSS.

59. *Manufacturer's Record*, 9 July 1897.

60. Fish to J. H. Norton, 19 April 1897, Fish MSS.

61. Fish to Theodore Roosevelt, 12 March 1898, Fish MSS.

62. Fish to William McKinley, 10 March 1898, Fish MSS.

63. Fish to Alexander Hogg, 19 March 1898; Fish to Welling, 11 March 1898: Fish MSS.

64. Fish to Gen. H. C. Corbin, 16 March 1898; Fish to Nelson A. Miles, 16 March 1898: Fish MSS.

65. Fish to M. J. Sanders, 17 March 1898; Fish to Alexander Hogg, 17 May 1898; Fish to R. H. Edmunds, 17 May 1898: Fish MSS.

66. Fish to Rev. John N. Roothan, 19 April 1898, Fish MSS.

67. Fish to H. I. Cleveland, editor of *Times-Herald*, December 1898, Fish MSS.

68. *Northwestern Miller*, 15 February 1899.

69. Fish to James Fentress, 16 February 1899, Fish MSS.

70. Fish to Walther Luttgen, 17 February 1899; Fish to R. H. Edmunds, 9 November 1899; Fish to Joseph Choate, 27 March 1899: Fish MSS.

71. Fish to Hon. T. C. Catchings, 23 December 1898, Fish MSS.

72. Fish to William B. Allison, 29 January 1900, William B. Allison Papers, Iowa State Historical Society, Des Moines, Iowa.

73. Frederic A. Ogg, "Railroad Rates and the Flow of Our Foreign Trade," *The American Monthly Review of Reviews*, XXXIII (1906), 458–463.

8

James J. Hill
and the Orient Trade

"THE HISTORY of our trade with the Orient is a tale of lost opportunity," wrote James J. Hill in 1910. Testifying in the antitrust suit brought by the federal government against the Northern Securities Company in 1902, the president of the Great Northern Railway indicated that the merger of his line with the Northern Pacific and the Chicago, Burlington & Quincy was intended to assist the three railroads in competing successfully with the transportation interests of European nations in the struggle to gain control of Asian markets. His statement was regarded by one business periodical as "furnishing one of the most interesting contributions to the history of transportation in the United States in its larger relations."[1]

The Supreme Court decision in 1904 favoring the government neither proved nor disproved that the Northern Securities Company was organized to expand the oriental trade. Had the decision gone the other way, it would not have meant disinterest in restricting trade and an end to competition between the railroads. The necessity for both sides to find the most convincing legal arguments oversimplified the historical problem. Unquestionably, a combination of motives was involved.[2] The purpose here is not to reopen the Northern Securities case. Rather, it is to demonstrate Hill's early conviction of the need for expanding oriental trade for the northern railroads, the influence of his ideas on public opinion, and the significance of his efforts in relation to American foreign policy.

A Transportation Philosophy

With the completion of the Great Northern Railway to Seattle in 1893, James J. Hill emerged as the foremost railroad man in the country. He differed from such well-known men in the western railroad industry as Henry Villard, Jay Gould, Charles E. Perkins, and John Murray Forbes in essential ways that gave him an influence beyond railroad circles. Leadership in the formative days of railroad building was generally assumed by financiers who were not knowledgeable about construction, tariff rates, traffic promotion, operating procedures, and related matters.[3] But from the moment he first became involved in railroading, Hill had immersed himself in the details of the day-to-day operations of his road. Moreover, he developed a carefully thought-out set of principles of transportation and an ideology that infused his public statements with a force and sense of vision that set him apart from other railroad executives.

Hill's belief in the importance of the oriental trade derived from three general tenets to which he subscribed throughout his career. First and fundamentally, he thought that the profits of trade, transportation, and manufacturing came out of the land. "Land without population is a wilderness, and population without land is a mob," he often repeated. His romantic, nostalgic emphasis on the virtues of land paralleled physiocratic doctrines of the eighteenth century and echoed the agrarianism present in the Midwest.[4]

Second, Hill acted upon the conviction that the prosperity of his enterprise hinged upon the prosperity of the settlers along the line of his railroad. The encouragement of immigrants to settle the Northwest is a well-known phase of Hill's activities. In order to produce more traffic, he provided free transportation to farmers wishing to visit North Dakota Agricultural College, ran demonstration trains, and established model farms to encourage cattle raising and other techniques of diversified farming.[5]

Finally, Hill understood that settlers producing great volumes of traffic did not suffice to make a prosperous region or railroad. He therefore sought enlarged markets for the surpluses of wheat, cattle, lumber, and minerals. The distribution of these surpluses was complicated by an additional factor—the need for balanced traffic. Low rates to consuming markets, and hence larger and more profitable traffic, could be achieved only if cars moving in each direction were loaded. To Hill, an empty car was a thief.[6]

Hill and the Canadian Pacific

These aspects of Hill's philosophy must be kept in mind in order to understand his growing interest in the oriental trade, first aroused by a brief term in the management of the Canadian Pacific Railroad. The key to that sequence of events was John A. Macdonald's return to power in Canada in 1878. By 1881 he had hammered through Parliament a new act that provided for construction of a transcontinental railroad by a private company aided by government grants, subsidies, and loans. Macdonald believed that the future of the Canadian Pacific lay in its possibilities as a fast through route to the Orient. While it would also be the means of settling the western prairies, promoting eastern industry, and ensuring political integration of the provinces, its success as a business in the first years depended on through traffic, especially import and export trade. The government would support a plan for the establishment of a steamship line on the Pacific with a subsidy for carrying the mails to Hong Kong and Yokohama once the railway was completed. The transcontinental line would develop ocean traffic on the Atlantic and Pacific coasts and provide year-round through business.[7]

To sponsor and direct the road, Macdonald wanted men of practical experience who shared his vision of the Canadian Pacific as a new route to the Far East. The prime minister had long been a close friend of George Stephen, president of the Bank of Montreal and one of the wealthiest men in Canada. Although reluctant at first, Stephen, along with his cousin Donald A. Smith, agreed to take up the tremendous financial burden of the Canadian Pacific project.[8]

Stephen did not find it hard to induce James J. Hill to join the Canadian Pacific syndicate and take on responsibility for routes and construction, for Stephen and Smith had supplied the major portion of the capital Hill needed to establish the St. Paul, Minneapolis, and Manitoba Railroad, predecessor of the Great Northern. Because the immediate task of the Canadian Pacific was to build the main line west from Winnipeg, much of the construction material would have to be carried over the St. Paul road, the only existing rail line to Winnipeg. In addition, Stephen knew that Hill would benefit from increased passenger traffic as immigrants moved into Manitoba.[9]

Fearing an approaching competitive clash in 1883, Hill resigned from the Canadian Pacific, and Stephen and Smith ceased their active roles in the management of the St. Paul, Minneapolis, and Manitoba. Nevertheless, Hill remained on friendly terms with Stephen, who worked incessantly to estab-

lish the Canadian Pacific as part of a fast through route be-
tween Europe and the Orient. Upon the completion of the
Canadian Pacific to Vancouver on the Pacific Coast, Hill asked
Stephen about the prospects of trade with Japan and China.
"We are, as you probably know, negotiating with the Imperial
Government with a view to establishing a first-class steamship
line across the Pacific," Stephen's vice-president, William C.
Van Horne, replied. "I think we will be in a position to pick
up a good deal of freight and a good many passengers to and
from Mississippi Valley points." Van Horne extended Hill an
invitation to take a trip to the Pacific. Whether he accepted
is not known, but his inquiry does indicate that Hill, who
by 1886 was already committed to reaching the Pacific himself, considered the oriental trade an integral part of his
plans.[10]

Preparations

The Great Northern did not reach Puget Sound until 1893.
Hill firmly believed that a railroad should not be built in advance of settlement and the development of traffic. Operating
without the advantage (or pressure) of a land grant and government loans, Hill struck out through North Dakota and
Montana, reaching Helena in 1887. He built grain elevators,
encouraged immigration, and established temporary low rates
to encourage shipment to market. The road had to pay for
itself as it advanced through a largely uninhabited region.[11]

Hill also guarded against his chief competitors, the Northern Pacific and Canadian Pacific. Under Henry Villard's direction, the Northern Pacific completed its lines from Duluth to
Tacoma in 1883. But Hill felt that the Northern Pacific had
cost too much to build, contained too many curves and heavy
grades, and—worst of all—had not protected its rear by short
branches off the main line. He correctly predicted the finan-

cial collapse of the road, and made certain that he did not repeat its mistakes.[12]

The Canadian Pacific enjoyed a government-backed monopoly on transportation from its main line to the international boundary west of Winnipeg. It did not extend branches into the United States, however, and Hill did not view it as a rival for the local business of the Northwest. But he did hope to compete with the Canadian Pacific for through business once the Great Northern reached Puget Sound. For this reason, the success of the Canadian Pacific steamships to the Orient after 1886, as well as that of smaller ships plying between American ports and Vancouver, aroused his grave concern.

Hill was not alone. The Canadian Pacific steamers, partially subsidized by Great Britain, transformed the complaint by railroad executives and shareholders against another competitor to a high-level issue of political significance. The United States Navy saw the ships as "vitally concerning British power in the future to command the sea on the other side of the world." The State Department worried over the impact of the Canadian steamships on the future status of Hawaii; it feared that the diversion of the carrying trade to Canadian ports and railways would lessen the chances for annexation of the island at a later time. In 1889, Congress began two investigations into the whole question of railroad aggression from the north.[13]

As the most important potential competitor of the Canadian Pacific for the through business to the Orient, Hill naturally took a part in these debates. In a little-known speech given in West Superior, Wisconsin, on 7 August 1889, he first formalized the intimate relation between the expansion of trade in Asia and American foreign policy. He emphasized that the most prosperous and most powerful nations were universally those "who controlled the commerce, and in controlling commerce they controlled it through transportation." The decline of the American merchant marine signified that the United States is "driven behind the ramparts of our own territorial boundaries."[14]

For many years the country had grown and prospered without much concern for the rest of the world. "We have to unlearn such ideas," Hill warned. "We must go back and take our place in the column and march to the music of the times." As an example of how America's vaunted progress was slowing down, Hill cited his own experience of seeing seventy carloads of cotton goods from New England going to China via the Canadian Pacific. No American transcontinental road would quote through rates because of inadequate steamship connections. He concluded (to great applause from his listeners), that the government should provide a million dollars a year for a line of regular steamships to South America and Asia in order to promote the foreign trade of the country.[15]

Because Hill had been an original member of the Canadian Pacific syndicate, he was a star witness at the Senate hearings of 1889 on Canadian competition with American transportation interests. He did nothing to lessen the concern of the Senators conducting the investigation. The British government, Hill explained, was doing everything it could to keep London the financial and commercial capital of the world. Subsidizing the Canadian Pacific steamships meant that the British did not have to rely solely on the Suez Canal to reach India. Hill suggested that the United States government provide steamship subsidies in order to compete with the British on equal terms.[16]

"When we built the Great Northern Railway to the Pacific coast, we knew that it was necessary to look to Asia for a part of our traffic," Hill recalled in 1897. As the Great Northern hammered its way through Marias Pass in the Rockies and down to Spokane, Hill made preparations for securing an adequate terminal at Seattle and for investigating the necessities of trade with the Orient. Judge Thomas Burke of Seattle handled the legal problems by working through local railways to purchase traffic facilities for the Great Northern on Puget Sound. Hill called Burke into his St. Paul office in 1891 and outlined "a system of transportation by land and by water which would reach from New York to Yokohama and Hong Kong." As the details of the project were laid before him, Burke remembered, "the boldness of the conception and the colossal character of the undertaking made me think that the author was dreaming."[17]

One of the details Hill may have mentioned to Burke was his intention to send Herman Rosenthal, a company representative, to visit Japan, China, and Korea before the Great Northern opened for transcontinental business. Rosenthal arrived in Japan in August 1892, remained in the Orient for eight months, and submitted his published report to Hill in May 1893. The feeling between Japanese and foreign merchants, Rosenthal observed, was not very pleasant. Nevertheless, the statistics on trade, commerce, and shipping indicated the United States had an important role to play in the Japanese economy. Rosenthal concluded that it would take a small effort "on the part of the American leading manufacturers and business firms to gain their share of the exports to Japan and China, while maintaining their present position as the leading importers from Japan."[18]

Matters in China did not appear very bright. Under the "rotten form of government" in China, foreign culture and trade were practically nonexistent. Rosenthal did predict, however, that fear of foreign intervention, especially from Russia, would force improvements in the army and navy, telegraphic communications, steam navigation, and railroads. In all these changes American firms might find a profitable business. Summing up, Rosenthal suggested to Hill that a steamship line under the control of the Great Northern, from Seattle to Hong Kong, Nagasaki, and Yokohama, would be a sound venture. Competition for the oriental trade was increasing, he warned; the Northern Pacific had just put on a line of steamers from Tacoma, the Santa Fe had made a contract with a Japanese steamship company for a run from San Diego, and the Canadian Pacific express steamers were diverting traffic away from the Great Northern. "I am fully convinced that you should lose no time in making a start for this purpose; and, as it takes considerable time to establish a regular steamship line, it would probably be advisable, in order to keep away unnecessary competition, to begin with chartered steamers."

Hill's intentions of entering the oriental trade were not secret. This was indicated by a huge, three-day celebration in St. Paul in June 1893 to mark the opening of 1,800 miles of the Great Northern tracks for through passenger and freight traffic to Seattle. "The products of the Orient will find their way over this line to St. Paul," predicted the *Pioneer Press* in a special supplement issued for the occasion. At the large banquet held in his honor, Hill spoke of the communications revolution that had brought the whole world closer together than the different states of the Union had been before the Civil War, and of its importance in conducting international trade.[19]

Building the Oriental Trade

The jubilation in St. Paul was short-lived. A parallel celebration in Seattle was canceled. The deteriorating financial situation, Hill explained in a public letter of regret, prevented him from keeping a commitment to bring three hundred businessmen to Seattle to show them the great resources of the Pacific Northwest. By the end of 1893, the downturn in the business cycle had culminated in a panic, throwing the Northern Pacific, Union Pacific, and Sante Fe into the hands of receivers. Only Hill's strict attention to grades, curves, and financing during the period of construction enabled the Great

Northern to survive the worst years of the depression and to continue to pay its stockholders dividends of more than 5 percent.[20]

Nevertheless, the depression created severe problems for Hill and delayed, until 1896, any active attempt to open the oriental trade. Nowhere were conditions worse than among the farmers of Minnesota and North Dakota. Hill wrote to President Grover Cleveland, in June 1893, that along 500 miles of the Great Northern line, farmers did not even have money to pay for binding twine. The next year the American Railway Union struck the Great Northern for higher wages. And even more serious than the agrarian and labor difficulties was the competition of the Northern Pacific. No longer responsible to stockholders and bondholders, the bankrupt road slashed its rates. Finally, despite an early setback, Hill and his banking ally, J. P. Morgan, purchased a controlling interest in the Northern Pacific and, in 1896, completely reorganized the line. For all practical purposes, the Northern Pacific thereafter became a second track of the Great Northern.[21]

Amid all these difficulties, a significant change in the traffic pattern of the Great Northern stimulated anew Hill's long-held hope of developing trade with the Orient. The Great Northern stretched through sparsely populated areas of Washington State where the chief natural resource was large forests of high-grade timber. "Unless I can move that crop," Hill had told Judge Burke in 1890, before the road ever reached Seattle, "I might as well not have built the railroad. First, it is a natural product which is in demand; second, unless it is moved there will be no room for farmers." Hill liked to tell the story of how he then called representatives of the lumber industry of Washington to discuss rates which would enable them to ship the product to the East. The going rate was ninety cents a hundredweight on lumber to St. Paul. Though extremely cheap, the rate was still prohibitive. The lumbermen told Hill that a rate of at least sixty cents was needed.

"They're crazy," Hill recalled telling a good friend. "At that rate they couldn't compete with southern pine. I think I'll have to make the rate fifty cents." In the end, the Great Northern rate on lumber from the tidewater area in Oregon and Washington to St. Paul was held at forty cents a hundred-weight for more than ten years, enabling the northwest product to compete successfully in the midwestern market against southern pine.[22]

The very success of the new rate policy for lumber created a serious traffic problem. In the early years of the Great Northern, westbound tonnage of local supplies for Montana, Washington, and Oregon stations was in excess of the eastward movement. But Hill estimated that sometime in 1895 (or, at the latest, in 1896) the eastbound quantity of lumber became so large that empty cars returned to the West Coast. Moreover, even with the addition of the merchandise trade of Alaska and Hawaii, the imbalance of east and west traffic remained. Only the oriental trade, Hill decided, provided the necessary market to restore the balance of traffic on the Great Northern.[23]

Thus, in February 1896, Hill sent a trusted associate, Capt. James Griffiths, to China and Japan to obtain a manifest of every ship that entered or left the Asian ports and to determine the feasibility of putting on his own line of steamers. "I was quite delighted at the prospect for trade with Asia," Hill reported in January 1897. But building his own steamships appeared out of the question. "I found that we could not do it profitably. I found that the little yellow man could do it a great deal cheaper than we could. Therefore we made an arrangement with the general steamship company of Japan to run its steamers to Puget Sound." As Hill recalled, once the contract was made in July 1896, "we had to consider how to give them loading back. There was no trouble about loading this way."[24]

One of the first items the Japanese told Hill they needed

was steel for the railroads of Japan. Orders had already been placed, however, in Antwerp, Belgium, and Middlesboro, England. Using the cable to London, Hill obtained quotations on rails from Europe to Japan. He then telegraphed to Chicago for prices on American rails. The outcome of those efforts was that a Chicago firm agreed to sell rails for $19.50 a ton, the Great Northern agreed to a forty cents per hundred carrying charge between Chicago and Yokohama, and the total cost to the Japanese was $1.50 lower than the English or Belgian quotations. The Japanese placed an initial order for 15,000 tons of the American product.[25]

The same year, Hill prevailed on a group of Japanese industrialists to meet him in Seattle, where he convinced them to buy a shipment of cotton to mix with the short-staple imports from India. He even guaranteed that, if the manufactured product did not satisfy them, he would pay for the cotton himself. But the Japanese apparently came to prefer the American product. Early in 1898, the *Manufacturers' Record* published data taken from congressional testimony given by Hill on raw cotton and cotton sheeting for export to the Orient over the Great Northern during the previous two years: Texas sources exported more than 33 million pounds of raw cotton; South Carolina shipped 25 million pounds of cotton sheeting; and the South as a region shipped 20 percent of its cotton goods on the Great Northern to China. Sen. Cushman K. Davis of Minnesota tied Hill's testimony directly to foreign policy. "Mr. Hill's statement demonstrates clearly the interest of the United States in the Asiatic trade and in the changes that may occur in European interventions in Chinese commerce."[26]

However, flour was more important to Hill than cotton, rails, or other exports. One of the first contracts with the Japanese steamship company was a three-dollar-per-ton rate on flour, four dollars less than on the Pacific Mail steamships out of San Francisco. The purpose of such a rate, as Hill first explained in 1897—and repeated in different forms for the rest of his life—was to "send all the export wheat of the entire Pacific coast to Asia, to be eaten by people who heretofore have lived almost wholly on rice." To the extent that this could be done, midwestern and eastern farmers would benefit because western wheat had formerly gone around Cape Horn to European markets in competition with wheat from the rest of the country. By withdrawing that grain from the European markets and sending it to Asia as flour, Hill predicted that the value of all the wheat in the country could be raised by a third.[27]

At the Farmers' National Congress in St. Paul in the summer of 1897, Hill asked rhetorically, "Could we get the people of China to displace some of their rice for our wheat? I interviewed many intelligent Chinamen on this subject." Hill explained to Chinese merchants in Seattle and Portland how bread should be baked from wheat flour and provided them with Chinese language literature teaching the use of flour. "I will make wheat flour as cheap as rice for the millions of the Orient," Hill boasted, "and our farmers will profit by a new demand." Total flour exports to Asia from 1897 to 1901 increased from 1.2 to 2 million barrels, a large proportion of which came from the Puget Sound terminal of the Great Northern Railroad.[28]

Hill's active and profitable trade with the Orient before the Spanish-American War and the accession of the Philippines in 1898 helps to explain his response to those events. He publicly and vehemently opposed going to war with Spain in Cuba. But he told a reporter for the Seattle *Post-Intelligencer* on 1 June 1898 that he did favor the annexation of the Philippines. "If you go back in the commercial history of the world you will find that the people who controlled the trade of the Orient have been the people who held the purse strings of nations."[29] The war served as an important fillip to Hill's efforts; it was not the origin of his interest in the Far East.

Hill, the Northwest, and the Oriental Trade

The five years after the Spanish-American War were the most active in Hill's career as an exponent of the expansion of trade with the Orient. He joined the American Asiatic Association, a powerful pressure group formed to encourage government assistance in opening Asian markets. One of his first plans was to work with Phillip D. Armour and Marshall Field, two of Chicago's leading businessmen, in purchasing the Baltimore and Ohio Railroad. The *Manufacturers' Record* explained that the negotiations were based on the extensive "interests abroad" of the three men and on Hill's hope of establishing a major world trade operation in connection with steamships from Puget Sound to Asia. No public explanation apparently was ever given for the failure of this effort.[30]

The need for more ships outweighed the need for additional railroad connections in developing the oriental trade. By 1899, the increase in traffic had begun to exceed the capacity of the Japanese ships. In addition, the war had taken many of the tramp steamers away from the Pacific coast, and exports were much curtailed for want of tonnage. Not too surprisingly, therefore, Hill vigorously joined in the campaign to secure federal subsidies for the American merchant marine. He testified on 12 January before the Senate Committee on Commerce in favor of the Hanna-Payne bill, which was designed to restore the service to its former status. The great increase in cotton and flour exports to Asia, he said, had even inclined him to build his own steamships.[31]

As the demand for flour increased in the first few months of 1899, Hill became even more sanguine about the prospects for trade and more anxious to secure adequate shipping facilities. He tried to explain to one western Senator the importance of voting for the Hanna-Payne bill. It was not outside the range of possibility, he suggested, that the Great Northern could ship wheat from Devils Lake in the eastern portion of North Dakota to the Pacific Coast and China. Pulling Washington wheat out of the European markets accounted for fifteen to eighteen cents of the twenty to twenty-five cent rise in the average price of wheat for 1899.[32]

The Hanna-Payne bill failed to pass the Congress, but early in 1900 Sen. William P. Frye of Maine proposed another subsidy bill. Hill bitterly opposed that legislation, however, because it stipulated that no more than 30 percent of the total amount could be used for Pacific coast steamers. Touching on what the press had come to call his favorite theme, Hill told the Minnesota Agricultural Society that the new bill was a "national scandal and disgrace" because it did not help to enlarge Asian markets. It would not give "a particle of relief to depressed agriculture. Its benefits would be absorbed by Atlantic greyhounds carrying passengers and not commodities." Hill favored subsidies for the merchant marine that were based on the value of "products carried to new markets, markets whose development would afford agriculture its only relief by increasing consumption, absorbing any possible surplus, and making the product scarcer." A few weeks later the Tri-State Grain Growers' convention elected Hill to testify before Congress against the Frye bill. The opposition of such friends of the Hanna-Payne subsidy bill was a deciding factor in the defeat of the Frye measure.[33]

Impatient with Congress, Hill proposed to his stockholders on 30 June 1900 the construction of Great Northern's own line of Pacific steamers. "The growth of the lumber and timber business from west of the Rocky Mountains begins to call for more cars than are loaded westbound. The growing Oriental trade has already reached a point where the traffic is practically limited to the ships which can be secured to carry the commodities seeking an outlet to China and Japan." Applying the principles of transportation he had found successful on land, Hill planned ships of much greater carrying capacity than anything afloat in order to offer the lowest carrying rates from the Pacific Coast to the Orient. The Great Northern Steamship Company was organized in 1900 at a capitalization of over $6 million, and contracts were placed for the construction of two huge steamships. The "Minnesota," launched in 1903, and the "Dakota," launched the next year, had a capacity of 28,000 tons each, more than the entire capacity of the five steamers in the Canadian Pacific fleet. Hill described the vessels as "the greatest carriers in the world."[34]

Hill would not have contemplated such ambitious plans for expanding trade with the Orient if he had not been sure of the cooperation of the producers, manufacturers, and politicians in the states through which the Great Northern crossed. To weigh the influence of these groups on his thinking would be impossible, but there is no question that Hill, whose name was a household word in the Northwest, dramatically shaped public opinion on the importance of the oriental market to the prosperity of the nation.

The Seattle Chamber of Commerce, for example, reviewed Hill's efforts in opening oriental markets for Washington wheat in 1903 and asserted that "it is a matter of common knowledge here that more has been done by the Great Northern . . . to open up, develop and extend our trans-Pacific trade than by all other agencies combined." Hill appears to have impressed deeply on farmers of the Northwest the need for greater overseas markets. Representing the National Farmers' Alliance and Industrial Union of America and the National Grain Growers' Association, John C. Hanley of St. Paul testified before the federal Industrial Commission on Agriculture and Agricultural Labor in August 1899, that he had worked with Hill on problems of the storage of grain. From that experience Hanley concluded that, in order for farming to be profitable through the country, but one thing was necessary: "I can sum the whole thing up in two words—oriental markets. Give us oriental markets."[35]

At the highest level of influence, Hill, a lifelong Democrat, came into close contact with President Cleveland. Cleveland thought Hill one of the most remarkable men he had known. "He knew more about Oriental trade and its relations to the business of this country than any man I ever saw," Cleveland revealed. "My surprise disappeared when I learned that for ten years he had spent more money than the Government in sending competent men to Japan and China to study the need of those countries." Not only did Hill dispatch agents to the Orient, but he had checked all their reports and absorbed the important information in them.[36]

At the Northern Securities trial, Hill argued that it had been necessary to purchase the Burlington line to provide both a market for western lumber and a supply source of meat products, raw cotton, textiles, iron, and steel for shipment to the Orient. The premise is plausible when one considers the expensive commitment to the expansion of Far Eastern trade and the widespread popularity achieved by the policy of redirecting the course of exports from Europe to Asia. Throughout the lengthy litigation, Hill spoke out in favor of enlarged markets in the Orient for agricultural and manufactured surpluses, usually implying that this was the motive for the formation of the Northern Securities Company. He always pointed to the challenge of European competition in the new markets and the necessity of meeting it with low transportation rates.

At Fargo, North Dakota, in January 1902, Hill told farmers that, while the favorable balance of trade depended on the export of agricultural commodities, the government had not reciprocated by helping farmers to open new markets. In Crookston, later the same year, he argued that the future of farming in the state depended on finding a new market for Pacific Coast wheat in Asia. And in Chicago, he encouraged the Illinois Manufacturers' Association to challenge Great Britain in the sale of manufactured goods in the Orient. So

often and so forcefully did he speak on the topic during the
Northern Securities case that Hill remarked, early in 1904,
that he had been charged with everything "from being 'an
Oriental dreamer' to a crank, but I am ready at all times to
plead guilty to any intelligent effort within my power that will
result in getting new markets for what we produce."[37]

Collapse

There is little doubt that the dissolution of the Northern Securities Company disappointed the president of the Great
Northern. The opposition forces, led by Edward H. Harriman
of the Union Pacific, received a paper profit of approximately
$58 million. But control of the Burlington—the principal ob-
jective of the merger—remained in the hands of Hill and
J. P. Morgan. "Two certificates of stock are now issued instead
of one," Hill remarked. "They are printed in different colors.
That is the main difference." And he complained mildly of
"keeping track of two different sets of securities."[38]

But the Supreme Court decision against the Northern Securities Company did not, at least in Hill's view, prove a serious obstacle in the development of the oriental business of
the Great Northern Railway. The decline and ultimate collapse of these efforts he blamed on a decision of the Interstate
Commerce Commission of 5 February 1904. Since its founding,
the ICC had assumed—and, in several instances had ruled—
that railroads were obliged to publish and file import and
export rates just as domestic rates were published and filed.
But until the passage of the Elkins Act of 19 February 1903,
no effective means existed to implement this regulation. Fearing that such enforcement might be injurious to the carrier
and public alike, the commission held two hearings in the
winter of 1903–1904. They were attended by representatives of

railroads, export and foreign trade associations, and shippers from all sections of the country.[39]

The leaders of the transcontinental lines were the most vehement opponents of the requirement of publishing export and import rates. Hill argued that the market for American products was not yet established, whereas European governments supported the efforts of the railroads and steamship lines in making the lowest possible rates to the Orient. "They do not say to them: 'Publish your rates so that the Yankees will know what your rates are, and then keep them there until they have a chance to make a rate under you.' They don't do that. What we are asked to do is to make a rate that we cannot change without publishing it . . . thus giving these people long enough to make a rate that will take the business. That is what is before the interstate commerce commission at this time." Since the search for new markets was a joint venture between the producer and the railroad, Hill concluded, the latter must be permitted to adjust transportation rates in order to meet competition in foreign markets.[40]

The decision confirming the requirement that export and import rates be published and filed with the ICC emphasized that there was no intention to limit the foreign market for American products. Railroads having connections to Atlantic or Gulf ports, however, abused the privilege of making such rates by discriminating between shippers and indirectly making concessions on domestic shipments. The opinion argued that more elastic rates were necessary to compete for the oriental market. Moreover, the transcontinentals had their own lines of steamers. The commission admitted that the new requirement might work a "substantial hardship" on Pacific Coast shippers and carriers. Despite these disclaimers, however, the new regulation carried heavy fines for its violation.[41]

The growing flour business from Minnesota to Australia, China, and Japan ceased entirely, due to the new ICC regulation, Hill told the members of the Hepburn Committee in

1905. His plea for a change in the ruling claimed that the oriental trade was not crucial to the Great Northern. He emphasized that it "was an advantage to everybody—to the country and the railroad and to the people of our section—to have the additional markets and to extend our trade."[42]

Although Hill dated the decline of his oriental business from the ICC decision of 1904, he enjoyed the most prosperous trans-Pacific trade of any of his competitors until 1907. In addition to his own steamers, the Great Northern was linked to the Orient by three Japanese liners and the services of the Boston Tow Boat Company to Manila. But a series of difficulties beset the steamship venture, including the sinking of the *Dakota* in 1907, thoroughly disenchanting Hill with that aspect of his railroad business.[43] He turned over the day-to-day operation of the Great Northern to his son and devoted his time to writing and speaking on the best methods of building up American foreign trade. He repeatedly attacked the government policy of forbidding the railroads to make competitive export rates, and only a few weeks before his death in 1916 lamented that such requirements had been an "effectual barrier to any activity of importance or value on the part of the railroads to build up American foreign trade."[44] Although Hill kept his vision of reversing the trade routes of the world in a westerly direction to the Orient, he had been unable to realize those dreams to the extent that he had hoped.

NOTES

1. James J. Hill, *Highways of Progress* (New York, 1910), p. 156. *Bradstreet's*, 25 October 1902.

2. In the Northern Securities case, the federal government charged that the holding company was acting in violation of the Sherman Antitrust Act of 1890. For the full account of the case see Balthasar H.

Meyer, "A History of the Northern Securities Case," *Bulletin of the University of Wisconsin*, no. 142, I, 217–349.

3. Julius Grodinsky, *Transcontinental Railway Strategy, 1869–1893* (Philadelphia: University of Pennsylvania Press, 1962), p. 141. Thomas C. Cochran, *Railroad Leaders, 1845–1890*, pp. 79–125. Hill's personal papers are not yet open for study.

4. Hill, *Highways of Progress*, p. 45.

5. Roy V. Scott, "American Railroads and Agricultural Extension, 1900–1914: A Study in Railway Development Techniques," *Business History Review*, XXXIX (Spring 1965), 74–98.

6. Hill, *Highways of Progress*, p. 159.

7. Macdonald, Canada's first prime minister, had been in office from 1867 to 1873. See Donald Creighton, *John A. Macdonald, The Old Chieftain*, II, 441 (Toronto, 1955); Heather Gilbert, *Awakening Continent: The Life of Lord Mount Stephen* (Aberdeen, Scotland: Aberdeen University Press, 1965), I, 65, 79. For the fullest statement of this thesis, see John M. Gibbon, *Steel of Empire: The Romantic History of the Canadian Pacific, The Northwest Passage of Today* (New York, 1935).

8. Gilbert, *Awakening Continent*, I, 19, 68–73.

9. Stewart M. Holbrook, *James J. Hill: A Great Life in Brief* (New York, 1955), pp. 69–74.

10. U.S., Congress, Senate, Reports, No. 847, p. 168 (serial 2706), 51st Cong., 1st sess., Van Horne to Hill, 21 April 1886, Van Horne letterbook, no. 16, pp. 268–270, William C. Van Horne Papers, Public Archives of Canada, Ottawa.

11. Holbrook, *James J. Hill*, pp. 86–112, 123.

12. Ibid., p. 90.

13. Ensign W. I. Chambers, "The Reconstruction and Increase of the Navy," United States Naval Institute, 1885, Proceedings, XI (3 April 1884), 9; Merze Tate, "Canada's Interest in Hawaii," *Canadian Historical Review*, XLIV (March 28, 1963), U.S. Congress, Senate, Reports, 51st Cong., 1st sess., no. 1530, X, Part I, p. 1, *Relations with Canada* (serial 2712); Senate, Reports, 51st Cong., 1st sess., No. 847, p. 2.

14. *Proceedings of the Waterways Convention*, held at Superior, Wisconsin (West Superior, 1890), pp. 11 and 12.

15. Ibid., p. 13.

16. U.S., Congress, Senate, Reports, 51st Cong., 1st sess., No. 847, p. 179.

17. James J. Hill, "History of Agriculture in Minnesota," *Minnesota Historical Collections*, VIII (1898), 289. Clarence B. Bagley, *History of Seattle from the Earliest Settlement to the Present Time* (Chicago, 1916), I, 262; Joseph G. Pyle, *The Life of James J. Hill* (New York: Doubleday, Page & Co., 1916), I, 458.

18. The quotations here and in the following paragraph are from a seventy-two-page report prepared for Hill. See Herman Rosenthal, *Report on Japan, Korea and China* (St. Paul, 1893), pp. 4, 5, 8.

19. *Daily Pioneer Press* (St. Paul), 8 June 1893.

20. *Post-Intelligencer* (Seattle), 9 June 1893; Edward G. Campbell, *The Reorganization of the American Railroad System, 1893–1900*, pp. 292–297.

21. Horace S. Merrill, *Bourbon Democracy of the Middle West, 1865–1896* (Baton Rouge, La.: Louisiana State University Press, 1953), p. 240; Holbrook, *James J. Hill*, pp. 120, 127–129.

22. Bagley, *History of Seattle*, p. 258; Ralph W. Hidy, Frank E. Hill, Allan Nevins, *Timber and Men: The Weyerhaeuser Story* (New York: Macmillan, 1963), p. 212.

23. Northern Securities Company et al. v. United States, *Transcript of Record*, No. 277, appeal from the Circuit Court of the United States for the District of Minnesota, I, 667, in the Supreme Court of the United States, October term, 1903.

24. Hill, *Minnesota Historical Collections*, VIII, 289. W. Kaye Lamb, "The Trans-Pacific Venture of James J. Hill: A History of the Great Northern Steamship Company," *The American Neptune*, III (July 1943), 186–187.

25. Northern Securities Company, et al. v. United States, *Transcript of Record*, No. 277, I, 669.

26. *Manufacturers' Record*, XXXIII, 19 (18 February 1898).

27. Hill, *Minnesota Historical Collections*, VIII, 290.

28. James J. Hill, "Farming from a Business Standpoint," *Proceedings of the 17th Annual Session of the Farmers' National Congress* (St. Paul, 1897), p. 36; John Foster Carr, "Creative Americans: A Great Railway Builder," *Outlook*, LXXXVII (26 October 1907), 397. *Statistical Abstract of the United States, 1901* (Washington, 1902), pp. 295, 300.

29. Quoted in Julius W. Pratt, *Expansionists of 1898* (Baltimore, 1936), p. 271. For a complete statement of Hill's view of the Spanish-American War, see Pyle, *The Life of James J. Hill*, II, 77.

30. Charles S. Campbell, Jr., *Special Business Interests and the Open Door Policy* (New Haven, 1951), p. 22; *Manufacturers' Record*, XXXIV, 142 (23 September 1898), 142.

31. *Daily Pioneer Press*, 13 January 1899.

32. Mary H. Severance, "James J. Hill: A Builder of the Northwest," *American Monthly Review of Reviews*, XXI (June 1900), 673.

33. U.S., Congress, Senate, Reports, 56th Cong., 1st sess., no. 473, 5 (serial 3887); Marguerite M. McKee, "The Ship Subsidy Question in United States Politics," *Smith College Studies in History*, VIII (October 1922), 50; *Daily Pioneer Press*, 10 and 27 January 1900. The Frye bill was Senate bill No. 727.

34. Great Northern Railway Company, *Eleventh Annual Report* (June 1900), p. 27; James J. Hill, "The Future of Our Oriental Trade," *World's Work*, X (August 1905), 6465–6467; Hill, *Highways of Progress*, p. 166; John H. Kemble, "The Transpacific Railroads, 1869–1915," *Pacific Historical Review*, XVIII (August 1949), 339–341.

35. The Seattle group was quoted in St. Paul *Globe*, 14 January

1904; U.S., Congress, House, Documents, 57th Cong., 1st sess., no. 179 (serial 4340), pp. 287–293.

36. George F. Parker, *Recollections of Grover Cleveland* (New York, 1909), p. 326.

37. James J. Hill, "The West and Its Railroads," *Northwest Magazine*, XX (January 1902), 15; James J. Hill, "The Minnesota Farmer and His Future," *Northwest Magazine*, XX (November 1902), 10; *Pioneer Press* (5 June 1902); St. Paul *Globe* (14 January 1904).

38. Holbrook, *James J. Hill*, p. 144.

39. Interstate Commerce Commission, *Eighteenth Annual Report* (Washington, 1904), p. 49.

40. St. Paul *Globe*, 14 January 1904.

41. Interstate Commerce Commission, *Decisions of the Interstate Commerce Commission, January 1904 to April 1905* (Rochester, N. Y., 1905), X, 79.

42. U.S., Congress, Senate, Documents, 59th Cong., 1st sess., no. 243, p. 1476.

43. Lamb, "The Trans-Pacific Venture of James J. Hill," III, 196.

44. Pyle, *James J. Hill*, II, 63–65.

PART FOUR

Conclusion

9

Consensus on Expansionism

ONE OF THE central themes of James J. Hill's involvement in trade with the Orient was his growing awareness of the community of interest among farmers, merchants, and railroad men in the effort to hold and extend the overseas market for American surplus production. Despite the intense and bitter conflicts within and between those interest groups, the available evidence points to the development of a clear majority in favor of expanded foreign markets. Moreover, if the United States hoped to gain supremacy in those markets, cheap and certain transportation from the point of production to the final consumer was essential. Hill's remark that the most prosperous and powerful nations were "those who controlled commerce, and in controlling commerce they controlled it through transportation," captured a prevailing aspect of the expansionist ideology of the 1890s.

Western agrarians and their merchant allies had been the first to formulate the problem of transportation to the seaboard in its global context. In the debates over internal improvements throughout the West, it was repeatedly stated

237

that any action which tended to cheapen transportation to the seaboard contributed to the growth and strength of the American market position for agricultural exports. Southern merchants and planters joined in the demand for increased appropriations for internal improvements on similar grounds. The culmination in the 1870s of this agitation was the Senate Committee on Transportation to the Seaboard and the organization of a congressional internal improvements coalition of southern Democrats and northwestern Republicans. The recommendation by these bodies for appropriations was made to "assure our imperiled position in the markets of the world" and thereby restore prosperity at home.

Although such arguments were advanced in the 1880s, the focus of the transportation debate shifted to national regulation of the railroads. The expansion of the railroad network and competitive rate clashes increasingly diverted bulk commodities from the waterways to the railroads and created concern over relatively high local rates and various discriminatory practices. Nevertheless, the question of the impact of regulation on rates for export commodities, and foreign trade generally, stirred up considerable controversy. The unanimous opposition of the trunk-line railroads to the Reagan bill, for example, was based on grounds that through rates would be raised and thereby decrease the export trade. This argument had to be countered by proponents of regulation who hoped to sustain and increase agricultural exports. The debate over regulation, therefore, found railroad men, merchants, and farmers agreeing on the necessity of overseas market expansion while differing over what methods would or would not accomplish that objective.

Railroad men had joined farmers and merchants in emphasizing the importance of agricultural exports to prosperity —their own and the nation's—as early as the depression of the 1870s. The famous trunk-line pool of 1877 formalized what trunk-line presidents had come to believe: their roads were simply links in a through route between points in the United States and foreign countries. By the 1880s, the railroads with terminals on the Gulf and Pacific coasts sought to increase their agricultural export trade by diverting a portion away from the east-west trunk lines and developing new markets in Latin America and Asia.

The involvement of the railroad men in the expanding export trade intensified a growing economic nationalism in the post-Civil War era. Several times they petitioned Congress to bar Canadian roads from carrying through traffic from the United States and, failing that, used the Canadian roads as an excuse for evading provisions of the Interstate Commerce Act. They joined hands with many farmer and merchant organizations in advocating subsidies for an American merchant marine, reciprocal trade treaties, the Nicaragua Canal, and a first class navy. They comprised a portion of the membership of the American Asiatic Association, a powerful pressure group formed to encourage government assistance in opening new markets in Asia. And such key figures as Stuyvesant Fish, James J. Hill, Collis P. Huntington, and Chauncey Depew, acting from both narrow-interest motives and broad-gauged world views, helped create a militant sentiment for economic and political expansion overseas.

Agrarians, merchants, and railroad interests agitated for a consideration of the transportation problem as part of a world-wide phenomenon after the Civil War. They believed that if America was to extend its economic and political interests abroad, then it must lead in transportation developments. The common assumption among foreign-policy makers by 1900—that the United States possessed preponderant economic power over other nations in the world—rested, in part, on the conviction that America was in fact the vanguard of a "transportation revolution."

Selected Bibliography

Archival and Manuscript Sources

CHARLES FRANCIS ADAMS, JR., PAPERS. Massachusetts Historical Society. Boston, Massachusetts.

EDWARD A. ATKINSON PAPERS. Massachusetts Historical Society. Boston, Massachusetts.

BALTIMORE & OHIO RAILROAD ARCHIVES. Maryland Historical Society. Baltimore, Maryland.

CHICAGO, BURLINGTON & QUINCY RAILROAD ARCHIVES. Newberry Library. Chicago, Illinois.

WILLIAM E. CURTIS PAPERS. Princeton University Library. Princeton, New Jersey.

GRENVILLE DODGE PAPERS. Iowa State Historical Society. Des Moines, Iowa.

STEPHEN B. ELKINS PAPERS. University of West Virginia Library. Morgantown, West Virginia.

JOHN W. GARRETT PAPERS. Library of Congress. Washington, D.C.

ILLINOIS CENTRAL RAILROAD ARCHIVES. Newberry Library. Chicago, Illinois.

CYRUS H. MCCORMICK PAPERS. McCormick Collection. Wisconsin State Historical Society. Madison, Wisconsin.

241

MISSISSIPPI VALLEY TRADING COMPANY LTD. PAPERS. Library of the Co-operative Union. Manchester, England. On microfilm at Minnesota State Historical Society. St. Paul, Minnesota.

NATIONAL ARCHIVES OF THE UNITED STATES. Legislative Records. Washington, D.C.

JOSEPH H. OSBORN PAPERS. Wisconsin State Historical Society. Madison, Wisconsin.

JOHN SAMUEL PAPERS. Wisconsin State Historical Society. Madison, Wisconsin.

JAMES W. TAYLOR PAPERS. Minnesota Historical Society. St. Paul, Minnesota.

WILLIAM VAN HORNE PAPERS. Public Archives of Canada. Ottawa, Canada.

HENRY VILLARD PAPERS. Houghton Library. Harvard University. Cambridge, Massachusetts.

JAMES HARRISON WILSON PAPERS. Library of Congress. Washington, D.C.

WILLIAM WINDOM PAPERS. Minnesota Historical Society. St. Paul, Minnesota.

Public Documents

CONGRESSIONAL

Congressional Record. 1865–1885.

U.S. Congress. House. Committee on Commerce. *Arguments and Statements.* Miscellaneous Document No. 55. 47th Cong., 1st sess., 1882.

————. House Miscellaneous Document No. 80. 39th Cong., 2d sess., 1867.

————. House Miscellaneous Document No. 379. 45th Cong., 2d sess., 1877.

U.S. Congress. Senate. Committee on Interstate Commerce. *Hearings, Regulation of Railway Freight Rates.* Document No. 243, 59th Cong., 1st sess., 1906.

————. *Report of the Select Committee on the Mississippi River Improvements.* No. 36. 48th Cong., 1st sess., 1884.

————. *Report on the Transportation Interests of the United States and Canada.* No. 847. 51st Cong., 1st sess., 1890.

————. *Report of the Select Committee on Relations with Canada.* No. 1530. 51st Cong., 1st sess., 1890.

————. *Report of the Select Committee on Transportation Routes to the Seaboard.* Report No. 307. 43d Cong., 31st sess., 1874.

————. Senate Miscellaneous Document No. 51. 42d Cong., 2d sess., 1872.

————. Senate Miscellaneous Document No. 55. 42d Cong., 2d sess., 1872.

————. Senate Miscellaneous Document No. 160. 51st Cong., 1st sess., 1889.

OTHER FEDERAL

U.S. Department of Agriculture. *Annual Reports of the Commissioner of Agriculture.* 1862–1880.

————. Bureau of Statistics. *Crop Export Movement and Port Facilities.* Bulletin 38. Washington, 1905.

————. *Yearbook of the United States Department of Agriculture, 1899.* Washington, 1900.

U.S. Department of Commerce. Bureau of Statistics. *Historical Statistics of the United States, Colonial Times to 1957.* Washington, 1960.

U.S. Department of State. *Consular Reports.* 1880–1895.

U.S. Industrial Commission. *Report of the Industrial Commission on Transportation v. 10.* Washington, 1900.

U.S. Interstate Commerce Commission. *Annual Reports.* 1887–1893.

————. *Railways in the United States in 1902: A Forty Year Review of Charges in Freight Tariffs.* Washington, 1903.

————. Tariff Commission. *Preferential Transportation Rates and Their Relation to Import and Export Traffic of the United States.* Washington, 1922.

STATE

State of Iowa. *Legislative Documents.* 1886–1880.

State of Minnesota. *Minnesota Executive Documents.* 1868–1880.

State of Wisconsin. *Governor's Message and Accompanying Documents*. 1865–1880.
State of Wisconsin. *Report of Railroad Commission*. 1874–1880.

Trade Journals and Newspapers

American Railroad Journal.
Banker's Magazine.
Bradstreet's.
Bulletin of the Executive Committee of the State Grange of Wisconsin, Patrons of Husbandry.
Commercial and Financial Chronicle.
Louisville *Courier-Journal.*
St. Paul *Daily Pioneer Press.*
DeBow's Review.
Farmer's Review.
Manufacturers' Record.
National Economist.
Northwestern Magazine.
Northwestern Miller.
Poor's Manual of Railroads in the United States.
Seattle *Post-Intelligencer.*
Railway Age.
Railroad Gazette.
New York *Sun.*
Oshkosh *Times.*
New York *Tribune.*
Western Rural.

Pamphlets and Proceedings

ATKINSON, EDWARD A. *The Railroads of the United States*. Boston: A. Williams & Co., 1880.
Advisory Commission. *Report of Messrs. Thurman, Washburne & Cooley, Constituting an Advisory Commission on Differential Rates by Railroads*. New York, 1882.

ELDER, WILLIAM. *How the Western States Can Become the Imperial Power of the Nation.* Philadelphia, 1865.

FINK, ALBERT. *Report Upon the Adjustment of Railroad Transportation Rates to the Seaboard, 1881.* New York, 1882.

Iowa State Agricultural Society. *Annual Report of the Secretary, 1872.* Des Moines, 1873.

Iowa State Grange. *Proceedings.* 1873–1877.

Minnesota State Grange. *Proceedings.* 1874–1877.

National Grange. *Proceedings.* 1874–1879.

Proceedings of the Mississippi River Improvement Convention. Dubuque, Iowa, 14–15 February 1866.

Proceedings of the Mississippi River Improvement Convention. St. Louis, Mo., 26–29 October 1881.

Proceedings of the National Ship Canal Convention. Chicago, Ill., 2–3 June 1863.

Proceedings of the Northwestern Waterways Convention. St. Paul, Minn., 3 September 1885.

Proceedings of the River Improvement Convention. St. Louis, Mo., 12–13 February 1867.

Proceedings of the Waterways Convention. Superior, Wis., 7–8 August 1889.

Trans-Mississippi Commercial Congress. *Proceedings.* 1891–1900.

Western States Commercial Congress. *Proceedings.* 1890.

Wisconsin State Agricultural Society. *Transactions.* 1872–1880.

Wisconsin State Grange. *Proceedings.* 1874–1879.

Unpublished Sources

CRAPOL, EDWARD. " 'America for Americans': Economic Nationalism and Anglophobia, 1876–1896." Ph.D. dissertation, University of Wisconsin, 1968.

ERLENBORN, JAMES L. "American Meat and Livestock Industry and American Foreign Policy, 1880–1896." Master's thesis, University of Wisconsin, 1966.

HARRIS, CARL V. "The Confederate Brigadiers: Congressmen of the New South." Master's thesis, University of Wisconsin, 1965.

JENSON, HELEN M. "Internal Improvements and Wisconsin Republicanism, 1865–1873." Master's thesis, University of Wisconsin, 1937.

MCCLUGGAGE, ROBERT. "The Fox-Wisconsin Waterway, 1836–1876: Land Speculation and Regional Rivalries." Ph.D. dissertation, University of Wisconsin, 1954.

MILLER, GEORGE H. "The Granger Laws: A Study of the Origins of State Railway Control in the Upper Mississippi Valley." Ph.D. dissertation, University of Michigan, 1951.

MURRAY, STANLEY M. "A History of Agriculture in the Red River Valley of the North, 1812–1920." Ph.D. dissertation, University of Wisconsin, 1963.

PROSS, EDWARD L. "A History of Rivers and Harbors Appropriations Bills, 1866–1930." Ph.D. dissertation, University of Ohio, 1938.

SCHONBERGER, HOWARD B. "Transportation to the Seaboard: A Case Study in the 'Communication Revolution' and American Foreign Policy, 1865–1900." Ph.D. dissertation, University of Wisconsin, 1968.

WRIGHT, GEORGE A. "William Windom, 1827–1890." Master's thesis, University of Wisconsin, 1911.

Articles

ADAMS, CHARLES F., JR. "The Granger Movement." *North American Review,* CXX (April 1875), 394–424.

ALLEN, WILLIAM V. "Western Feeling Towards the East." *North American Review,* CLXII (April 1896), 588–593.

ANDREW, A. PIATT. "The Influence of the Crops upon Business in America." *Quarterly Journal of Economics,* XX (1906), 323–352.

BEARD, EARL S. "The Background of State Railroad Regulation in Iowa." *Iowa Journal of History,* LI (January 1953), 1–36.

CARR, JOHN FOSTER. "Creative Americans: A Great Railway Builder." *Outlook,* LXXXVII (1907), 391–398.

CUMMINGS, RICHARD O. "American Interest in World Agriculture, 1861–1865." *Agricultural History,* XXIII (April 1949), 116–123.

DALAND, ROBERT T. "Enactment of the Potter Law." *Wisconsin Magazine of History,* XXXIII (September 1949), 45–54.

DESTLER, CHESTER M. A. "Western Radicalism, 1865–1901: Concepts and Origins." *Mississippi Valley Historical Review*, XXXI (December 1944), 335–368.

FITE, EMERSON D. "The Agricultural Development of the West in the Civil War." *Quarterly Journal of Economics*, XX (1906), 259–278.

GROSVENOR, WILLIAM M. "The Railroads and the Farms." *Atlantic*, XXXII (November 1873), 591–610.

HARBESON, R. W. "The North Atlantic Port Differentials." *Quarterly Journal of Economics*, XLVI (1932), 644–670.

HILL, JAMES J. "The Future of Our Oriental Trade." *World's Work*, X (August 1905), 6465–6467.

————. "History of Agriculture in Minnesota." *Minnesota Historical Society Collections*, VIII (1898), 275–290.

JENCKS, LELAND H. "Railroads as an Economic Force in American Development." *Journal of Economic History*, IV (May 1944), 1–20.

KEMBLE, JOHN H. "The Transpacific Railroads, 1869–1915." *Pacific Historical Review*, XVIII (August 1949), 331–343.

LAMB, W. KAYE. "The Transpacific Venture of James J. Hill: A History of the Great Northern Steamship Company." *American Neptune*, III (July 1943), 185–204.

LIPPINCOTT, ISAAC. "A History of River Improvement." *Journal of Political Economy*, XXII (1914), 630–660.

LOWREY, WALTER M. "The Engineers and the Mississippi." *Louisiana History*, V (Summer 1964), 233–255.

MCCLUGGAGE, ROBERT. "Joseph H. Osborn, Grange Leader." *Wisconsin Magazine of History*, XXXV (Spring 1952), 178–184.

MCKEE, SAMUEL, JR. "Canada's Bid for the Traffic of the Middle West." *Canadian Historical Association Reports* (1940), 26–35.

MILLER, GEORGE H. "The Iowa Granger Law." *Mississippi Valley Historical Review*, XL (March 1954), 657–680.

MORGAN, JOHN T. "The Political Alliance of the South with the West." *North American Review*, CXXVI (1878), 309–322.

NASH, GERALD. "Origins of the Interstate Commerce Act of 1887." *Pennsylvania History*, XXIV (July 1957), 181–190.

OGG, FREDERIC A. "Railroad Rates and the Flow of Our Foreign Trade." *American Monthly Review of Reviews*, XXXIII (1906), 458–463.

ROACH, HANNAH G. "Sectionalism in Congress, 1870–1890." *American Political Science Review,* XIX (August 1925), 500–526.

ROTHSTEIN, MORTON. "America in the International Rivalry for the British Wheat Market, 1860–1914." *Mississippi Valley Historical Review,* XLVII (December 1960), 401–418.

SCHMIDT, LOUIS B. "The Internal Grain Trade of the United States, 1860–1890." *Iowa Journal of History and Politics,* XIX (1921), 196–245, 414–455; XX (1922), 70–131.

SCOTT, ROY V. "American Railroads and Agricultural Extension, 1900–1914: A Study in Railway Development Techniques." *Business History Review,* XXXIX (Spring 1965), 74–98.

SEVERANCE, MARY H. "James J. Hill: A Builder of the Northwest." *American Monthly Review of Reviews,* XXI (June 1900), 669–678.

SHARROW, WALTER G. "William Henry Seward and the Basis for the American Empire." *Pacific Historical Review,* XXXVI (April 1967), 325–342.

TATE, MERZE. "Canada's Interest in the Trade and Sovereignty of Hawaii." *Canadian Historical Review,* XLIV (March 1963), 20–42.

THORNE, MILDRED. "The Grange in Iowa." *Iowa Journal of History.* XLVII (October 1949), 289–324.

TUNNELL, GEORGE G. "The Diversion of the Flour and Grain Traffic from the Great Lakes to Railroads." *Journal of Political Economy,* V (1897), 340–375.

WILCOX, BENTON H. "An Historical Definition of Northwestern Radicalism." *Mississippi Valley Historical Review,* XXVI (December 1939), 377–394.

WILLIAMS, WILLIAM A. "The Vicious Circle of American Imperialism." *New Politics,* IV (Fall 1965), 48–55.

YEARLY, CLIFTON K. "Baltimore and Ohio Railroad Strike of 1877." *Maryland Historical Magazine,* LI (1966), 188–211.

Books

BAKER, GEORGE E., ed. *The Works of William H. Seward.* Boston: Houghton Mifflin & Co., 1886.

BANCROFT, FREDERIC. *The Life of William H. Seward.* New York: Harper & Brothers, 1900.

BARROWS, CHESTER L. *William M. Evarts.* Chapel Hill: University of North Carolina Press, 1941.

BELCHER, WYATT W. *The Economic Rivalry Between St. Louis and Chicago, 1850–1880.* New York: Columbia University Press, 1947.

BEMIS, EDWARD W., SHAW, ALBERT ET AL. *History of Cooperation in the United States.* Baltimore: Johns Hopkins University Press, 1888.

BENSON, LEE. *Merchants, Farmers, & Railroads: Railroad Regulation and New York Politics, 1850–1887.* Cambridge: Harvard University Press, 1955.

BUCK, SOLON J. *The Granger Movement, 1870–1880.* Cambridge: Harvard University Press, 1913.

CAMPBELL, EDWARD G. *The Reorganization of the American Railroad System, 1893–1900.* New York: Columbia University Press, 1938.

CARR, EZRA. *The Patrons of Husbandry on the Pacific Coast.* San Francisco: A. L. Bancroft Co., 1875.

CHANDLER, ALFRED D. *Henry Varnum Poor, Business Editor, Analyst, and Reformer.* Cambridge: Harvard University Press, 1956.

———, ed. *The Railroads, the Nation's First Big Business.* New York: Harcourt, Brace & World, 1965.

CLAPP, EDWIN J. *The Port of Boston.* New Haven: Yale University Press, 1916.

COCHRAN, THOMAS C. *Railroad Leaders, 1845–1890: The Business Mind in Action.* Cambridge: Harvard University Press, 1953.

CORLISS, CARLETON J. *Main-Line of Mid-America: The Story of the Illinois Central.* New York: Creative Age Press, 1950.

CREIGHTON, DONALD. *John A. Macdonald: The Old Chieftain.* Toronto: Macmillan Company of Canada, 1955.

CULLOM, SHELBY. *Fifty Years of Public Service.* Chicago: A. C. McClurg & Co., 1911.

CURRENT, RICHARD N. *Pine Logs and Politics: A Life of Philetus Sawyer, 1816–1900.* Madison: The State Historical Society of Wisconsin, 1950.

CURRIE, ARCHIBALD W. *The Grand Trunk Railway of Canada.* Toronto: University of Toronto Press, 1957.

DODGE, MARY ABIGAIL [GAIL HAMILTON]. *Biography of James G. Blaine.* Norwich: Henry Bill Publishing Co., 1895.

DORSEY, FLORENCE. *Road to the Sea: The Story of James B. Eads and the Mississippi River.* New York: Rinehart, 1947.

EADS, JAMES B. *Addresses and Papers of James B. Eads.* Edited by Estell McHenry. St. Louis: Slauson & Co., 1884.

FOGEL, ROBERT W. *Railroads and American Economic Growth.* Baltimore: Johns Hopkins Press, 1964.

FRANKLIN, JOHN H. *Reconstruction After the Civil War.* Chicago: University of Chicago Press, 1961.

GATES, PAUL W. *Agriculture and the Civil War.* New York: Alfred A. Knopf, 1965.

————. *The Illinois Central Railroad and Its Colonization Work.* Cambridge: Harvard University Press, 1934.

GIBBON, JOHN M. *Steel of Empire.* New York: Bobbs Merrill Co., 1935.

GILBERT, HEATHER. *Awakening Continent: The Life of Lord Mount Stephen.* Aberdeen: Aberdeen University Press, 1965.

GLAAB, CHARLES N. *Kansas City and the Railroads.* Madison: The State Historical Society of Wisconsin, 1962.

GLUEK, ALVIN C., JR. *Minnesota and the Manifest Destiny of the Canadian Northwest.* Toronto: University of Toronto Press, 1965.

GOODRICH, CARTER. *Government Promotion of American Canals and Railroads, 1800–1890.* New York: Columbia University Press, 1960.

GRODINSKY, JULIUS. *Transcontinental Railway Strategy, 1869–1893.* Philadelphia: University of Pennsylvania Press, 1962.

HARRISON, BENJAMIN. *Speeches of Benjamin Harrison.* Edited by Charles Hedges. New York: United States Book Co., 1892.

HAYNES, FREDERICK E. *Third Party Movements Since the Civil War with Special Reference to Iowa.* Iowa City: State Historical Society of Iowa, 1916.

HESSELTINE, WILLIAM B. *A History of the South.* New York: Prentice-Hall, 1936.

HICKS, JOHN D. *The Populist Revolt.* Minneapolis: University of Minnesota Press, 1931.

HILL, JAMES J. *Highways of Progress.* New York: Doubleday, Page & Co., 1910.

HOAR, GEORGE F. *Autobiography of Seventy Years.* New York: Charles Scribner's Sons, 1903.

HOLBROOK, STEWART H. *James J. Hill: A Great Life in Brief.* New York: Alfred A. Knopf, 1955.

HUBBART, HENRY C. *The Older Middle West, 1840–1880.* New York: D. Appleton-Century, 1936.

HUNGERFORD, EDWARD. *The Story of the Baltimore and Ohio Railroad, 1827–1927.* New York: G. P. Putnam's Sons, 1928.

HUTCHINS, JOHN G. B. *The American Maritime Industries and Public Policy, 1789–1914.* Cambridge: Harvard University Press, 1941.

HUTCHINSON, WILLIAM T. *Cyrus Hall McCormick.* New York: D. Appleton-Century Co., 1935.

KELLEY, OLIVER H. *Origin and Progress of the Order of Patrons of Husbandry in the United States: A History from 1866 to 1873.* Philadelphia: J. A. Wagenseller, Publisher, 1875.

KENNAN, GEORGE. *E. H. Harriman, a Biography.* Boston: Houghton Mifflin Company, 1922.

KLEMENT, FRANK L. *The Copperheads in the Middle West.* Chicago: University of Chicago Press, 1960.

KOLKO, GABRIEL. *Railroads and Regulation, 1877–1916.* Princeton: Princeton University Press, 1965.

LAFEBER, WALTER. *The New Empire: An Interpretation of American Expansion, 1860–1898.* Ithaca: Cornell University Press, 1963.

LARRABEE, WILLIAM. *The Railroad Question.* Chicago: Schulte Publishing Co., 1898.

LARSON, HENRIETTA M. *The Wheat Market and the Farmer in Minnesota, 1858–1900.* New York: Columbia University Press, 1926.

MARTIN, EDWARD W. *History of the Grange Movement; or the Farmers' War Against Monopoly; . . . etc.* Chicago: National Publishing Co., 1874.

MAY, ERNEST R. *Imperial Democracy: The Emergence of America as a Great Power.* New York: Harcourt, Brace & World, 1961.

MERK, FREDERICK. *Economic History of Wisconsin During the Civil War.* Madison: The Society, 1916.

MERRILL, HORACE S. *Bourbon Democracy of the Middle West, 1865–1896.* Baton Rouge: Louisiana State University Press, 1953.

MEYER, BALTHASAR H. *A History of the Northern Securities Case.* Madison, 1906.

MORGAN, W. SCOTT. *History of the Wheel and Alliance, and the Impending Revolution.* Fort Scott, Kan.: J. H. Rice & Sons, 1889.

MOULTON, HAROLD G. *Waterways versus Railways.* Boston, 1912.

NEILSON, JAMES W. *Shelby Cullom, Prairie State Republican.* Urbana: University of Illinois Press, 1962.

NEVINS, ALLAN. *Hamilton Fish: The Inner History of the Grant Administration.* New York: Frederick Ungar Co., 1957.

NORRIS, FRANK. *The Octopus.* New York: Bantam Books, 1963.

NOURSE, EDWIN G. *American Agriculture and the European Market.* New York: McGraw-Hill Book Company, 1924.

OLSON, JAMES C. *J. Sterling Morton.* Lincoln, Neb.: University of Nebraska Press, 1942.

OVERTON, RICHARD C. *Gulf to Rockies.* Austin: University of Texas Press, 1953.

PARRISH, WILLIAM E. *Missouri under Radical Rule, 1865–1870.* Columbia, Mo.: University of Missouri Press, 1965.

PERIAN, JONATHON. *The Groundswell: A History of the Origin, Aim and Progress of the Farmer's Movement.* Chicago: Hannaford & Thompson, 1874.

PERLOFF, HARVEY S. ET AL. *Regions, Resources, and Economic Growth.* Lincoln: University of Nebraska Press, 1960.

PIERCE, BESSE L. *A History of Chicago: From Town to City, 1848–1871.* New York: Alfred A. Knopf, 1940.

PORTER, KIRK, AND JOHNSON, DONALD B., eds. *National Party Platforms, 1840–1964.* Urbana: University of Illinois Press, 1966.

PRATT, JULIUS W. *A History of United States Foreign Policy.* Englewood Cliffs, N.J.: Prentice-Hall, 1955.

PROCTER, BEN H. *Not Without Honor: The Life of John H. Reagan.* Austin: University of Texas Press, 1962.

PYLE, JOSEPH G. *The Life of James J. Hill.* New York: Doubleday, Page & Co., 1916–17.

RICHARDSON, JAMES D., ed. *Messages and Papers of the Presidents, 1789–1897.* Washington, D.C.: Government Printing Office, 1898.

RIPLEY, WILLIAM Z. *Railroads: Rates and Regulations.* New York: Ginn & Co., 1912.

SAGE, LELAND L. *William Boyd Allison.* Iowa City: State Historical Society of Iowa, 1956.

SATTERLEE, HERBERT L. *J. Pierpont Morgan.* New York: Macmillan, 1939.

SEWARD, WILLIAM H. *Life and Public Services of John Quincy Adams.* Auburn, N.Y.: Derby, Miller & Co., 1851.

SHANNON, FRED A. *The Farmer's Last Frontier: Agriculture, 1860–1897.* New York: Farrar & Rinehart, Inc., 1945.

SHARFMAN, ISAIAH L. *The Interstate Commerce Commission.* New York: The Commonwealth Fund, 1931–1937.

SHARKEY, ROBERT P. *Money, Class, and Party: An Economic Study of the Civil War and Reconstruction.* Baltimore: Johns Hopkins University Press, 1959.

SHIPPEE, LESTER B. *Canadian-American Relations, 1849–1874.* New Haven: Yale University Press, 1939.

SMITH, HENRY NASH. *Virgin Land.* New York: Random House, 1957.

STOVER, JOHN F. *The Railroads of the South, 1865–1900.* Chapel Hill: University of North Carolina Press, 1955.

SUMMERS, FESTUS P. *The Baltimore and Ohio in the Civil War.* New York: G. P. Putnam's Sons, 1939.

TANSILL, CHARLES C. *Canadian-American Relations, 1875–1911.* New Haven: Yale University Press, 1943.

TAYLOR, GEORGE R., AND NEU, IRENE D. *The American Railroad Network, 1861–1890.* Cambridge: Harvard University Press, 1956.

THOMPSON, D. G. BRINTON. *Ruggles of New York: A Life of Samuel B. Ruggles.* New York: Columbia University Press, 1946.

TYLER, ALICE. *The Foreign Policy of James G. Blaine.* Minneapolis: University of Minnesota Press, 1927.

WEBB, BEATRICE POTTER. *The Cooperative Movement in Great Britain.* London: George Allen & Unwin Ltd., 1930.

WEBER, THOMAS. *The Northern Railroads in the Civil War, 1861–1865.* New York: King's Crown Press, 1952.

WHEDBEE, T. COURTENAY J. *The Port of Baltimore in the Making, 1828–1878.* Baltimore: Schneidereith & Sons, 1953.

WILLIAMS, WILLIAM A. *The Great Evasion.* Chicago: Quadrangle Books, 1964.

———. *The Roots of the Modern American Empire.* New York: Random House, 1969.

———. *Tragedy of American Diplomacy.* New York: Dell Publishing Co., 1961.

WILLIAMSON, HAROLD F. *Edward Atkinson: The Biography of an American Liberal, 1827–1905.* Cambridge: Riverside Press, 1934.

WILLOUGHBY, WILLIAM R. *The St. Lawrence Waterway.* Madison: University of Wisconsin Press, 1961.

WINTHER, OSCAR O. *The Great Northwest.* New York: Alfred A. Knopf, 1947.

WOOLFOLK, GEORGE R. *The Cotton Regency, the Northern Merchants, and Reconstruction.* New York: Bookman Associates, 1958.

WOODWARD, C. VANN. *Origins of the New South, 1877–1913.* Baton Rouge: Louisiana State University Press, 1951.

WORRALL, THOMAS D. *Manual of Practical Cooperation.* Louisville: American Cooperative Union, 1875.

YEARLEY, CLIFTON K., JR. *Britons in American Labor: A History of the Influence of the United Kingdom Immigrants on American Labor, 1820–1914.* Baltimore: Johns Hopkins Press, 1957.

Index

affiliation with English Cooperative Union, 79
organizing by Worrall, 72–75
Missouri State Grange, 47
Morgan, Edwin D., 14
Morgan, John Pierpont, 221, 229
Morgan, John T., 197
Morgan, Junius Spencer, 170, 172
Morton, J. Sterling, 145
Morton, Oliver P., 11
Murphy, Jerry H., 131

Nation, 31, 44, 109
National Antimonopoly League, 122
National Board of Railroad Commissioners, 122
National Board of Trade, 100
National Cheap Transportation Association, 44, 52
National Farmers' Alliance, 132, 227
National Grain Growers' Association, 227
National Grange, 54–55
  Charleston, S.C., meeting (1875), 60–61
  see also Grangers
National Grange Committee on Confederation, 43
National Grange Executive Committee, 67, 75
Neale, E. V., 74
Nelson, Knute, 143
Nelson, W. H., 138
New England, economic "hold" of, 29
New Orleans
  grain and other shipments from, 92–94, 97, 104–105

Illinois Central Railroad and, 189
New Orleans Chamber of Commerce, 71, 91, 97, 99, 106
New Orleans City Council, 201
New Orleans *Times,* 72
New Orleans *Times Democrat,* 109–110, 203
New Orleans *Times-Picayune,* 202
Newton, Isaac, 12
New York Central Railroad, 121, 125, 128, 148, 169, 171
New York Chamber of Commerce, 141
New York *Herald,* 54, 186
New York *Tribune,* 103, 109
Niagara ship canal, 21, 28
Nicaragua canal, 185, 197, 200, 207, 239
Nicaragua Canal Co., 197
Nickel Plate Railroad, 181
Nimmo, Joseph, 150–152
Northern Pacific Railroad, 16, 167
Northern Securities Co. case, 212, 228–229
North German Lloyd Line, 164, 167
Northwestern Miller, 194
Northwestern Waterways Convention, 131

Oglesby, Joseph H., 71, 97
Ohio and Mississippi Railroad, 165
Ohio canals, improvement of, 16
Ohio River, railroad junction at, 11, 163, 187
Open Door Policy, ix–x
Orient trade, 7, 212–231, 237

Transportation to the Seaboard was composed in Linotype Baskerville with Bulmer display type by The Book Press, Brattleboro, Vermont. The entire book was printed by offset lithography.